AFTER THE VALKYRIES — ASGARDIAN WARRIORS CHARGED WITH [...]
DEAD TO THEIR ETERNAL REWARD — WERE ALL KILLED IN THE WAR [...]
FOSTER TOOK UP UNDRJARN, THE ALL-WEAPON, AND BECAME [...] KNOWN VALKYRIE.

BUT THERE WAS ACTUALLY ANOTHER VALKYRIE OUT THERE — ONE LOST TO TIME AND TRAGEDY.
JANE FREED THIS LEGENDARY WARRIOR AND HELPED HER RECLAIM HER ORIGINAL WEAPON — THE
ENCHANTED AX JARNBJORN — AND TOGETHER THEY DESTROYED THE CORRUPTED CELESTIAL THAT
HAD KEPT THIS ANCIENT VALKYRIE AND INNUMERABLE OTHER SOULS TRAPPED FOR CENTURIES.

NOW JANE RETURNS TO HER LIFE AS A MORTICIAN ON MIDGARD WHILE HER NEWFOUND ALLY
SETS OUT TO REDISCOVER HERS. EONS AGO, SHE LEFT ASGARD, INTENDING NEVER TO RETURN.
BUT SHE LEFT BEHIND MORE THAN JUST A LEGEND — SHE LEFT PIECES OF HERSELF, INCLUDING A
PIECE OF KNOWLEDGE SO OLD EVEN SHE HAS FORGOTTEN IT: HER OWN NAME.

THE MIGHTY VALKYRIES

All Hel Let Loose

JANE STORY

**JASON AARON &
TORUNN GRØNBEKK**
WRITERS

MATTIA DE IULIS
ARTIST/COLOR ARTIST

NEW VALKYRIE STORY

TORUNN GRØNBEKK
WRITER

ERICA D'URSO
ARTIST

MARCIO MENYZ
COLOR ARTIST

VC's JOE SABINO LETTERER

MATTIA DE IULIS COVER ART

JAY BOWEN LOGO DESIGN

WIL MOSS & SARAH BRUNSTAD EDITORS

COLLECTION EDITOR **JENNIFER GRÜNWALD**   **DANIEL KIRCHHOFFER** ASSISTANT EDITOR
ASSISTANT MANAGING EDITOR **MAIA LOY**   **LISA MONTALBANO** ASSISTANT MANAGING EDITOR
VP PRODUCTION & SPECIAL PROJECTS **JEFF YOUNGQUIST**   **JAY BOWEN** BOOK DESIGNER
SVP PRINT, SALES & MARKETING **DAVID GABRIEL**   **C.B. CEBULSKI** EDITOR IN CHIEF

THE MIGHTY VALKYRIES: ALL HEL LET LOOSE. Contains material originally published in magazine form as THE MIGHTY VALKYRIES (2021) #1-5. First printing 2021. ISBN 978-1-302-93019-6. Published by MARVEL WORLDWIDE, INC., a subsidiary of MARVEL ENTERTAINMENT, LLC. OFFICE OF PUBLICATION: 1290 Avenue of the Americas, New York, NY 10104. © 2021 MARVEL No similarity between any of the names, characters, persons, and/or institutions in this magazine with those of any living or dead person or institution is intended, and any such similarity which may exist is purely coincidental. Printed in Canada. KEVIN FEIGE, Chief Creative Officer; DAN BUCKLEY, President, Marvel Entertainment; JOE QUESADA, EVP & Creative Director; DAVID BOGART, Associate Publisher & SVP of Talent Affairs; TOM BREVOORT, VP, Executive Editor; NICK LOWE, Executive Editor, VP of Content, Digital Publishing; DAVID GABRIEL, VP of Print & Digital Publishing; JEFF YOUNGQUIST, VP of Production & Special Projects; ALEX MORALES, Director of Publishing Operations; DAN EDINGTON, Managing Editor; RICKEY PURDIN, Director of Talent Relations; JENNIFER GRÜNWALD, Senior Editor, Special Projects; SUSAN CRESPI, Production Manager; STAN LEE, Chairman Emeritus. For information regarding advertising in Marvel Comics or on Marvel.com, please contact Vit DeBellis, Custom Solutions & Integrated Advertising Manager, at vdebellis@marvel.com. For Marvel subscription inquiries, please call 888-511-5480. Manufactured between 9/3/2021 and 10/5/2021 by SOLISCO PRINTERS, SCOTT, QC, CANADA.

10 9 8 7 6 5 4 3 2 1

1.

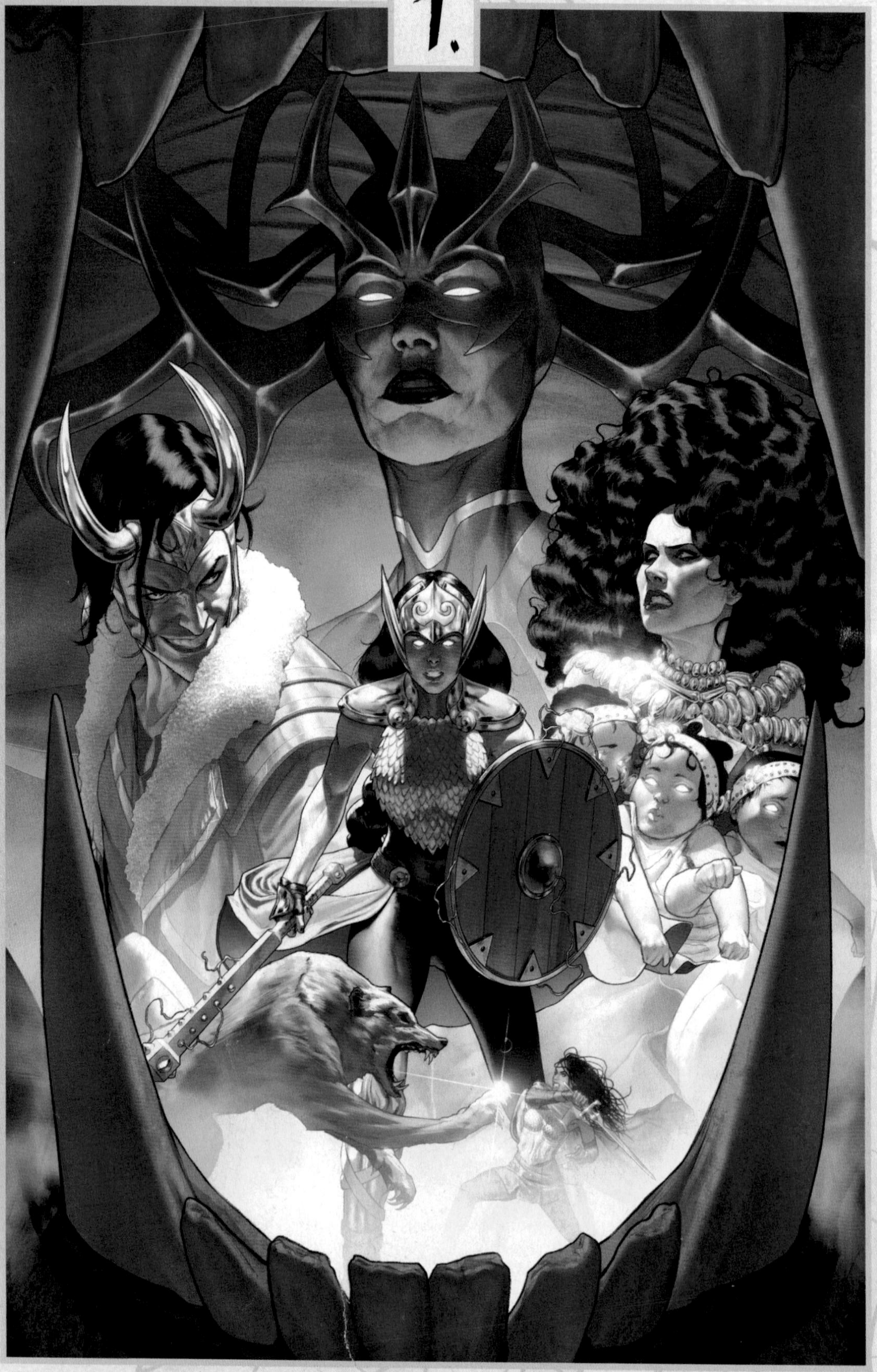

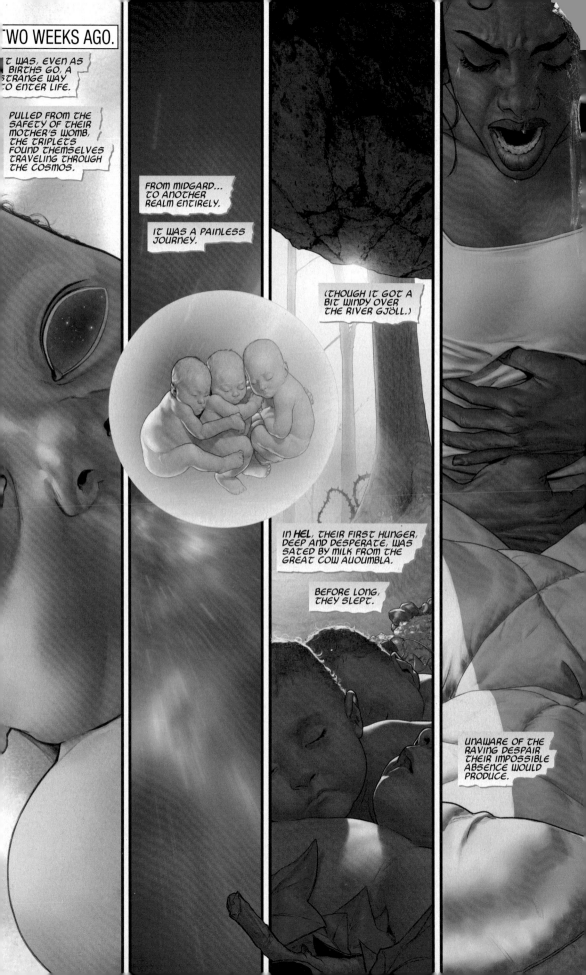

TWO WEEKS AGO.

IT WAS, EVEN AS BIRTHS GO, A STRANGE WAY TO ENTER LIFE.

PULLED FROM THE SAFETY OF THEIR MOTHER'S WOMB, THE TRIPLETS FOUND THEMSELVES TRAVELING THROUGH THE COSMOS.

FROM MIDGARD... TO ANOTHER REALM ENTIRELY.

IT WAS A PAINLESS JOURNEY.

(THOUGH IT GOT A BIT WINDY OVER THE RIVER GJÖLL.)

IN HEL, THEIR FIRST HUNGER, DEEP AND DESPERATE, WAS SATED BY MILK FROM THE GREAT COW AUDUMBLA.

BEFORE LONG, THEY SLEPT.

UNAWARE OF THE RAVING DESPAIR THEIR IMPOSSIBLE ABSENCE WOULD PRODUCE.

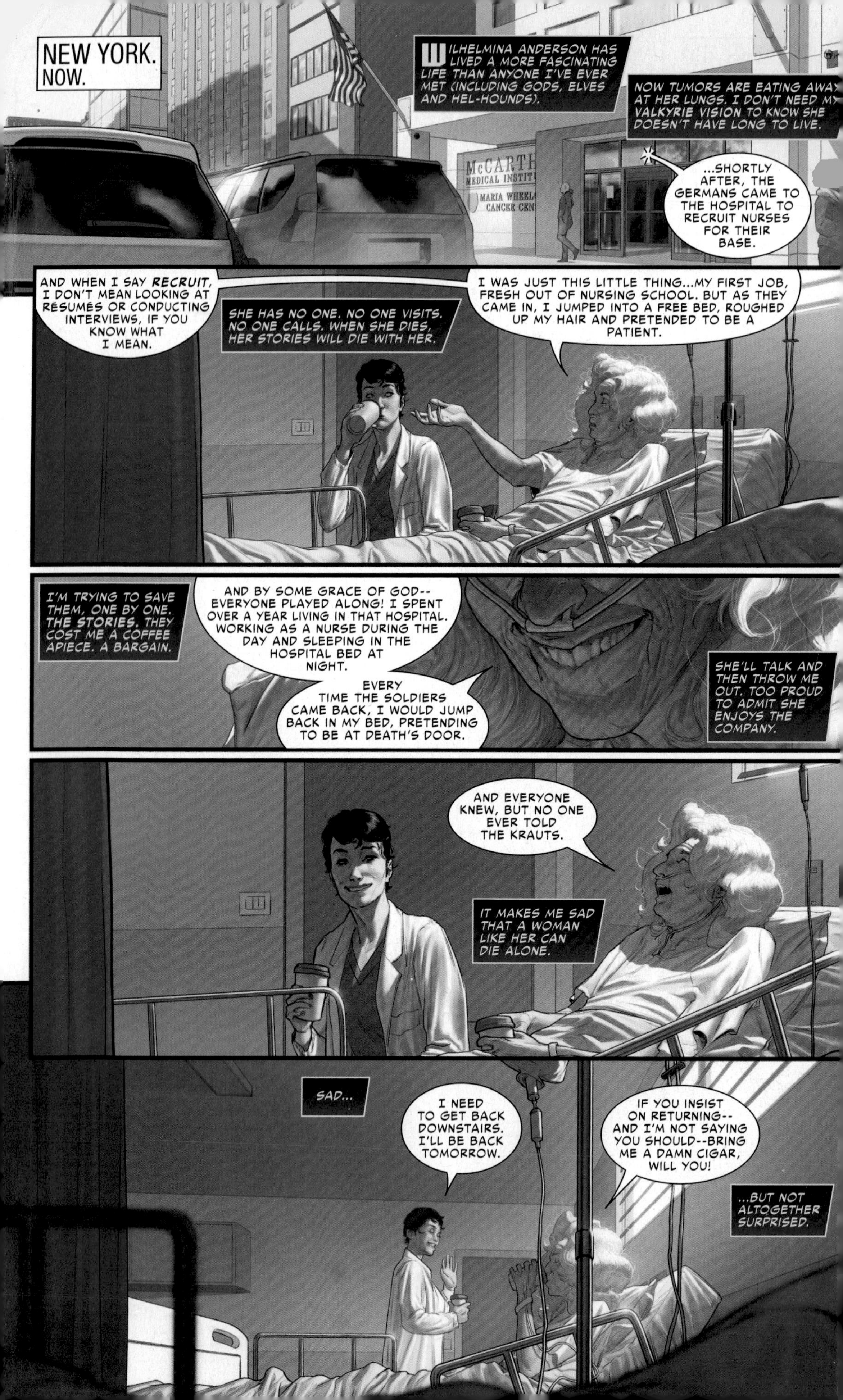
NEW YORK. NOW.
WILHELMINA ANDERSON HAS LIVED A MORE FASCINATING LIFE THAN ANYONE I'VE EVER MET (INCLUDING GODS, ELVES AND HEL-HOUNDS).
NOW TUMORS ARE EATING AWAY AT HER LUNGS. I DON'T NEED MY VALKYRIE VISION TO KNOW SHE DOESN'T HAVE LONG TO LIVE.
McCARTH MEDICAL INSTIT MARIA WHEEL CANCER CEN
...SHORTLY AFTER, THE GERMANS CAME TO THE HOSPITAL TO RECRUIT NURSES FOR THEIR BASE.
AND WHEN I SAY **RECRUIT**, I DON'T MEAN LOOKING AT RÉSUMÉS OR CONDUCTING INTERVIEWS, IF YOU KNOW WHAT I MEAN.
SHE HAS NO ONE. NO ONE VISITS. NO ONE CALLS. WHEN SHE DIES, HER STORIES WILL DIE WITH HER.
I WAS JUST THIS LITTLE THING...MY FIRST JOB, FRESH OUT OF NURSING SCHOOL. BUT AS THEY CAME IN, I JUMPED INTO A FREE BED, ROUGHED UP MY HAIR AND PRETENDED TO BE A PATIENT.
I'M TRYING TO SAVE THEM, ONE BY ONE. **THE STORIES.** THEY COST ME A COFFEE APIECE. A BARGAIN.
AND BY SOME GRACE OF GOD-- EVERYONE PLAYED ALONG! I SPENT OVER A YEAR LIVING IN THAT HOSPITAL. WORKING AS A NURSE DURING THE DAY AND SLEEPING IN THE HOSPITAL BED AT NIGHT.
EVERY TIME THE SOLDIERS CAME BACK, I WOULD JUMP BACK IN MY BED, PRETENDING TO BE AT DEATH'S DOOR.
SHE'LL TALK AND THEN THROW ME OUT. TOO PROUD TO ADMIT SHE ENJOYS THE COMPANY.
AND EVERYONE KNEW, BUT NO ONE EVER TOLD THE KRAUTS.
IT MAKES ME SAD THAT A WOMAN LIKE HER CAN DIE ALONE.
SAD...
I NEED TO GET BACK DOWNSTAIRS. I'LL BE BACK TOMORROW.
IF YOU INSIST ON RETURNING-- AND I'M NOT SAYING YOU SHOULD--BRING ME A DAMN CIGAR, WILL YOU!
...BUT NOT ALTOGETHER SURPRISED.

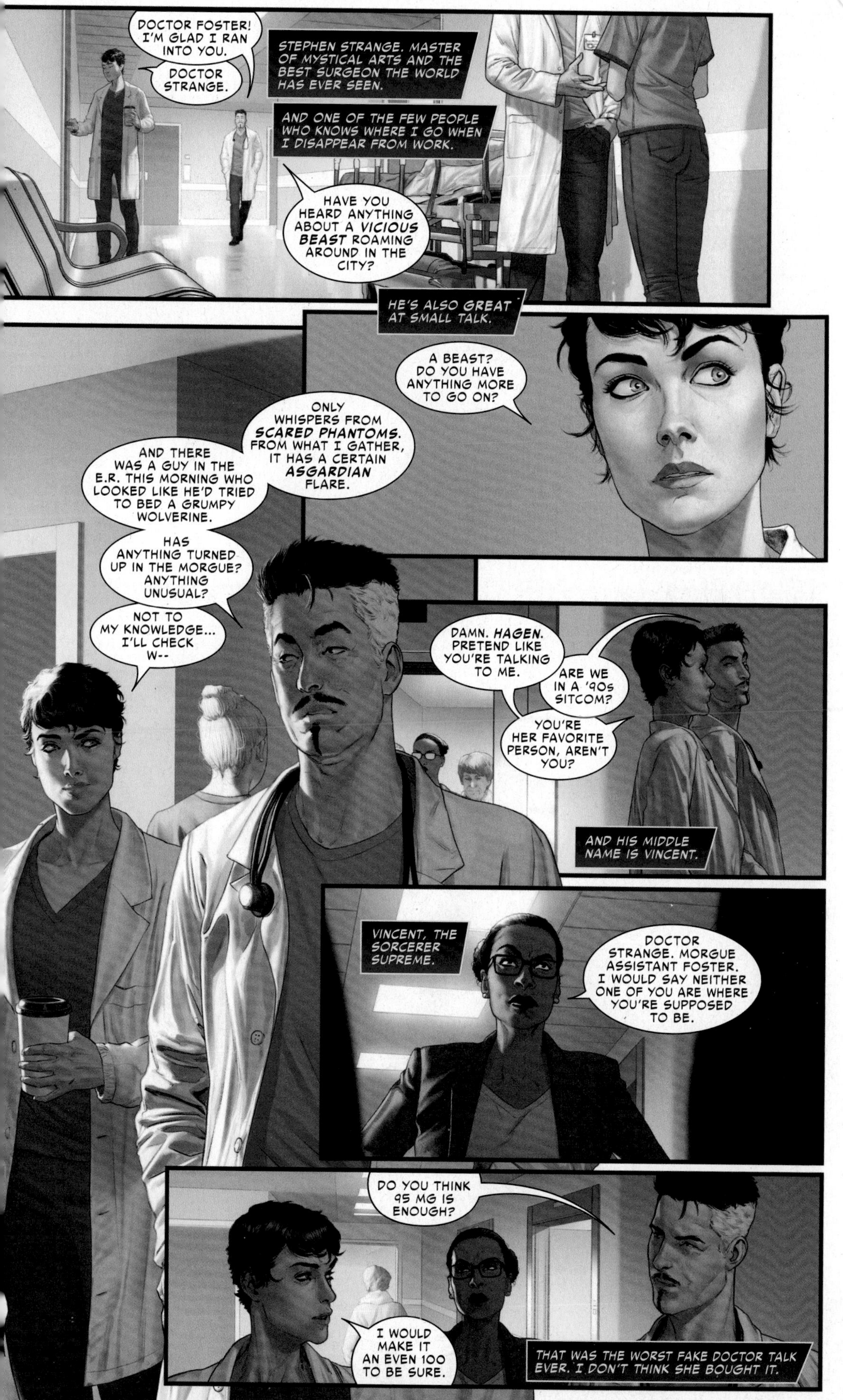

DOCTOR FOSTER! I'M GLAD I RAN INTO YOU.
DOCTOR STRANGE.
STEPHEN STRANGE. MASTER OF MYSTICAL ARTS AND THE BEST SURGEON THE WORLD HAS EVER SEEN.
AND ONE OF THE FEW PEOPLE WHO KNOWS WHERE I GO WHEN I DISAPPEAR FROM WORK.
HAVE YOU HEARD ANYTHING ABOUT A VICIOUS BEAST ROAMING AROUND IN THE CITY?
HE'S ALSO GREAT AT SMALL TALK.
A BEAST? DO YOU HAVE ANYTHING MORE TO GO ON?
ONLY WHISPERS FROM SCARED PHANTOMS. FROM WHAT I GATHER, IT HAS A CERTAIN ASGARDIAN FLARE.
AND THERE WAS A GUY IN THE E.R. THIS MORNING WHO LOOKED LIKE HE'D TRIED TO BED A GRUMPY WOLVERINE.
HAS ANYTHING TURNED UP IN THE MORGUE? ANYTHING UNUSUAL?
NOT TO MY KNOWLEDGE... I'LL CHECK W--
DAMN. HAGEN. PRETEND LIKE YOU'RE TALKING TO ME.
ARE WE IN A '90s SITCOM?
YOU'RE HER FAVORITE PERSON, AREN'T YOU?
AND HIS MIDDLE NAME IS VINCENT.
VINCENT, THE SORCERER SUPREME.
DOCTOR STRANGE. MORGUE ASSISTANT FOSTER. I WOULD SAY NEITHER ONE OF YOU ARE WHERE YOU'RE SUPPOSED TO BE.
DO YOU THINK 95 MG IS ENOUGH?
I WOULD MAKE IT AN EVEN 100 TO BE SURE.
THAT WAS THE WORST FAKE DOCTOR TALK EVER. I DON'T THINK SHE BOUGHT IT.

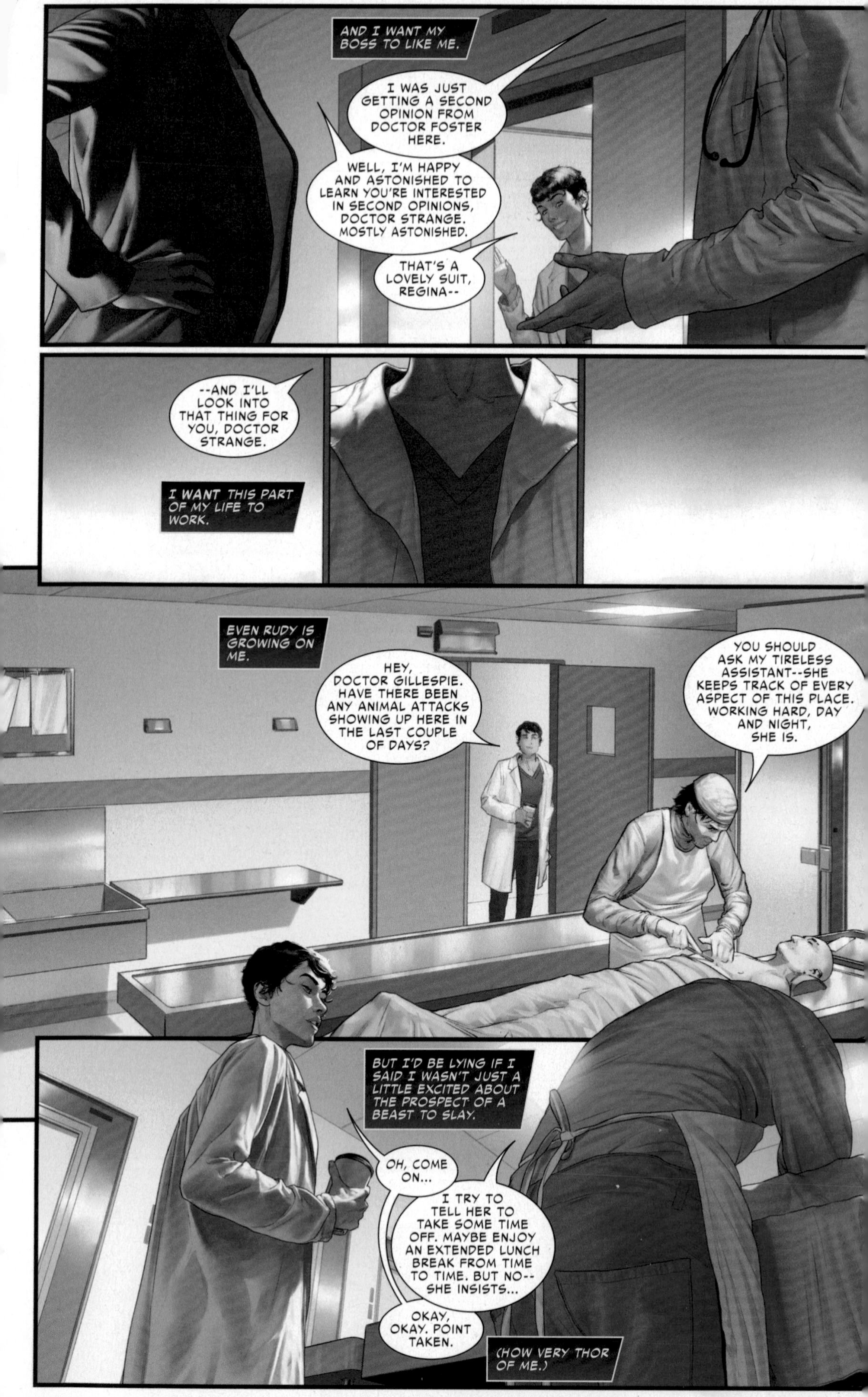
AND I WANT MY BOSS TO LIKE ME.
I WAS JUST GETTING A SECOND OPINION FROM DOCTOR FOSTER HERE.
WELL, I'M HAPPY AND ASTONISHED TO LEARN YOU'RE INTERESTED IN SECOND OPINIONS, DOCTOR STRANGE. MOSTLY ASTONISHED.
THAT'S A LOVELY SUIT, REGINA--
--AND I'LL LOOK INTO THAT THING FOR YOU, DOCTOR STRANGE.
I WANT THIS PART OF MY LIFE TO WORK.
EVEN RUDY IS GROWING ON ME.
HEY, DOCTOR GILLESPIE. HAVE THERE BEEN ANY ANIMAL ATTACKS SHOWING UP HERE IN THE LAST COUPLE OF DAYS?
YOU SHOULD ASK MY TIRELESS ASSISTANT--SHE KEEPS TRACK OF EVERY ASPECT OF THIS PLACE. WORKING HARD, DAY AND NIGHT, SHE IS.
BUT I'D BE LYING IF I SAID I WASN'T JUST A LITTLE EXCITED ABOUT THE PROSPECT OF A BEAST TO SLAY.
OH, COME ON...
I TRY TO TELL HER TO TAKE SOME TIME OFF. MAYBE ENJOY AN EXTENDED LUNCH BREAK FROM TIME TO TIME. BUT NO--SHE INSISTS...
OKAY, OKAY. POINT TAKEN.
(HOW VERY THOR OF ME.)

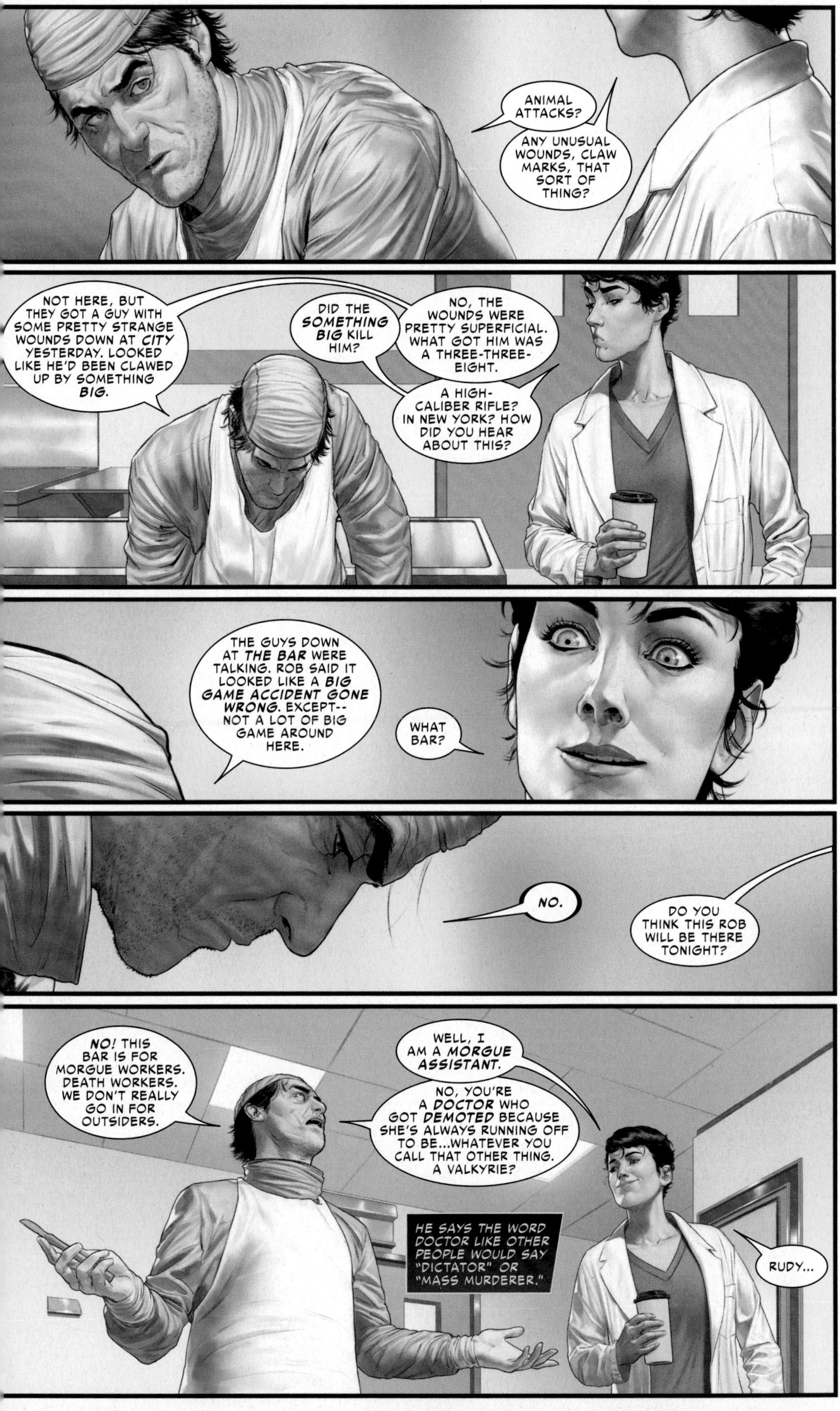
ANIMAL ATTACKS?
ANY UNUSUAL WOUNDS, CLAW MARKS, THAT SORT OF THING?
NOT HERE, BUT THEY GOT A GUY WITH SOME PRETTY STRANGE WOUNDS DOWN AT CITY YESTERDAY. LOOKED LIKE HE'D BEEN CLAWED UP BY SOMETHING BIG.
DID THE SOMETHING BIG KILL HIM?
NO, THE WOUNDS WERE PRETTY SUPERFICIAL. WHAT GOT HIM WAS A THREE-THREE-EIGHT.
A HIGH-CALIBER RIFLE? IN NEW YORK? HOW DID YOU HEAR ABOUT THIS?
THE GUYS DOWN AT THE BAR WERE TALKING. ROB SAID IT LOOKED LIKE A BIG GAME ACCIDENT GONE WRONG. EXCEPT--NOT A LOT OF BIG GAME AROUND HERE.
WHAT BAR?
DO YOU THINK THIS ROB WILL BE THERE TONIGHT?
NO.
NO! THIS BAR IS FOR MORGUE WORKERS. DEATH WORKERS. WE DON'T REALLY GO IN FOR OUTSIDERS.
WELL, I AM A MORGUE ASSISTANT.
NO, YOU'RE A DOCTOR WHO GOT DEMOTED BECAUSE SHE'S ALWAYS RUNNING OFF TO BE...WHATEVER YOU CALL THAT OTHER THING. A VALKYRIE?
HE SAYS THE WORD DOCTOR LIKE OTHER PEOPLE WOULD SAY "DICTATOR" OR "MASS MURDERER."
RUDY...

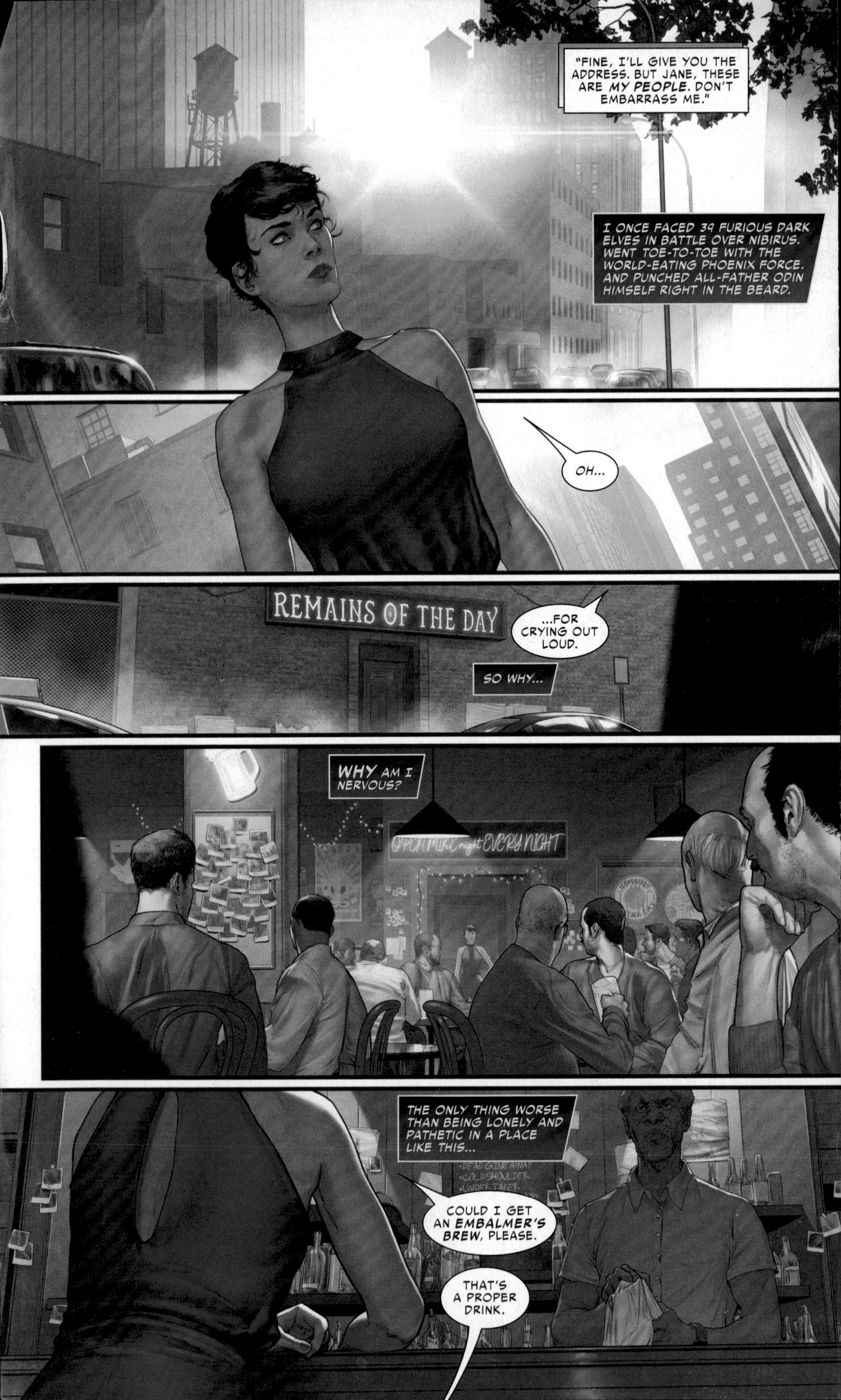

"FINE, I'LL GIVE YOU THE ADDRESS. BUT JANE, THESE ARE MY PEOPLE. DON'T EMBARRASS ME."
I ONCE FACED 39 FURIOUS DARK ELVES IN BATTLE OVER NIBIRUS. WENT TOE-TO-TOE WITH THE WORLD-EATING PHOENIX FORCE. AND PUNCHED ALL-FATHER ODIN HIMSELF RIGHT IN THE BEARD.
OH...
REMAINS OF THE DAY
...FOR CRYING OUT LOUD.
SO WHY...
WHY AM I NERVOUS?
OPEN MIKE night EVERY NIGHT
THE ONLY THING WORSE THAN BEING LONELY AND PATHETIC IN A PLACE LIKE THIS...
COULD I GET AN EMBALMER'S BREW, PLEASE.
THAT'S A PROPER DRINK.

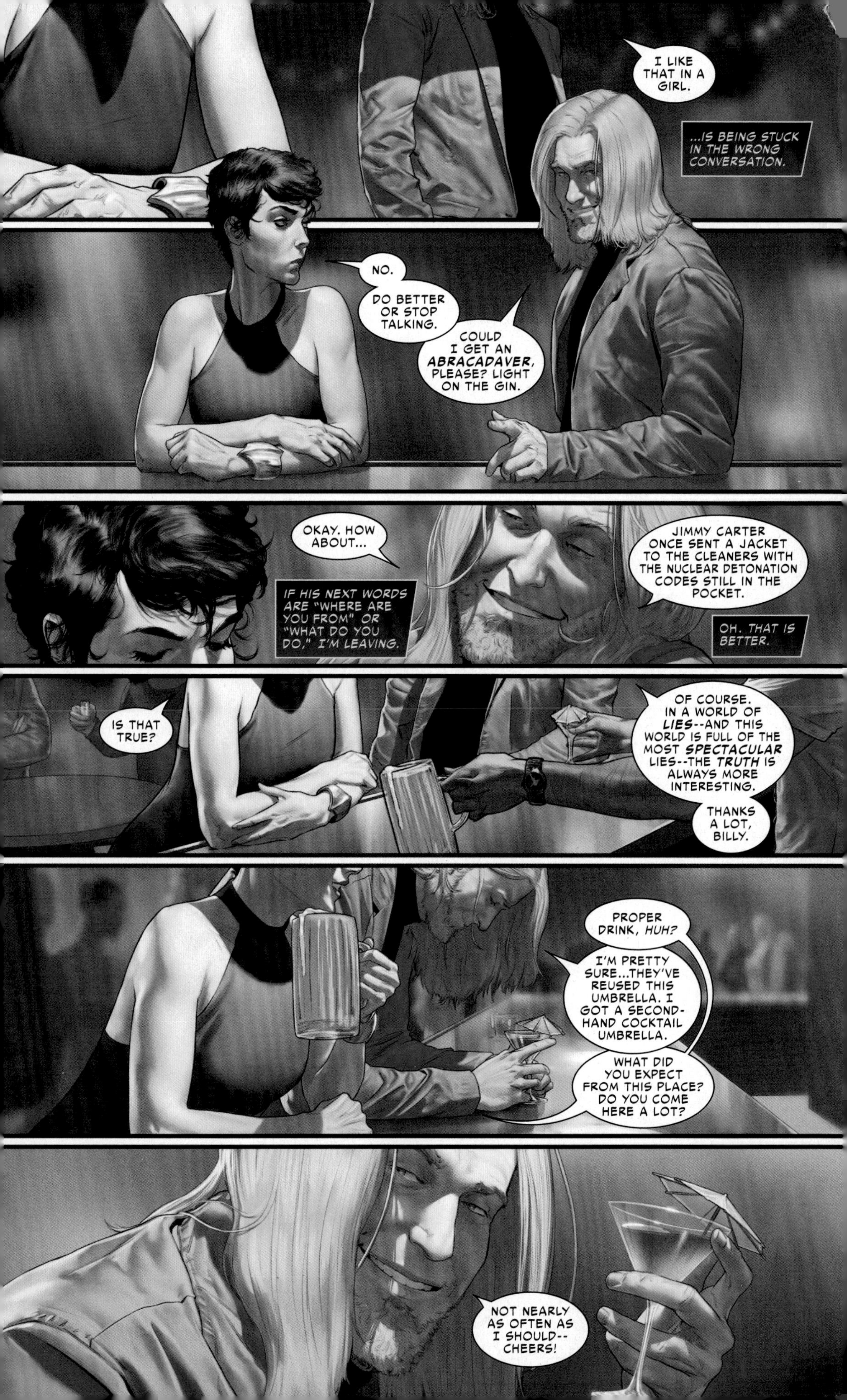
I LIKE THAT IN A GIRL.
...IS BEING STUCK IN THE WRONG CONVERSATION.
NO.
DO BETTER OR STOP TALKING.
COULD I GET AN ABRACADAVER, PLEASE? LIGHT ON THE GIN.
OKAY. HOW ABOUT...
IF HIS NEXT WORDS ARE "WHERE ARE YOU FROM" OR "WHAT DO YOU DO," I'M LEAVING.
JIMMY CARTER ONCE SENT A JACKET TO THE CLEANERS WITH THE NUCLEAR DETONATION CODES STILL IN THE POCKET.
OH. THAT IS BETTER.
IS THAT TRUE?
OF COURSE. IN A WORLD OF LIES--AND THIS WORLD IS FULL OF THE MOST SPECTACULAR LIES--THE TRUTH IS ALWAYS MORE INTERESTING.
THANKS A LOT, BILLY.
PROPER DRINK, HUH?
I'M PRETTY SURE...THEY'VE REUSED THIS UMBRELLA. I GOT A SECOND-HAND COCKTAIL UMBRELLA.
WHAT DID YOU EXPECT FROM THIS PLACE? DO YOU COME HERE A LOT?
NOT NEARLY AS OFTEN AS I SHOULD--CHEERS!

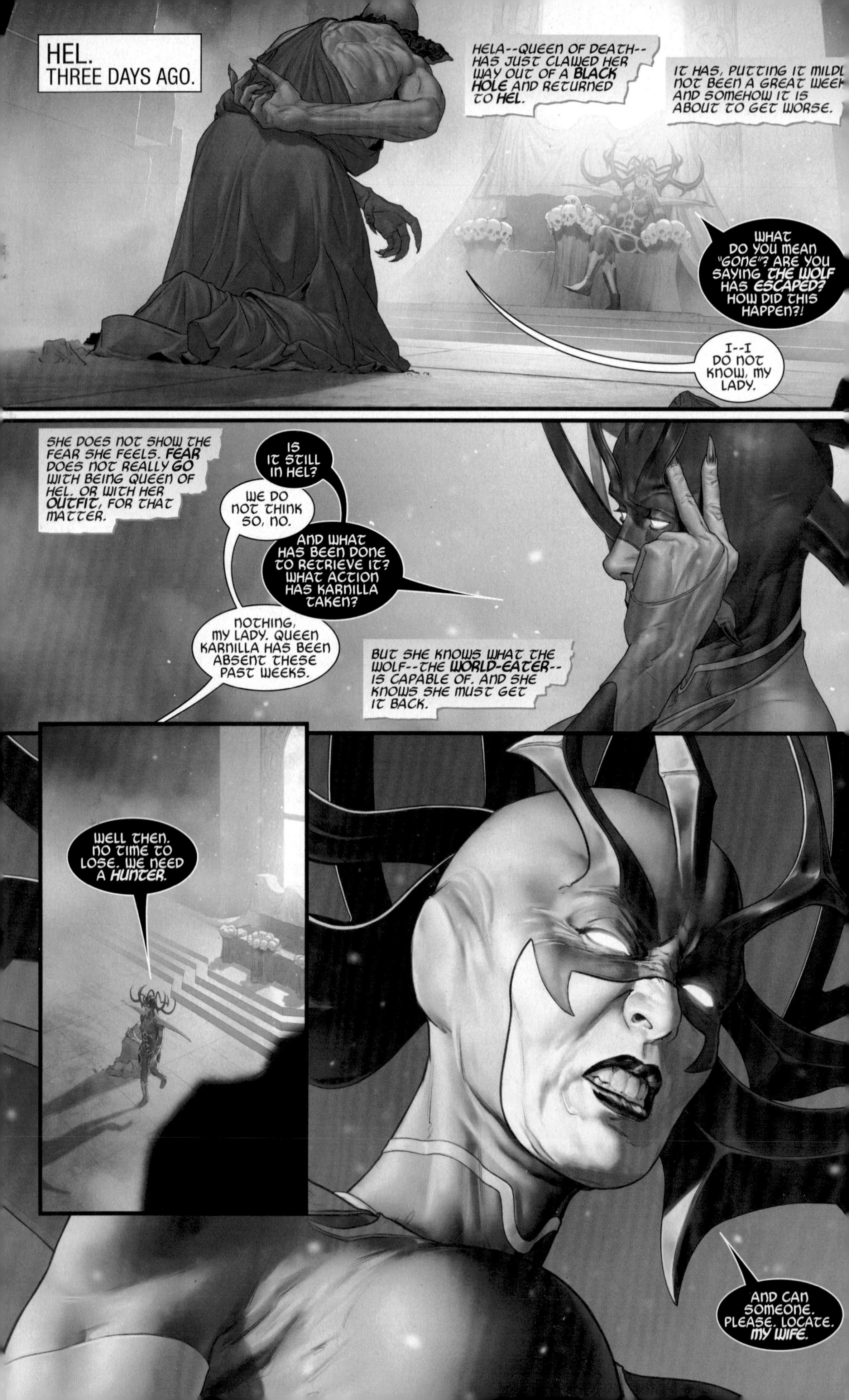
HEL.
THREE DAYS AGO.
HELA--QUEEN OF DEATH--HAS JUST CLAWED HER WAY OUT OF A BLACK HOLE AND RETURNED TO HEL.
IT HAS, PUTTING IT MILDL NOT BEEN A GREAT WEEK AND SOMEHOW IT IS ABOUT TO GET WORSE.
WHAT DO YOU MEAN "GONE"? ARE YOU SAYING THE WOLF HAS ESCAPED? HOW DID THIS HAPPEN?!
I--I DO NOT KNOW, MY LADY.
SHE DOES NOT SHOW THE FEAR SHE FEELS. FEAR DOES NOT REALLY GO WITH BEING QUEEN OF HEL. OR WITH HER OUTFIT, FOR THAT MATTER.
IS IT STILL IN HEL?
WE DO NOT THINK SO, NO.
AND WHAT HAS BEEN DONE TO RETRIEVE IT? WHAT ACTION HAS KARNILLA TAKEN?
NOTHING, MY LADY. QUEEN KARNILLA HAS BEEN ABSENT THESE PAST WEEKS.
BUT SHE KNOWS WHAT THE WOLF--THE WORLD-EATER--IS CAPABLE OF. AND SHE KNOWS SHE MUST GET IT BACK.
WELL THEN. NO TIME TO LOSE. WE NEED A HUNTER.
AND CAN SOMEONE. PLEASE. LOCATE. MY WIFE.

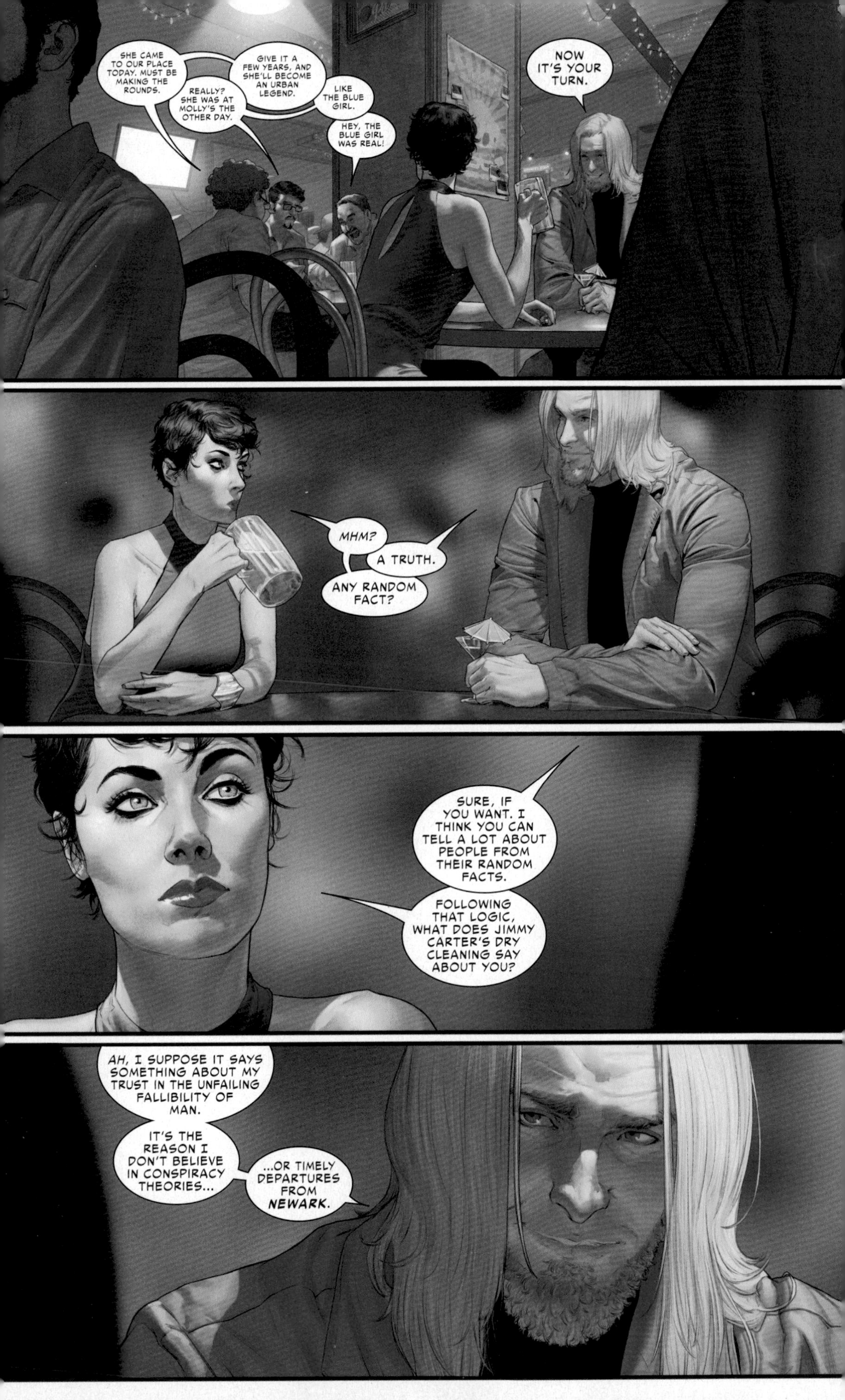
SHE CAME TO OUR PLACE TODAY. MUST BE MAKING THE ROUNDS.
REALLY? SHE WAS AT MOLLY'S THE OTHER DAY.
GIVE IT A FEW YEARS, AND SHE'LL BECOME AN URBAN LEGEND.
LIKE THE BLUE GIRL.
HEY, THE BLUE GIRL WAS REAL!
NOW IT'S YOUR TURN.
MHM?
A TRUTH.
ANY RANDOM FACT?
SURE, IF YOU WANT. I THINK YOU CAN TELL A LOT ABOUT PEOPLE FROM THEIR RANDOM FACTS.
FOLLOWING THAT LOGIC, WHAT DOES JIMMY CARTER'S DRY CLEANING SAY ABOUT YOU?
AH, I SUPPOSE IT SAYS SOMETHING ABOUT MY TRUST IN THE UNFAILING FALLIBILITY OF MAN.
IT'S THE REASON I DON'T BELIEVE IN CONSPIRACY THEORIES...
...OR TIMELY DEPARTURES FROM NEWARK.

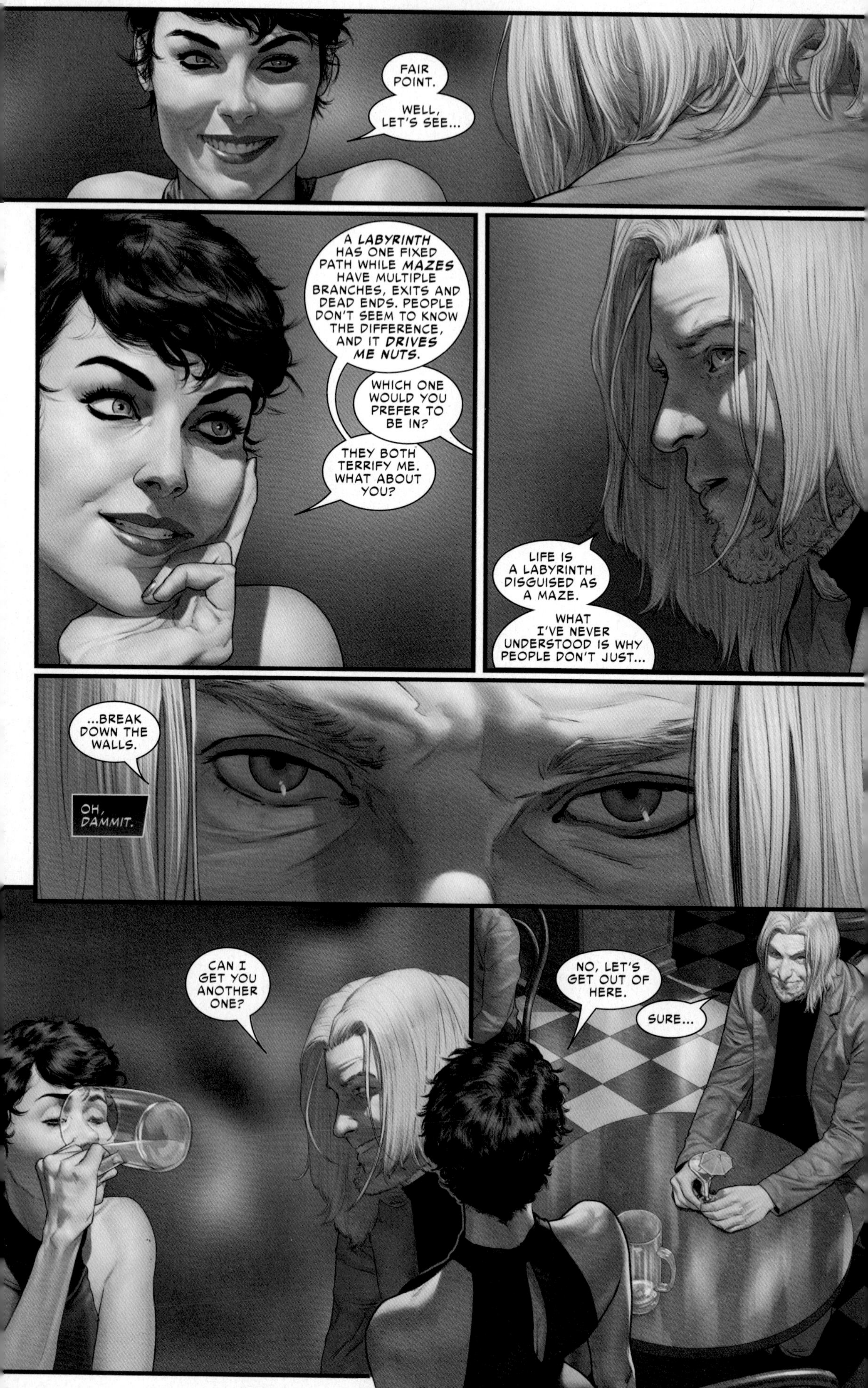
FAIR POINT.
WELL, LET'S SEE...
A *LABYRINTH* HAS ONE FIXED PATH WHILE *MAZES* HAVE MULTIPLE BRANCHES, EXITS AND DEAD ENDS. PEOPLE DON'T SEEM TO KNOW THE DIFFERENCE, AND IT *DRIVES ME NUTS*.
WHICH ONE WOULD YOU PREFER TO BE IN?
THEY BOTH TERRIFY ME. WHAT ABOUT YOU?
LIFE IS A LABYRINTH DISGUISED AS A MAZE.
WHAT I'VE NEVER UNDERSTOOD IS WHY PEOPLE DON'T JUST...
...BREAK DOWN THE WALLS.
OH, DAMMIT.
CAN I GET YOU ANOTHER ONE?
NO, LET'S GET OUT OF HERE.
SURE...

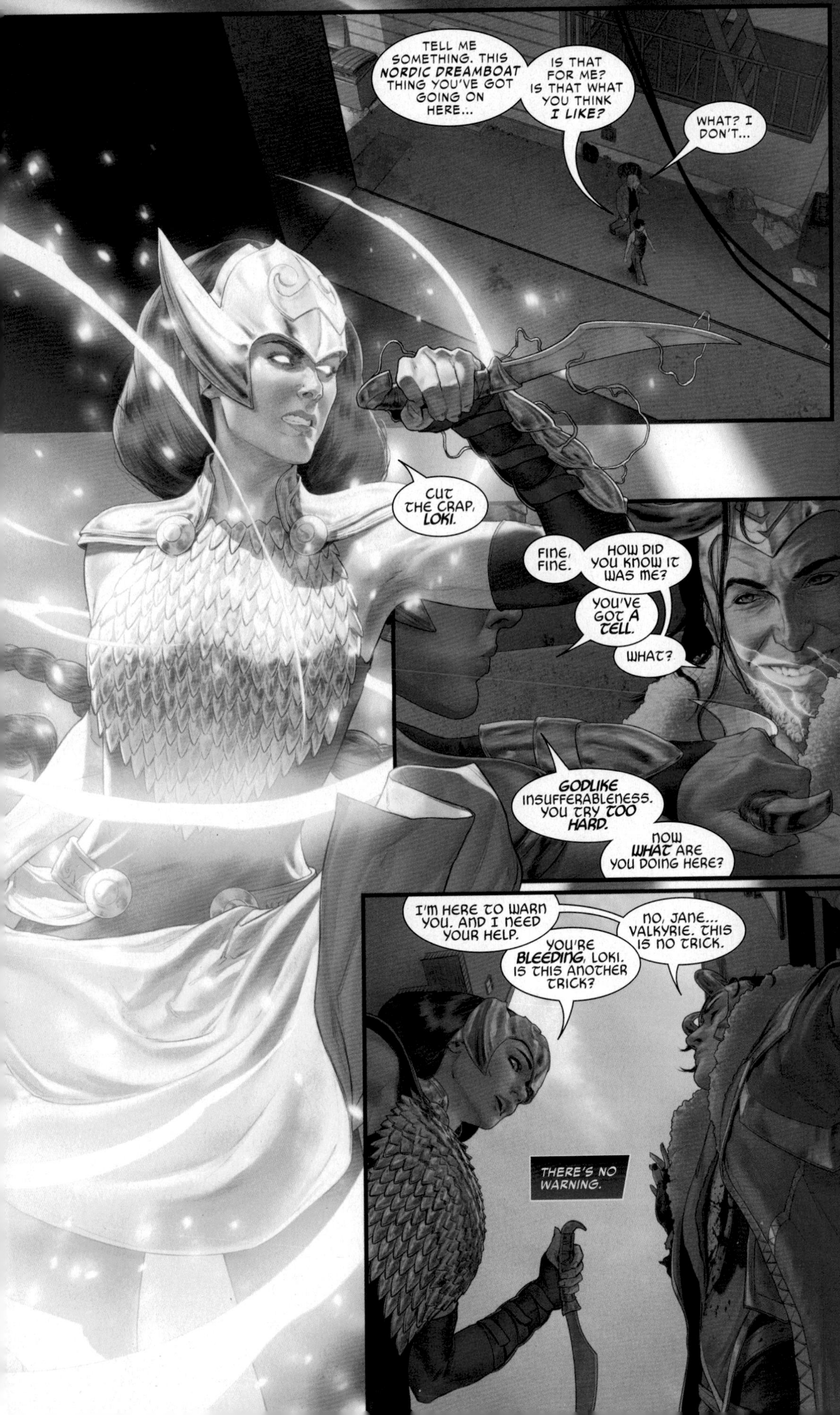
TELL ME SOMETHING. THIS NORDIC DREAMBOAT THING YOU'VE GOT GOING ON HERE...
IS THAT FOR ME? IS THAT WHAT YOU THINK I LIKE?
WHAT? I DON'T...
CUT THE CRAP, LOKI.
FINE, FINE.
HOW DID YOU KNOW IT WAS ME?
YOU'VE GOT A TELL.
WHAT?
GODLIKE INSUFFERABLENESS. YOU TRY TOO HARD.
NOW WHAT ARE YOU DOING HERE?
I'M HERE TO WARN YOU. AND I NEED YOUR HELP.
YOU'RE BLEEDING, LOKI. IS THIS ANOTHER TRICK?
NO, JANE... VALKYRIE. THIS IS NO TRICK.
THERE'S NO WARNING.

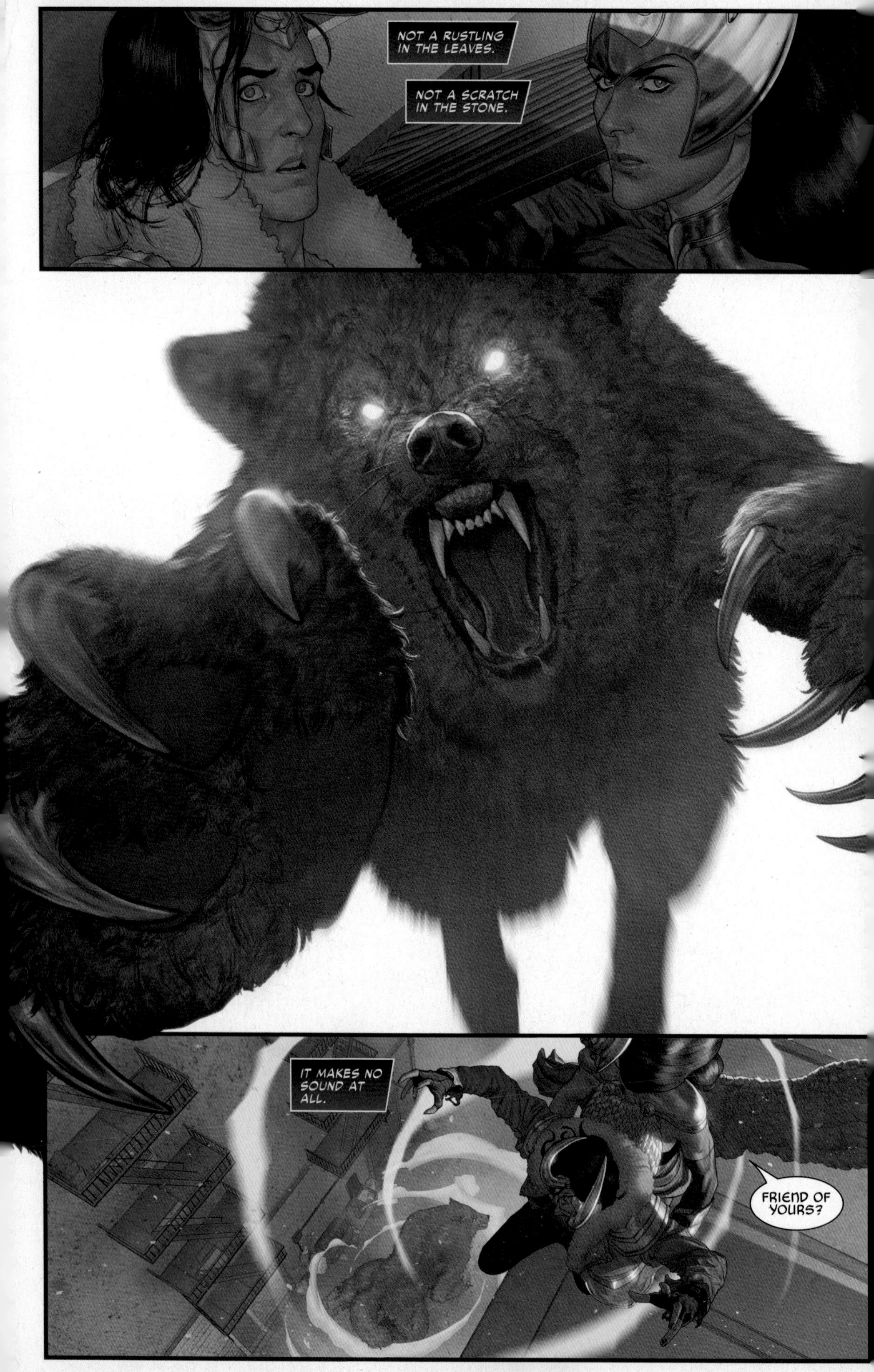
NOT A RUSTLING IN THE LEAVES.
NOT A SCRATCH IN THE STONE.
IT MAKES NO SOUND AT ALL.
FRIEND OF YOURS?

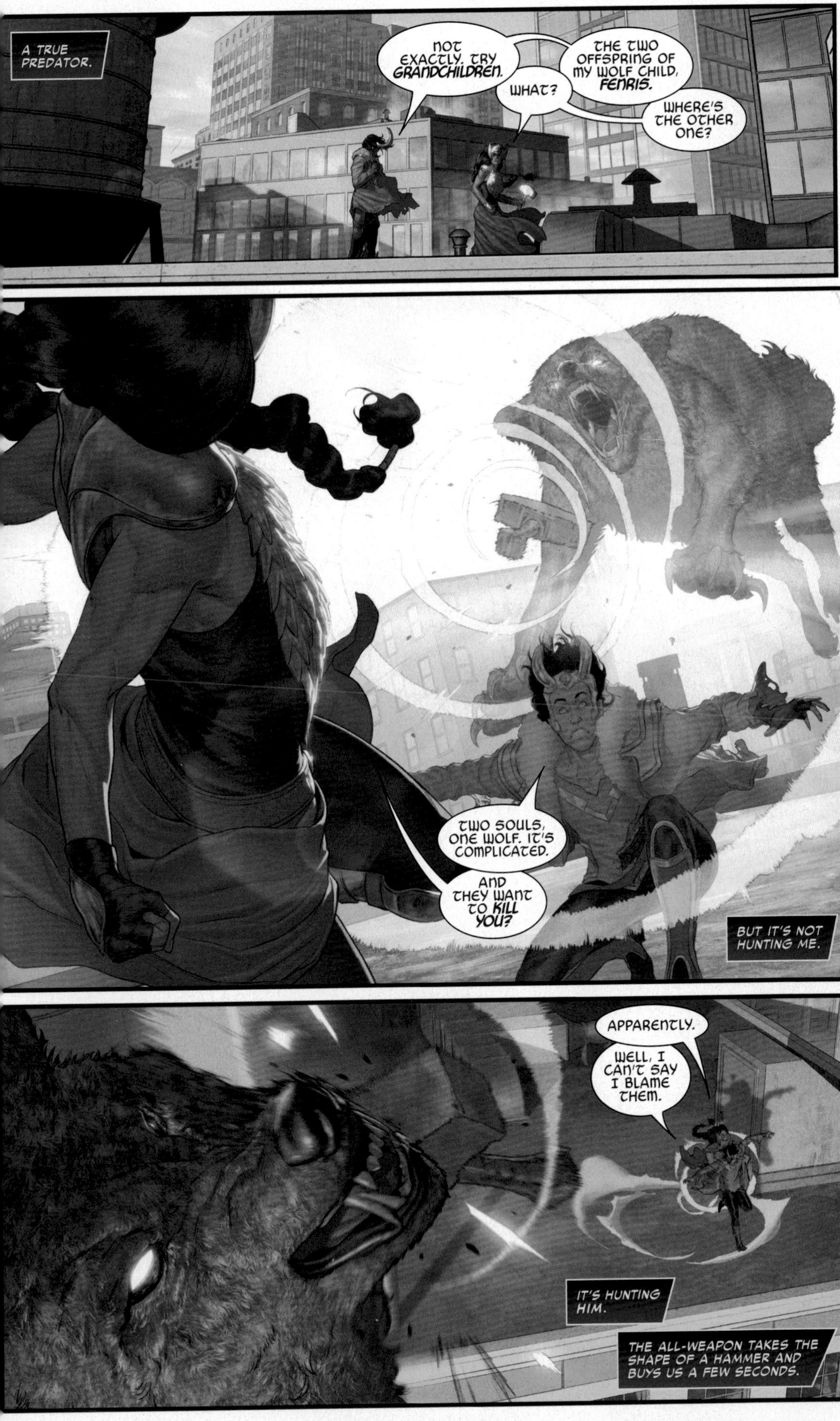
A TRUE PREDATOR.
NOT EXACTLY. TRY GRANDCHILDREN.
WHAT?
THE TWO OFFSPRING OF MY WOLF CHILD, FENRIS.
WHERE'S THE OTHER ONE?
TWO SOULS, ONE WOLF. IT'S COMPLICATED.
AND THEY WANT TO KILL YOU?
BUT IT'S NOT HUNTING ME.
APPARENTLY.
WELL, I CAN'T SAY I BLAME THEM.
IT'S HUNTING HIM.
THE ALL-WEAPON TAKES THE SHAPE OF A HAMMER AND BUYS US A FEW SECONDS.

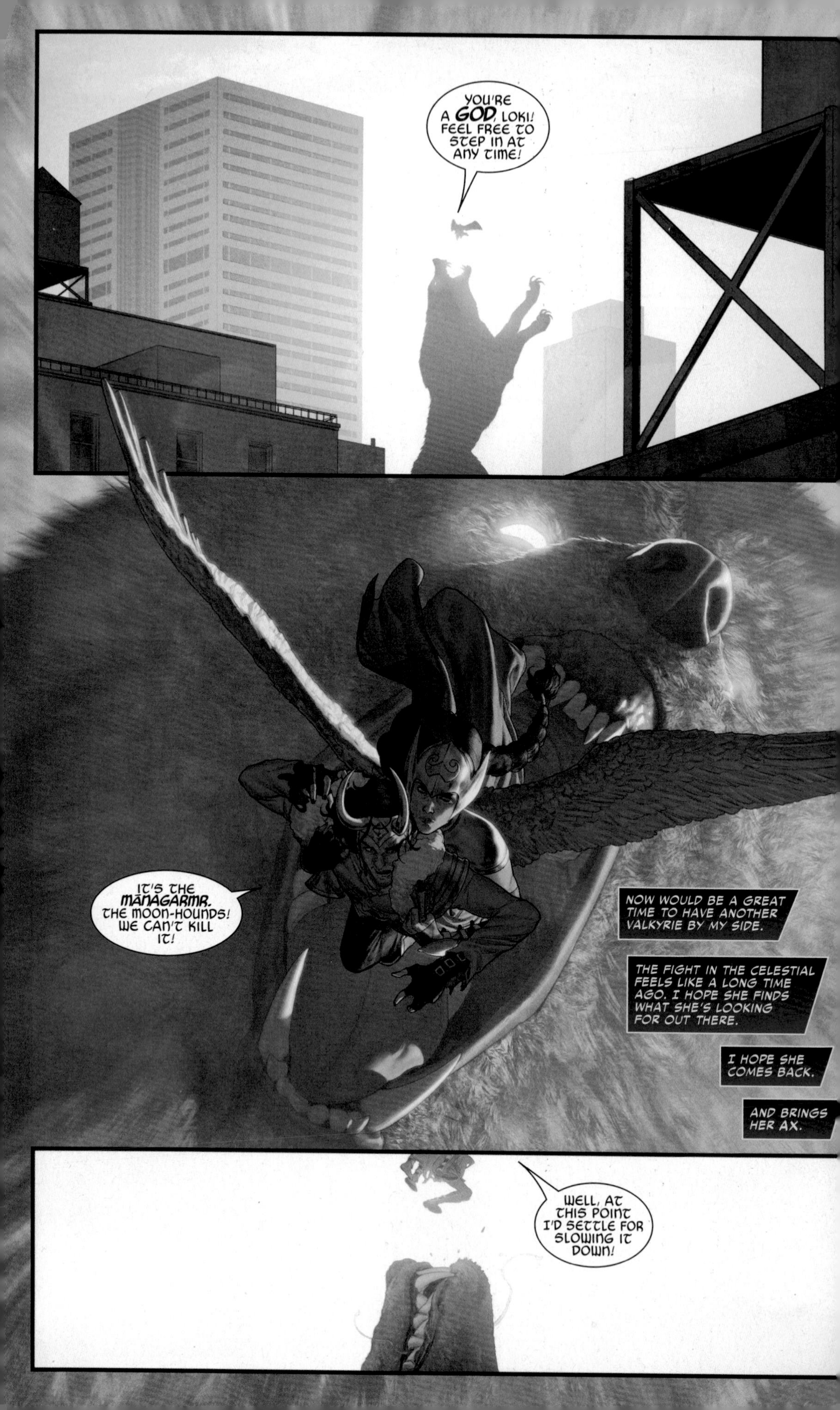

YOU'RE A GOD, LOKI! FEEL FREE TO STEP IN AT ANY TIME!
IT'S THE MÁNAGARMR. THE MOON-HOUNDS! WE CAN'T KILL IT!
NOW WOULD BE A GREAT TIME TO HAVE ANOTHER VALKYRIE BY MY SIDE.
THE FIGHT IN THE CELESTIAL FEELS LIKE A LONG TIME AGO. I HOPE SHE FINDS WHAT SHE'S LOOKING FOR OUT THERE.
I HOPE SHE COMES BACK.
AND BRINGS HER AX.
WELL, AT THIS POINT I'D SETTLE FOR SLOWING IT DOWN!

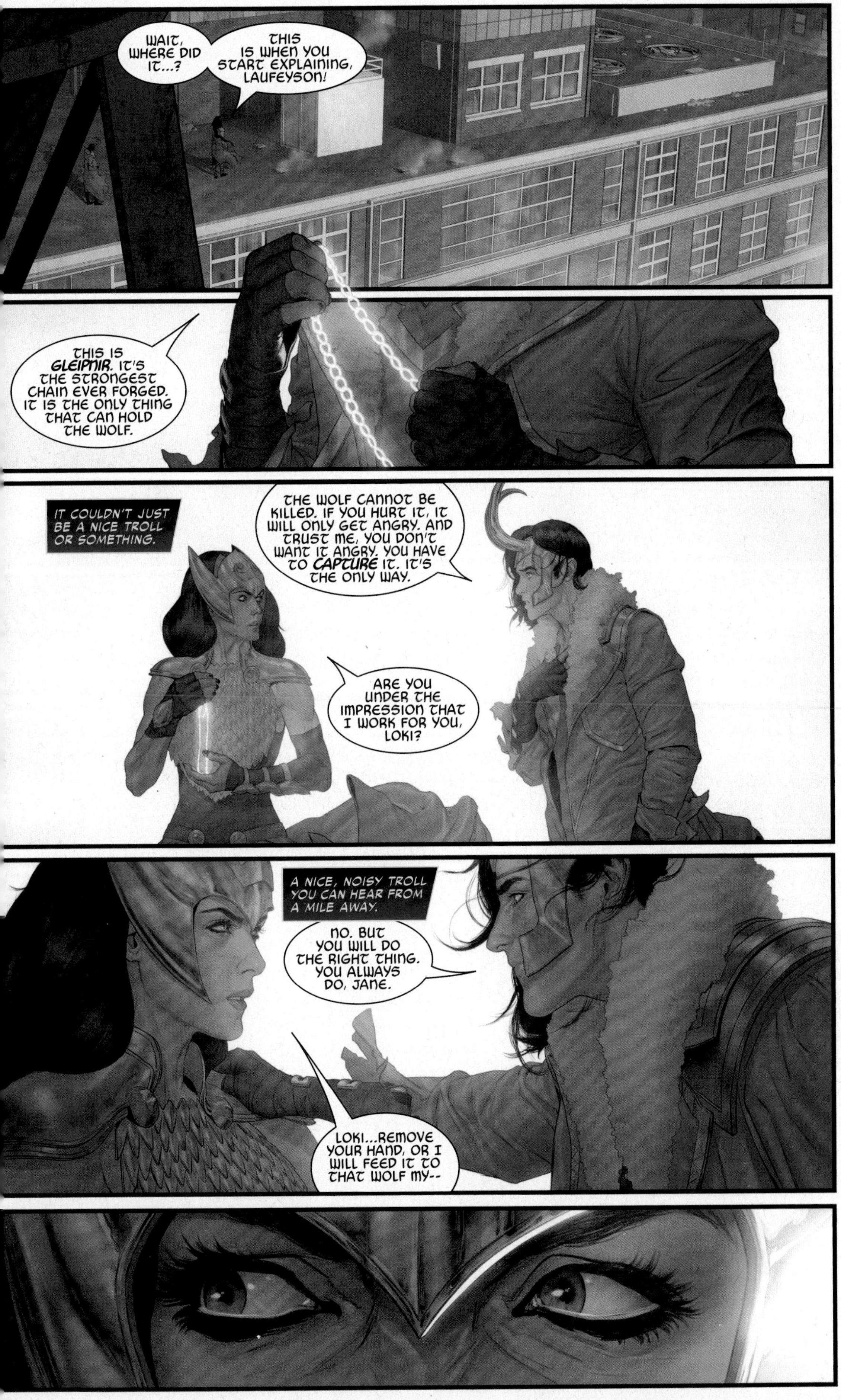

WAIT, WHERE DID IT...?
THIS IS WHEN YOU START EXPLAINING, LAUFEYSON!
THIS IS GLEIPNIR. IT'S THE STRONGEST CHAIN EVER FORGED. IT IS THE ONLY THING THAT CAN HOLD THE WOLF.
IT COULDN'T JUST BE A NICE TROLL OR SOMETHING.
THE WOLF CANNOT BE KILLED. IF YOU HURT IT, IT WILL ONLY GET ANGRY. AND TRUST ME, YOU DON'T WANT IT ANGRY. YOU HAVE TO CAPTURE IT. IT'S THE ONLY WAY.
ARE YOU UNDER THE IMPRESSION THAT I WORK FOR YOU, LOKI?
A NICE, NOISY TROLL YOU CAN HEAR FROM A MILE AWAY.
NO. BUT YOU WILL DO THE RIGHT THING. YOU ALWAYS DO, JANE.
LOKI...REMOVE YOUR HAND, OR I WILL FEED IT TO THAT WOLF MY--

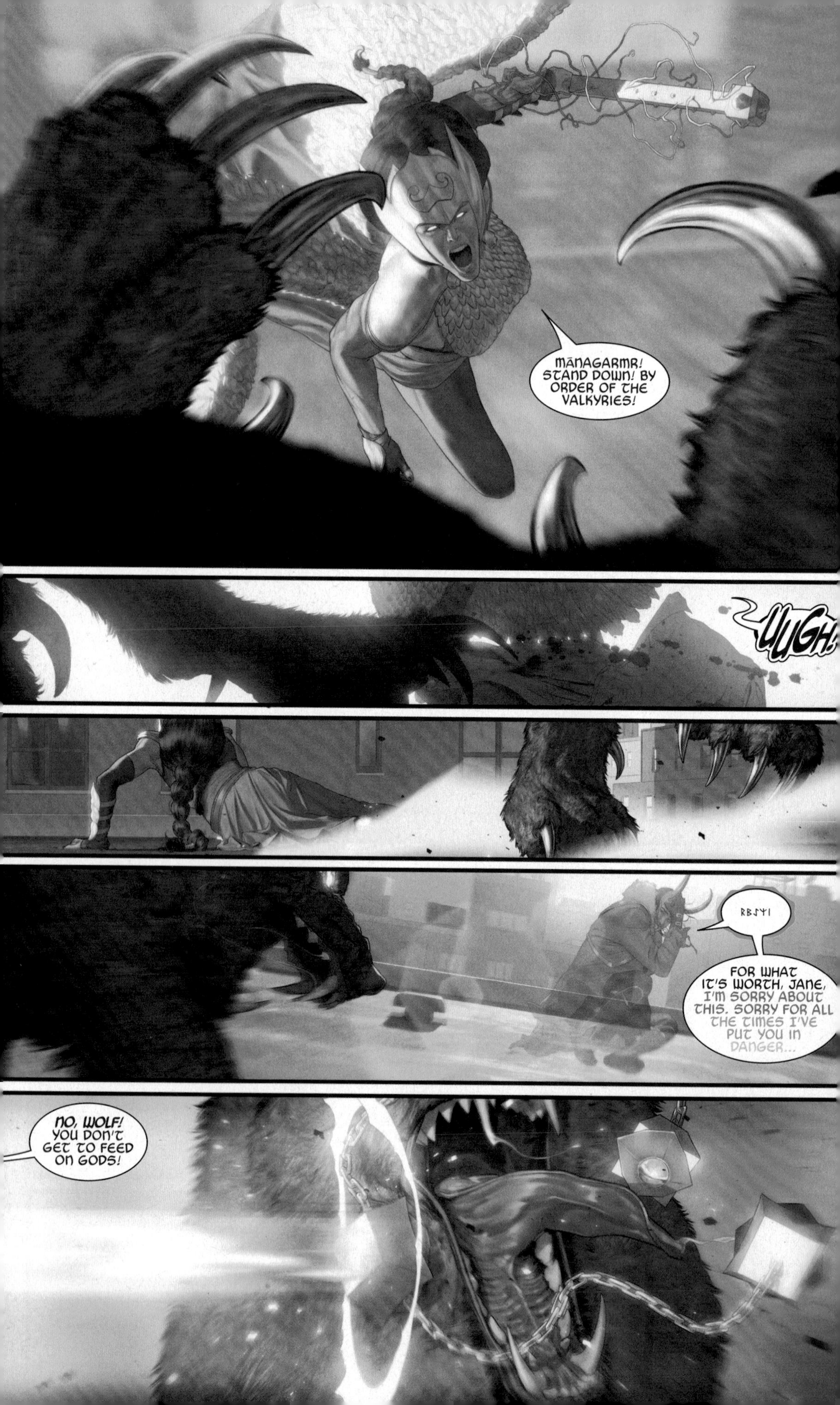
MĀNAGARMR! STAND DOWN! BY ORDER OF THE VALKYRIES!
UUGH!
RBSYI
FOR WHAT IT'S WORTH, JANE, I'M SORRY ABOUT THIS. SORRY FOR ALL THE TIMES I'VE PUT YOU IN DANGER...
NO, WOLF! YOU DON'T GET TO FEED ON GODS!

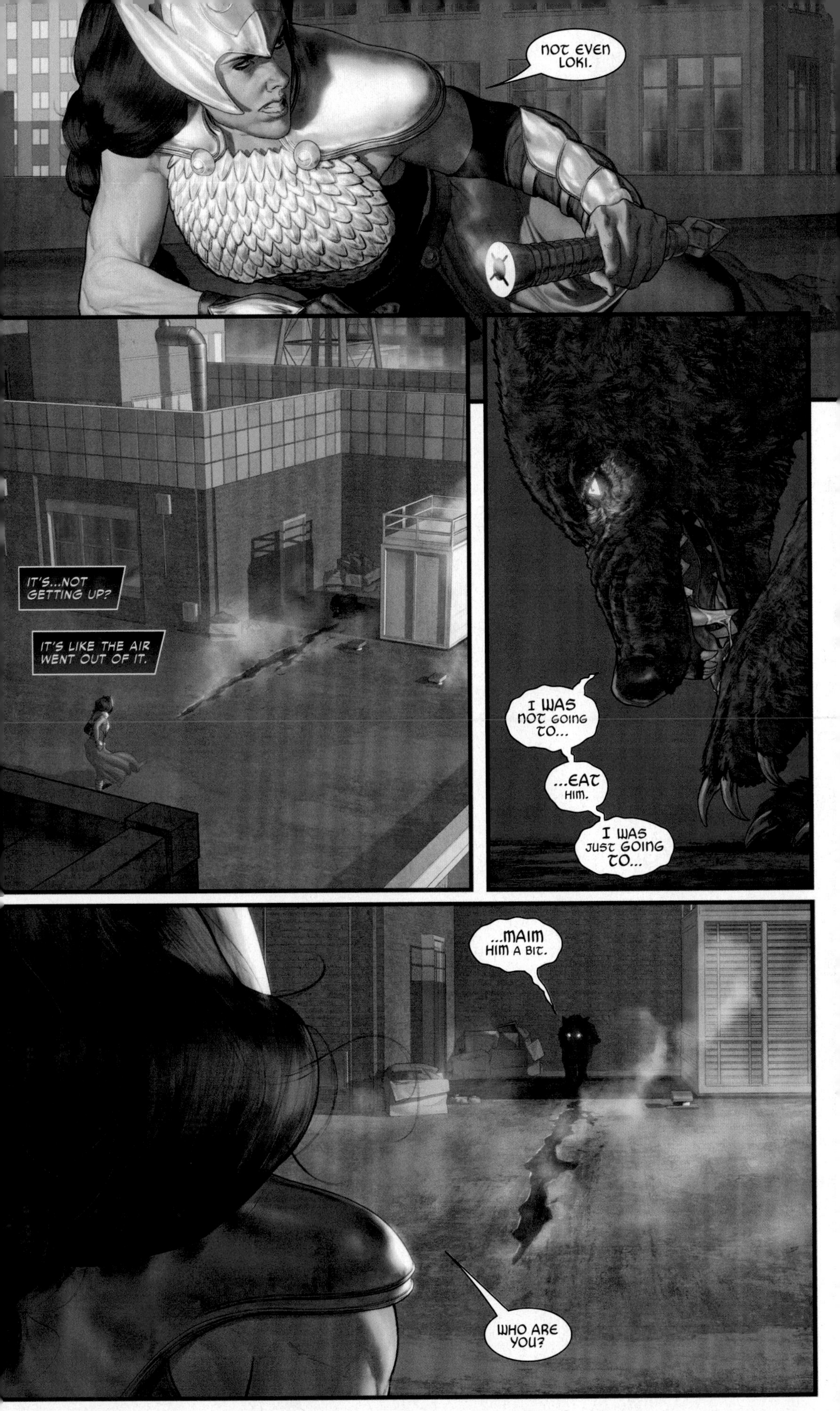

NOT EVEN LOKI.
IT'S...NOT GETTING UP?
IT'S LIKE THE AIR WENT OUT OF IT.
I WAS NOT GOING TO...
...EAT HIM.
I WAS JUST GOING TO...
...MAIM HIM A BIT.
WHO ARE YOU?

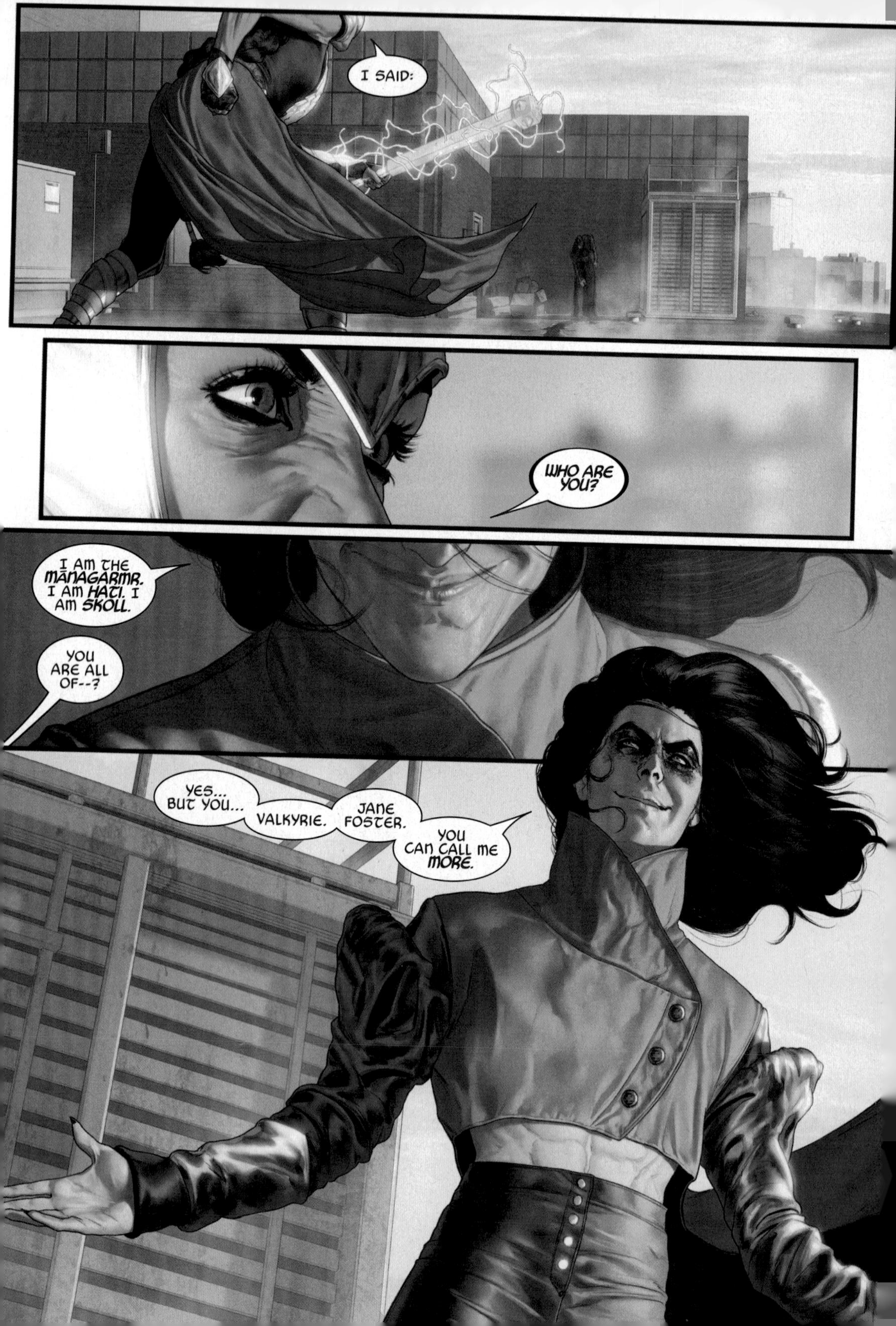
I SAID:
WHO ARE YOU?
I AM THE MÁNAGARMR. I AM HATI. I AM SKOLL.
YOU ARE ALL OF--?
YES... BUT YOU...
VALKYRIE.
JANE FOSTER.
YOU CAN CALL ME MORE.

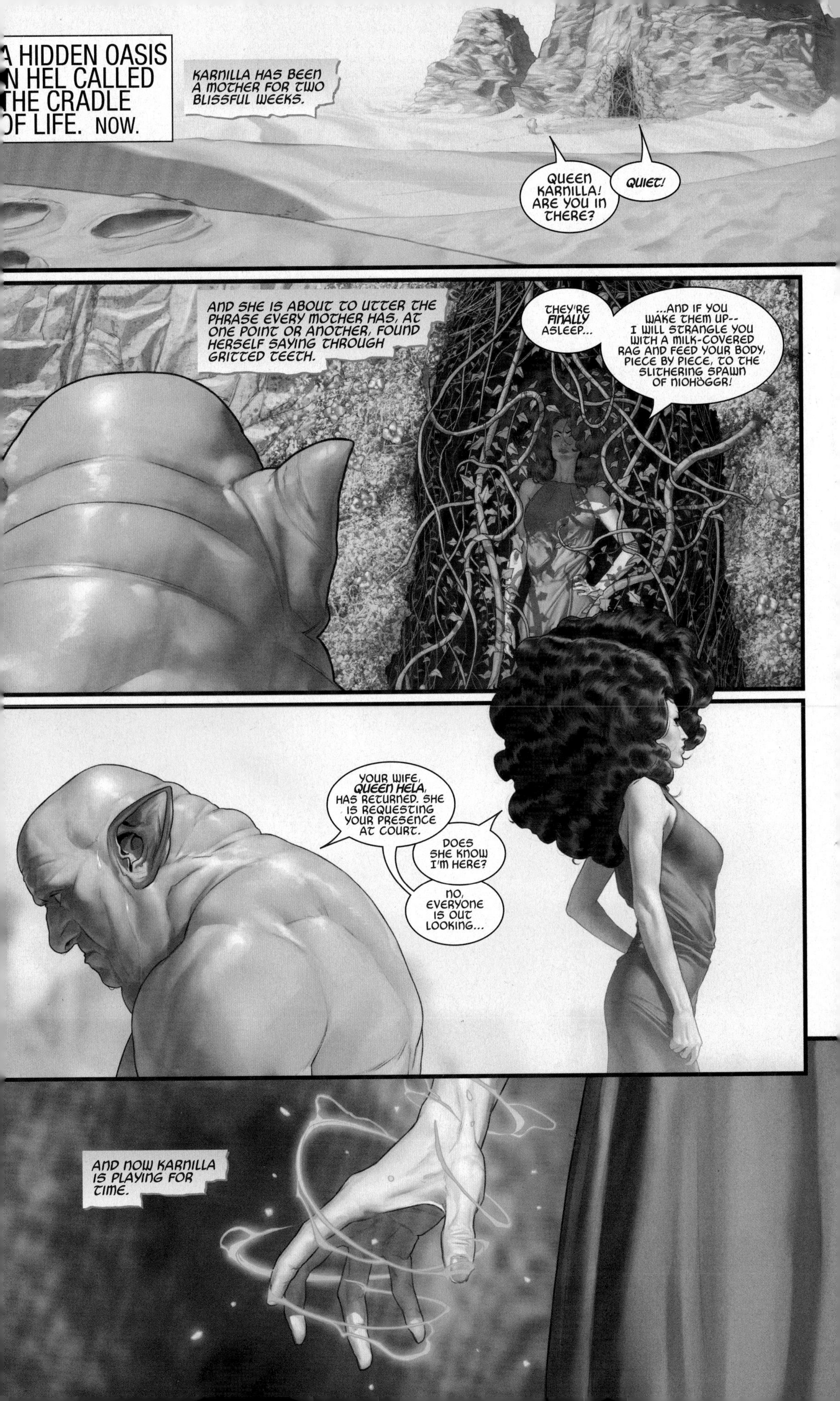
A HIDDEN OASIS
N HEL CALLED
THE CRADLE
OF LIFE. NOW.
KARNILLA HAS BEEN A MOTHER FOR TWO BLISSFUL WEEKS.
QUEEN KARNILLA! ARE YOU IN THERE?
QUIET!
AND SHE IS ABOUT TO UTTER THE PHRASE EVERY MOTHER HAS, AT ONE POINT OR ANOTHER, FOUND HERSELF SAYING THROUGH GRITTED TEETH.
THEY'RE FINALLY ASLEEP...
...AND IF YOU WAKE THEM UP-- I WILL STRANGLE YOU WITH A MILK-COVERED RAG AND FEED YOUR BODY, PIECE BY PIECE, TO THE SLITHERING SPAWN OF NIÐHÖGGR!
YOUR WIFE, QUEEN HELA, HAS RETURNED. SHE IS REQUESTING YOUR PRESENCE AT COURT.
DOES SHE KNOW I'M HERE?
NO, EVERYONE IS OUT LOOKING...
AND NOW KARNILLA IS PLAYING FOR TIME.

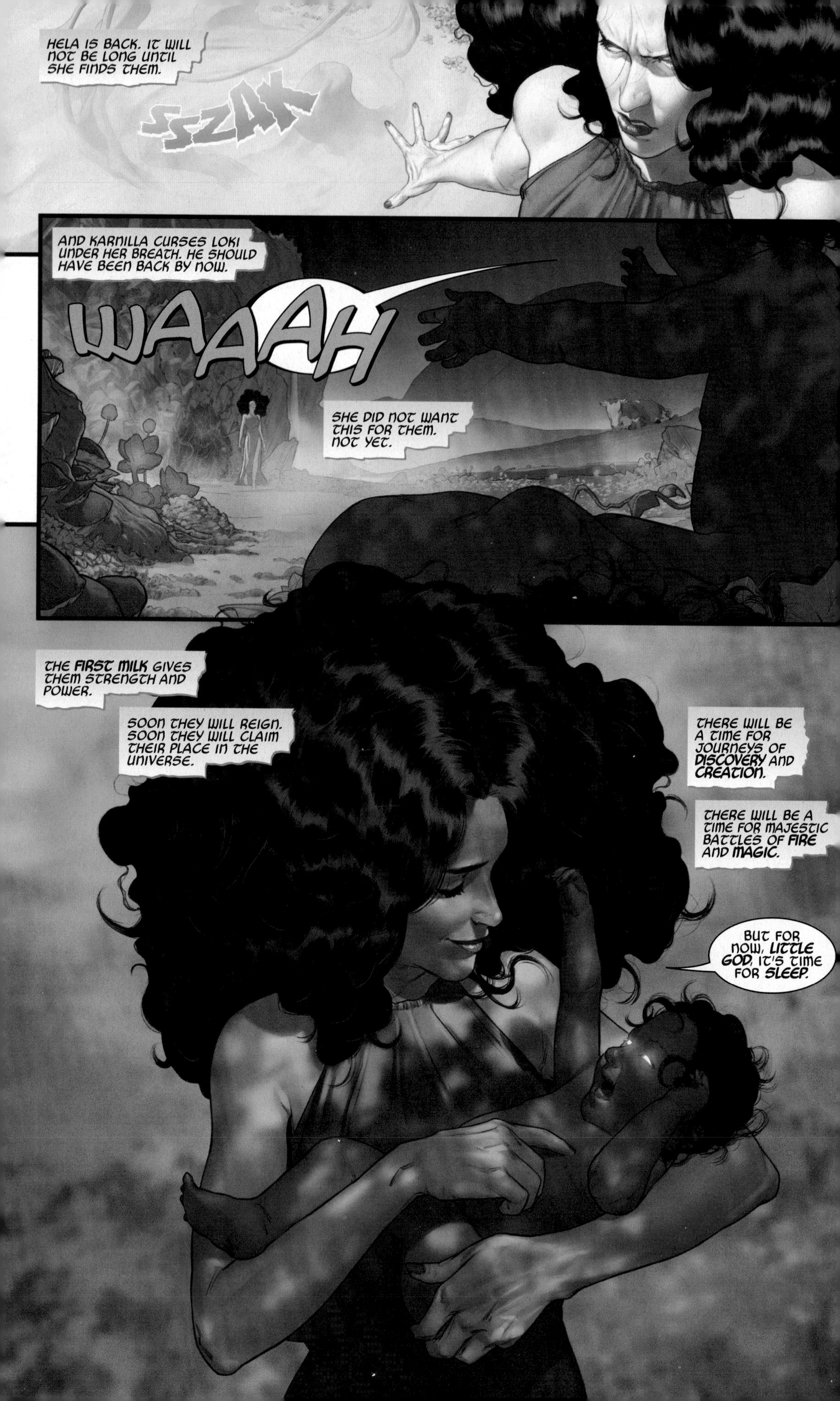
HELA IS BACK. IT WILL NOT BE LONG UNTIL SHE FINDS THEM.
SSZAK
AND KARNILLA CURSES LOKI UNDER HER BREATH. HE SHOULD HAVE BEEN BACK BY NOW.
WAAAH
SHE DID NOT WANT THIS FOR THEM. NOT YET.
THE FIRST MILK GIVES THEM STRENGTH AND POWER.
SOON THEY WILL REIGN. SOON THEY WILL CLAIM THEIR PLACE IN THE UNIVERSE.
THERE WILL BE A TIME FOR JOURNEYS OF DISCOVERY AND CREATION.
THERE WILL BE A TIME FOR MAJESTIC BATTLES OF FIRE AND MAGIC.
BUT FOR NOW, LITTLE GOD, IT'S TIME FOR SLEEP.

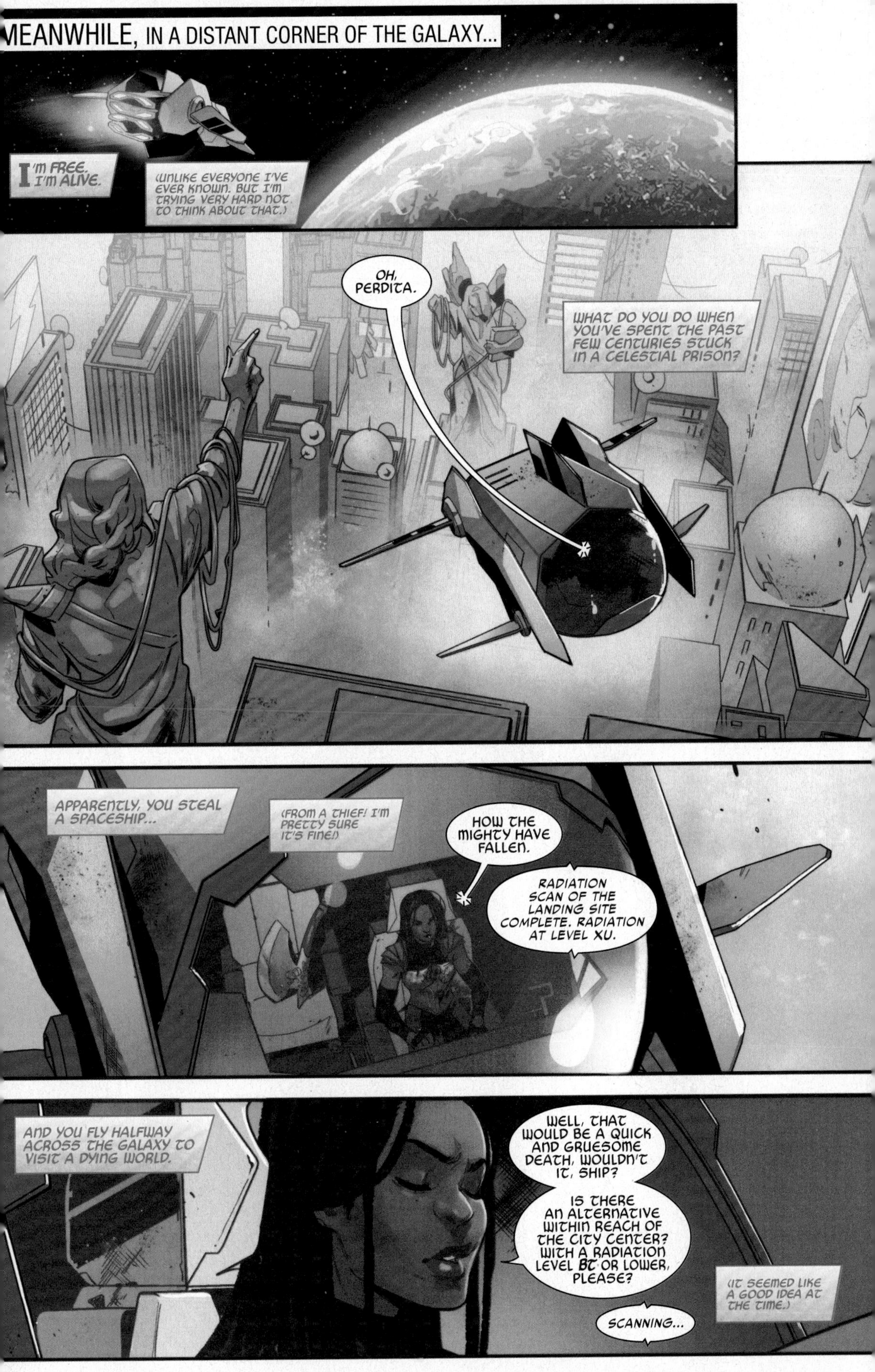
MEANWHILE, IN A DISTANT CORNER OF THE GALAXY...
I'M FREE. I'M ALIVE.
(UNLIKE EVERYONE I'VE EVER KNOWN. BUT I'M TRYING VERY HARD NOT TO THINK ABOUT THAT.)
OH, PERDITA.
WHAT DO YOU DO WHEN YOU'VE SPENT THE PAST FEW CENTURIES STUCK IN A CELESTIAL PRISON?
APPARENTLY, YOU STEAL A SPACESHIP...
(FROM A THIEF! I'M PRETTY SURE IT'S FINE!)
HOW THE MIGHTY HAVE FALLEN.
RADIATION SCAN OF THE LANDING SITE COMPLETE. RADIATION AT LEVEL XU.
AND YOU FLY HALFWAY ACROSS THE GALAXY TO VISIT A DYING WORLD.
WELL, THAT WOULD BE A QUICK AND GRUESOME DEATH, WOULDN'T IT, SHIP?
IS THERE AN ALTERNATIVE WITHIN REACH OF THE CITY CENTER? WITH A RADIATION LEVEL BT OR LOWER, PLEASE?
(IT SEEMED LIKE A GOOD IDEA AT THE TIME.)
SCANNING...

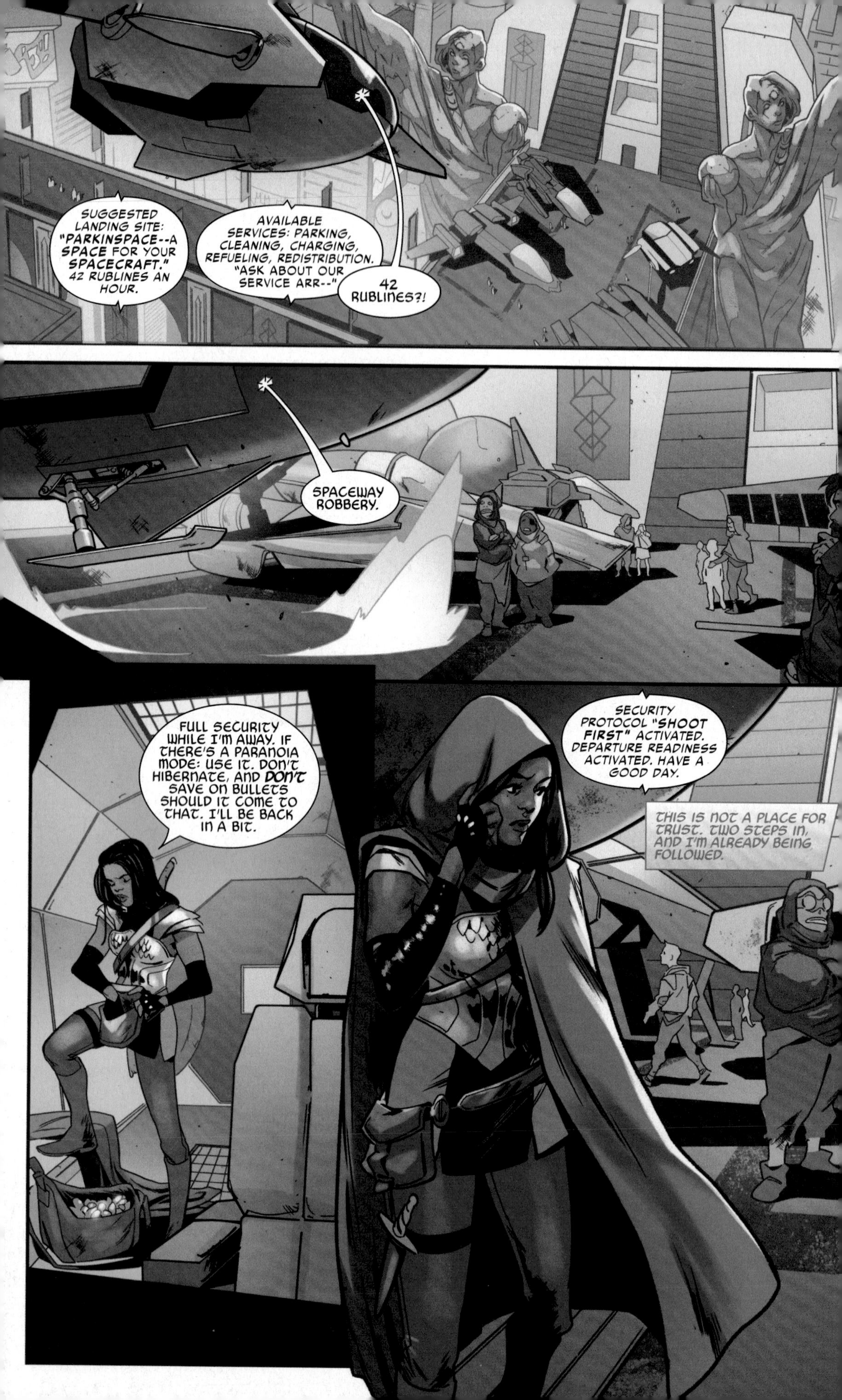
SUGGESTED LANDING SITE: "PARKINSPACE--A SPACE FOR YOUR SPACECRAFT." 42 RUBLINES AN HOUR.
AVAILABLE SERVICES: PARKING, CLEANING, CHARGING, REFUELING, REDISTRIBUTION. "ASK ABOUT OUR SERVICE ARR--"
42 RUBLINES?!
SPACEWAY ROBBERY.
FULL SECURITY WHILE I'M AWAY. IF THERE'S A PARANOIA MODE: USE IT. DON'T HIBERNATE, AND DON'T SAVE ON BULLETS SHOULD IT COME TO THAT. I'LL BE BACK IN A BIT.
SECURITY PROTOCOL "SHOOT FIRST" ACTIVATED. DEPARTURE READINESS ACTIVATED. HAVE A GOOD DAY.
THIS IS NOT A PLACE FOR TRUST. TWO STEPS IN, AND I'M ALREADY BEING FOLLOWED.

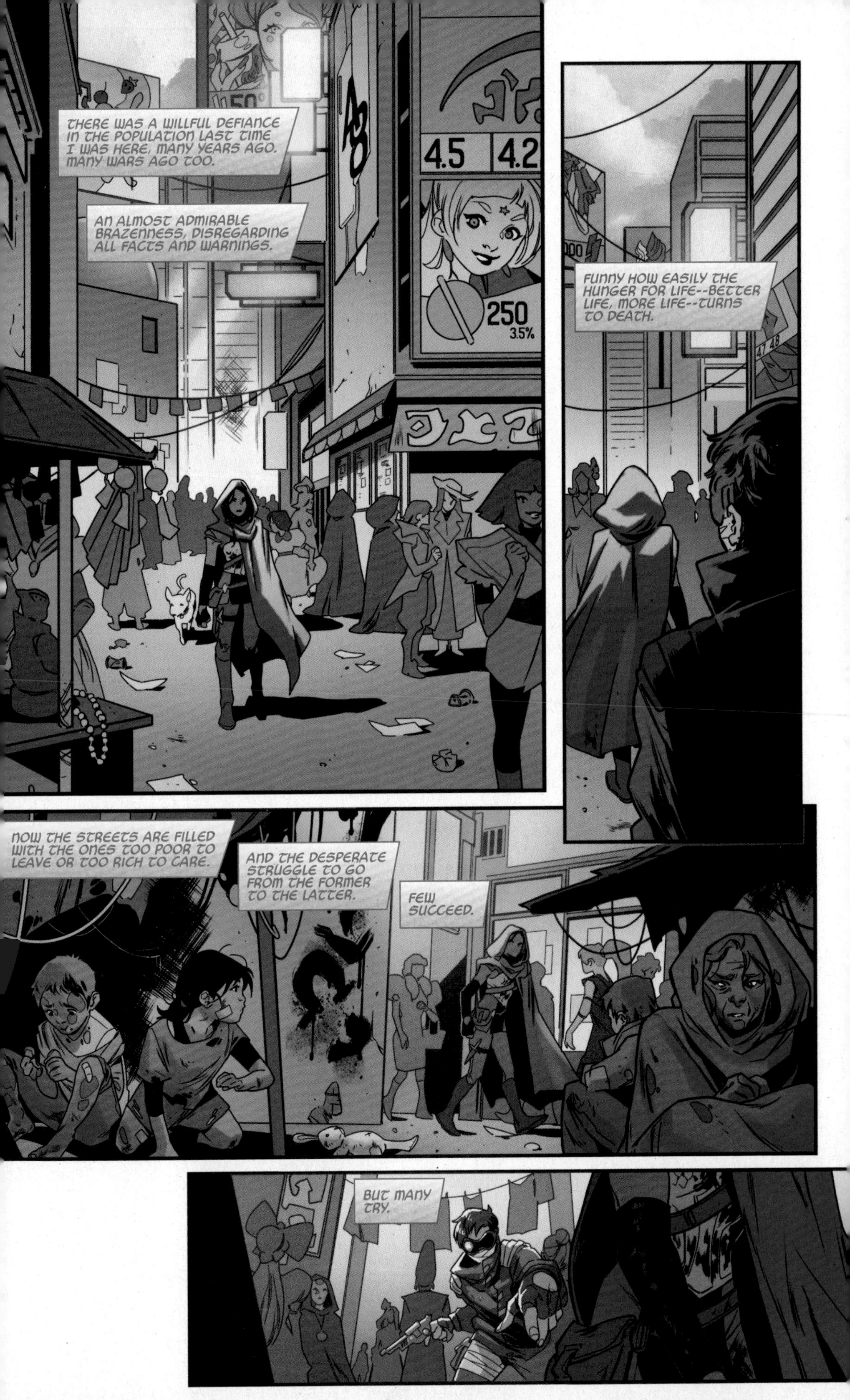

THERE WAS A WILLFUL DEFIANCE IN THE POPULATION LAST TIME I WAS HERE, MANY YEARS AGO. MANY WARS AGO TOO.
AN ALMOST ADMIRABLE BRAZENNESS, DISREGARDING ALL FACTS AND WARNINGS.
4.5
4.2
250
3.5%
FUNNY HOW EASILY THE HUNGER FOR LIFE--BETTER LIFE, MORE LIFE--TURNS TO DEATH.
NOW THE STREETS ARE FILLED WITH THE ONES TOO POOR TO LEAVE OR TOO RICH TO CARE.
AND THE DESPERATE STRUGGLE TO GO FROM THE FORMER TO THE LATTER.
FEW SUCCEED.
BUT MANY TRY.

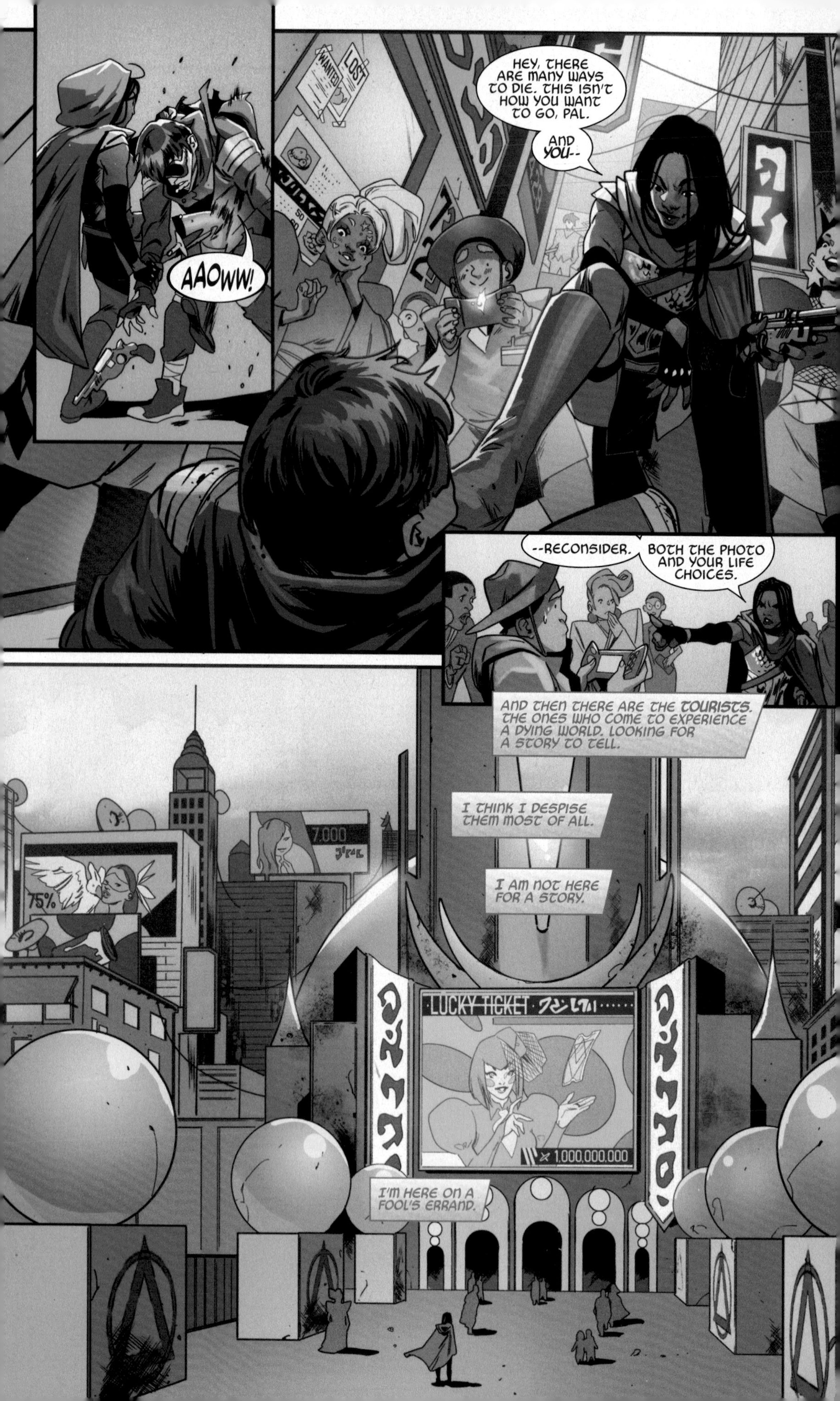
WANTED
LOST
AAOWW!
HEY, THERE ARE MANY WAYS TO DIE. THIS ISN'T HOW YOU WANT TO GO, PAL.
AND YOU--
--RECONSIDER.
BOTH THE PHOTO AND YOUR LIFE CHOICES.
AND THEN THERE ARE THE TOURISTS. THE ONES WHO COME TO EXPERIENCE A DYING WORLD. LOOKING FOR A STORY TO TELL.
I THINK I DESPISE THEM MOST OF ALL.
I AM NOT HERE FOR A STORY.
75%
7,000
LUCKY TICKET
1,000,000,000
I'M HERE ON A FOOL'S ERRAND.

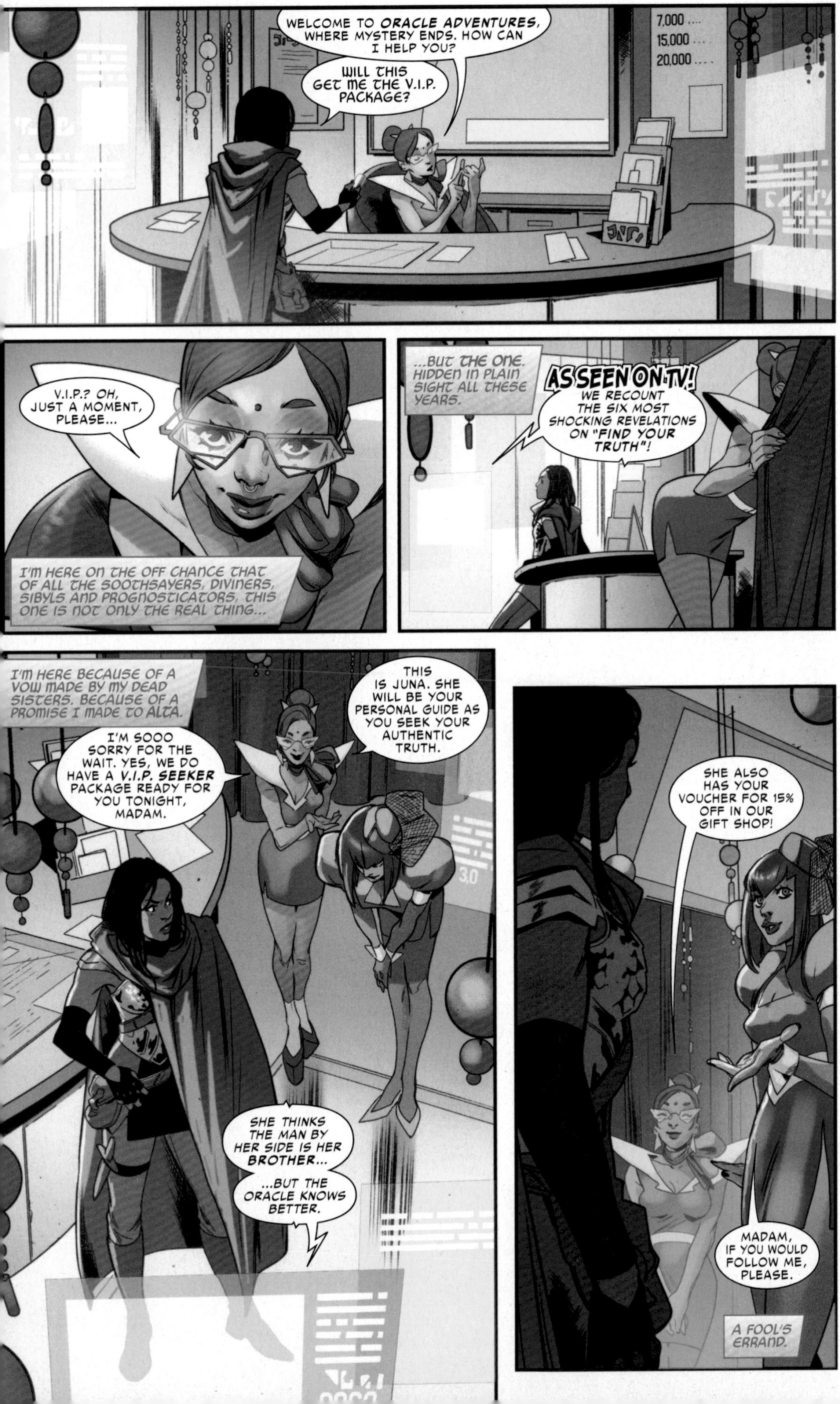
WELCOME TO ORACLE ADVENTURES, WHERE MYSTERY ENDS. HOW CAN I HELP YOU?
WILL THIS GET ME THE V.I.P. PACKAGE?
7,000 ....
15,000 ....
20,000 ....
V.I.P.? OH, JUST A MOMENT, PLEASE...
I'M HERE ON THE OFF CHANCE THAT OF ALL THE SOOTHSAYERS, DIVINERS, SIBYLS AND PROGNOSTICATORS, THIS ONE IS NOT ONLY THE REAL THING...
...BUT THE ONE. HIDDEN IN PLAIN SIGHT ALL THESE YEARS.
AS SEEN ON TV! WE RECOUNT THE SIX MOST SHOCKING REVELATIONS ON "FIND YOUR TRUTH"!
I'M HERE BECAUSE OF A VOW MADE BY MY DEAD SISTERS. BECAUSE OF A PROMISE I MADE TO ALTA.
I'M SOOO SORRY FOR THE WAIT. YES, WE DO HAVE A V.I.P. SEEKER PACKAGE READY FOR YOU TONIGHT, MADAM.
THIS IS JUNA. SHE WILL BE YOUR PERSONAL GUIDE AS YOU SEEK YOUR AUTHENTIC TRUTH.
3.0
SHE THINKS THE MAN BY HER SIDE IS HER BROTHER...
...BUT THE ORACLE KNOWS BETTER.
SHE ALSO HAS YOUR VOUCHER FOR 15% OFF IN OUR GIFT SHOP!
MADAM, IF YOU WOULD FOLLOW ME, PLEASE.
A FOOL'S ERRAND.

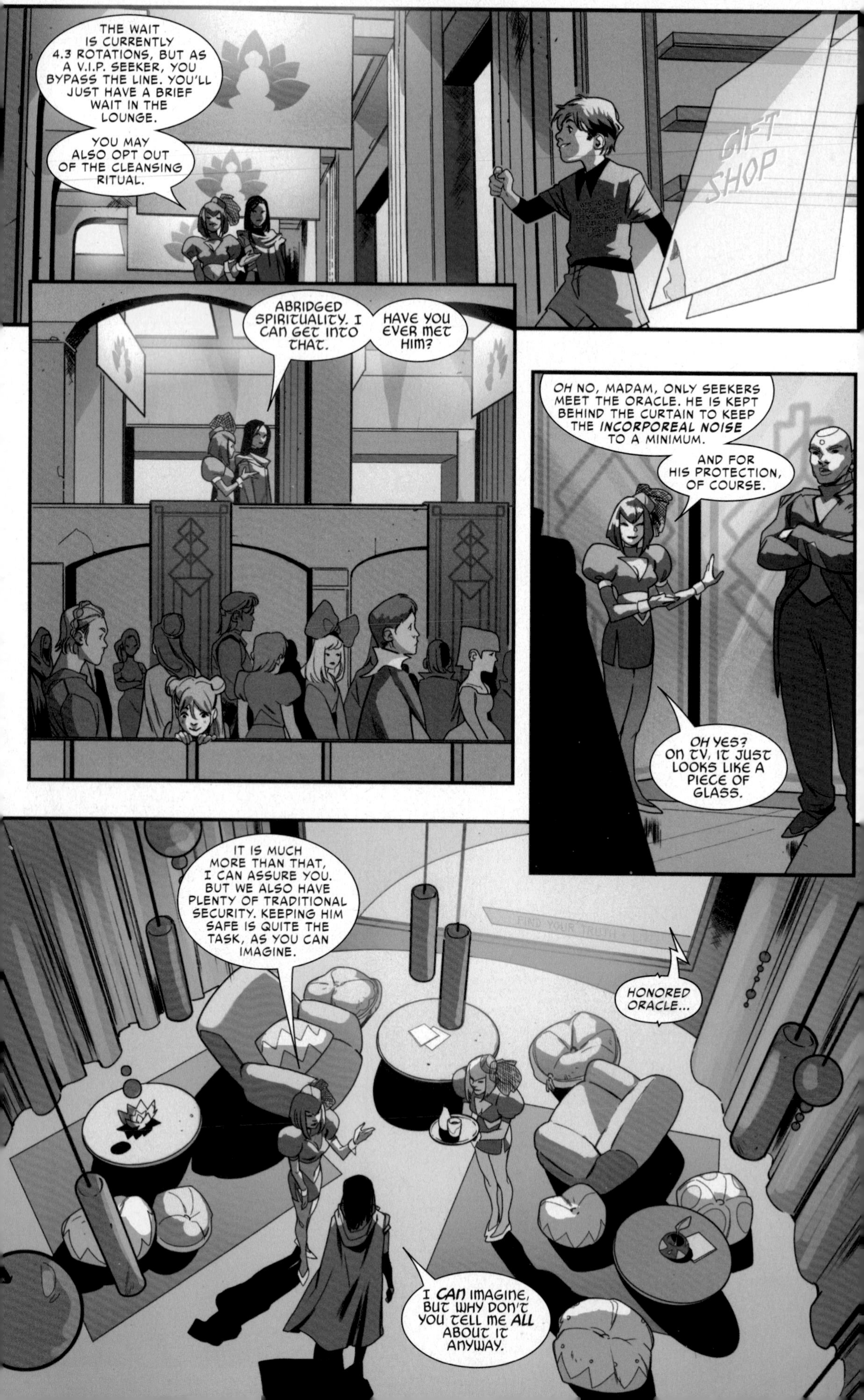

THE WAIT IS CURRENTLY 4.3 ROTATIONS, BUT AS A V.I.P. SEEKER, YOU BYPASS THE LINE. YOU'LL JUST HAVE A BRIEF WAIT IN THE LOUNGE.
YOU MAY ALSO OPT OUT OF THE CLEANSING RITUAL.
GIFT SHOP
ABRIDGED SPIRITUALITY. I CAN GET INTO THAT.
HAVE YOU EVER MET HIM?
OH NO, MADAM, ONLY SEEKERS MEET THE ORACLE. HE IS KEPT BEHIND THE CURTAIN TO KEEP THE INCORPOREAL NOISE TO A MINIMUM.
AND FOR HIS PROTECTION, OF COURSE.
OH YES? ON TV, IT JUST LOOKS LIKE A PIECE OF GLASS.
IT IS MUCH MORE THAN THAT, I CAN ASSURE YOU. BUT WE ALSO HAVE PLENTY OF TRADITIONAL SECURITY. KEEPING HIM SAFE IS QUITE THE TASK, AS YOU CAN IMAGINE.
HONORED ORACLE...
I CAN IMAGINE, BUT WHY DON'T YOU TELL ME ALL ABOUT IT ANYWAY.

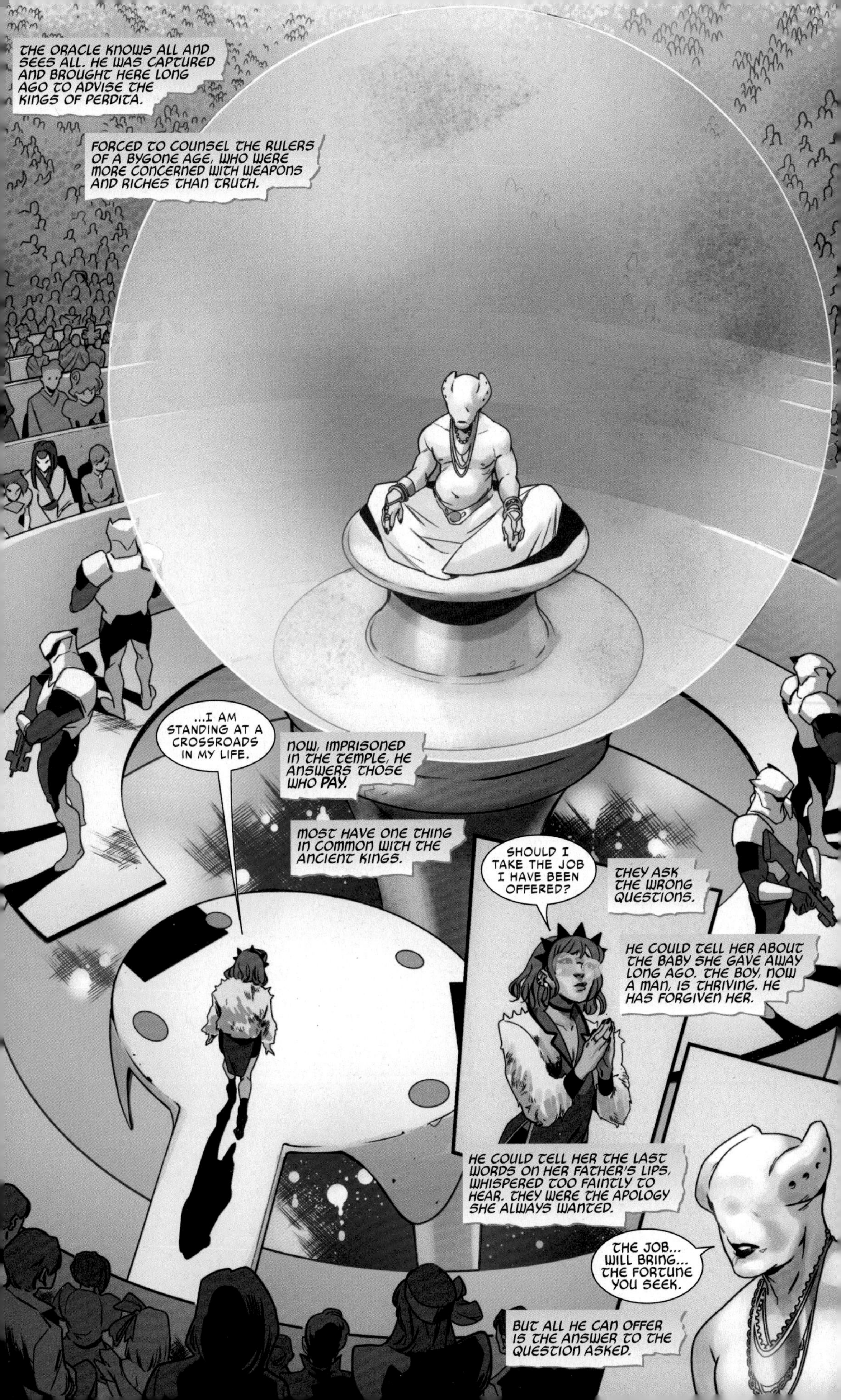
THE ORACLE KNOWS ALL AND SEES ALL. HE WAS CAPTURED AND BROUGHT HERE LONG AGO TO ADVISE THE KINGS OF PERDITA.
FORCED TO COUNSEL THE RULERS OF A BYGONE AGE, WHO WERE MORE CONCERNED WITH WEAPONS AND RICHES THAN TRUTH.
...I AM STANDING AT A CROSSROADS IN MY LIFE.
NOW, IMPRISONED IN THE TEMPLE, HE ANSWERS THOSE WHO PAY.
MOST HAVE ONE THING IN COMMON WITH THE ANCIENT KINGS.
SHOULD I TAKE THE JOB I HAVE BEEN OFFERED?
THEY ASK THE WRONG QUESTIONS.
HE COULD TELL HER ABOUT THE BABY SHE GAVE AWAY LONG AGO. THE BOY, NOW A MAN, IS THRIVING. HE HAS FORGIVEN HER.
HE COULD TELL HER THE LAST WORDS ON HER FATHER'S LIPS, WHISPERED TOO FAINTLY TO HEAR. THEY WERE THE APOLOGY SHE ALWAYS WANTED.
THE JOB... WILL BRING... THE FORTUNE YOU SEEK.
BUT ALL HE CAN OFFER IS THE ANSWER TO THE QUESTION ASKED.

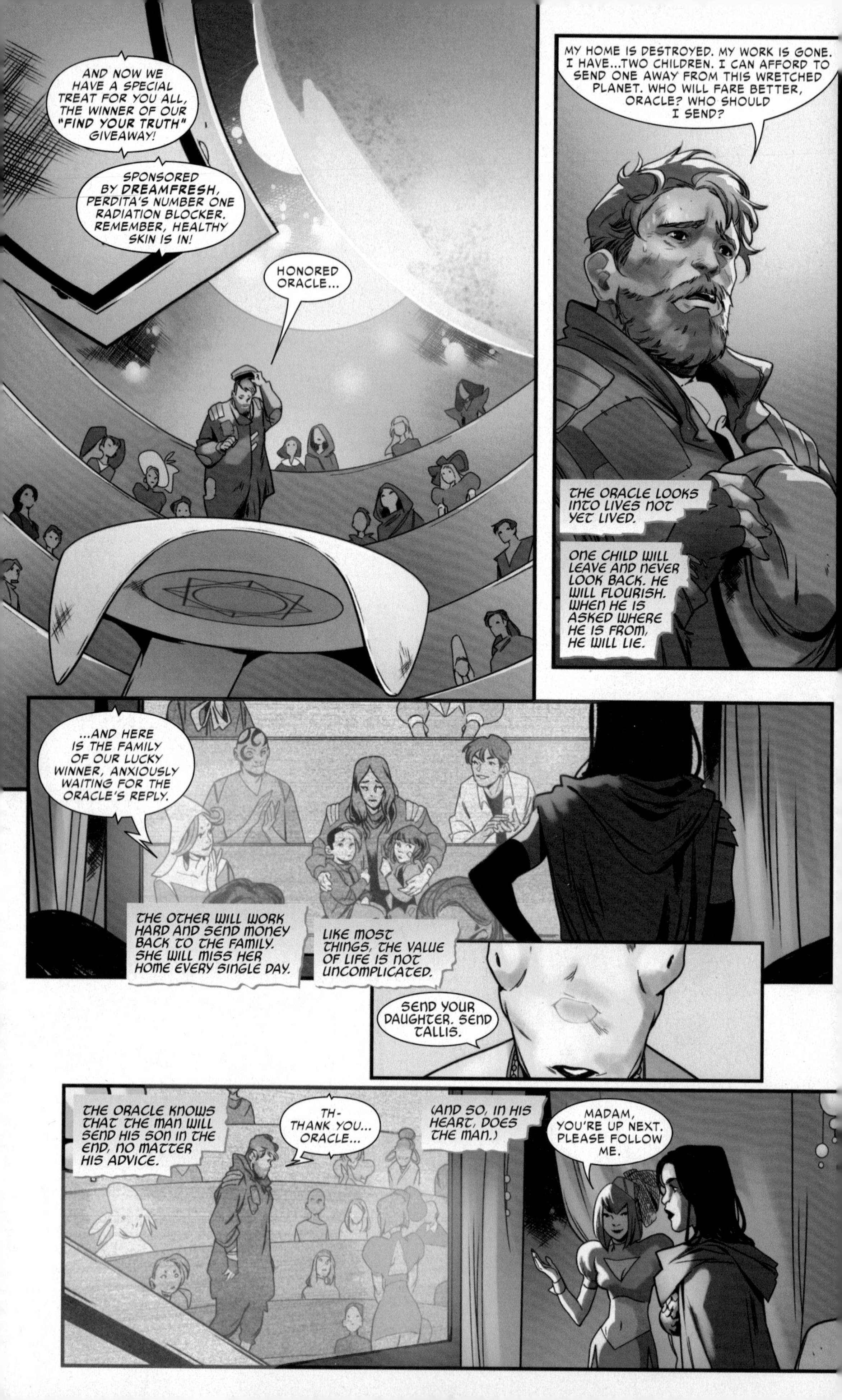
AND NOW WE HAVE A SPECIAL TREAT FOR YOU ALL, THE WINNER OF OUR "FIND YOUR TRUTH" GIVEAWAY!
SPONSORED BY DREAMFRESH, PERDITA'S NUMBER ONE RADIATION BLOCKER. REMEMBER, HEALTHY SKIN IS IN!
HONORED ORACLE...
MY HOME IS DESTROYED. MY WORK IS GONE. I HAVE...TWO CHILDREN. I CAN AFFORD TO SEND ONE AWAY FROM THIS WRETCHED PLANET. WHO WILL FARE BETTER, ORACLE? WHO SHOULD I SEND?
THE ORACLE LOOKS INTO LIVES NOT YET LIVED.
ONE CHILD WILL LEAVE AND NEVER LOOK BACK. HE WILL FLOURISH. WHEN HE IS ASKED WHERE HE IS FROM, HE WILL LIE.
...AND HERE IS THE FAMILY OF OUR LUCKY WINNER, ANXIOUSLY WAITING FOR THE ORACLE'S REPLY.
THE OTHER WILL WORK HARD AND SEND MONEY BACK TO THE FAMILY. SHE WILL MISS HER HOME EVERY SINGLE DAY.
LIKE MOST THINGS, THE VALUE OF LIFE IS NOT UNCOMPLICATED.
SEND YOUR DAUGHTER. SEND TALLIS.
THE ORACLE KNOWS THAT THE MAN WILL SEND HIS SON IN THE END, NO MATTER HIS ADVICE.
TH- THANK YOU... ORACLE...
(AND SO, IN HIS HEART, DOES THE MAN.)
MADAM, YOU'RE UP NEXT. PLEASE FOLLOW ME.

ORACLE...

TELL ME-- WHAT IS MY *NAME*, AND *WHY* AM I HERE.

‡GASP‡ YOU ARE ONLY ALLOWED *ONE* QUESTION!

THE BREACH OF PROTOCOL IS ENOUGH TO ALERT THE GUARDS.

Y... YOU ARE HERE BECAUSE YOU MADE A PROMISE TO A WOMAN YOU LOVED.

THE ORACLE'S REACTION ALERTS THE REST.

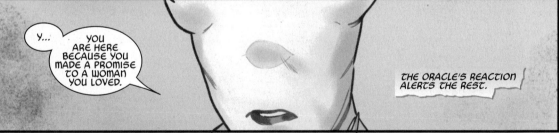

A WOMAN I RAISED. A WOMAN WHO DIED WITH REGRET IN HER HEART.

YOU ARE HERE TO HONOR THE COVENANT THE VALKYRIES ONCE MADE.

YOUR NAME IS KNOWN TO NO LIVING BEING, LOST IN TIME AND DEATH.

I AM THE ONE YOU SEEK. I AM *KVASIR*. AND YOUR NAME IS...

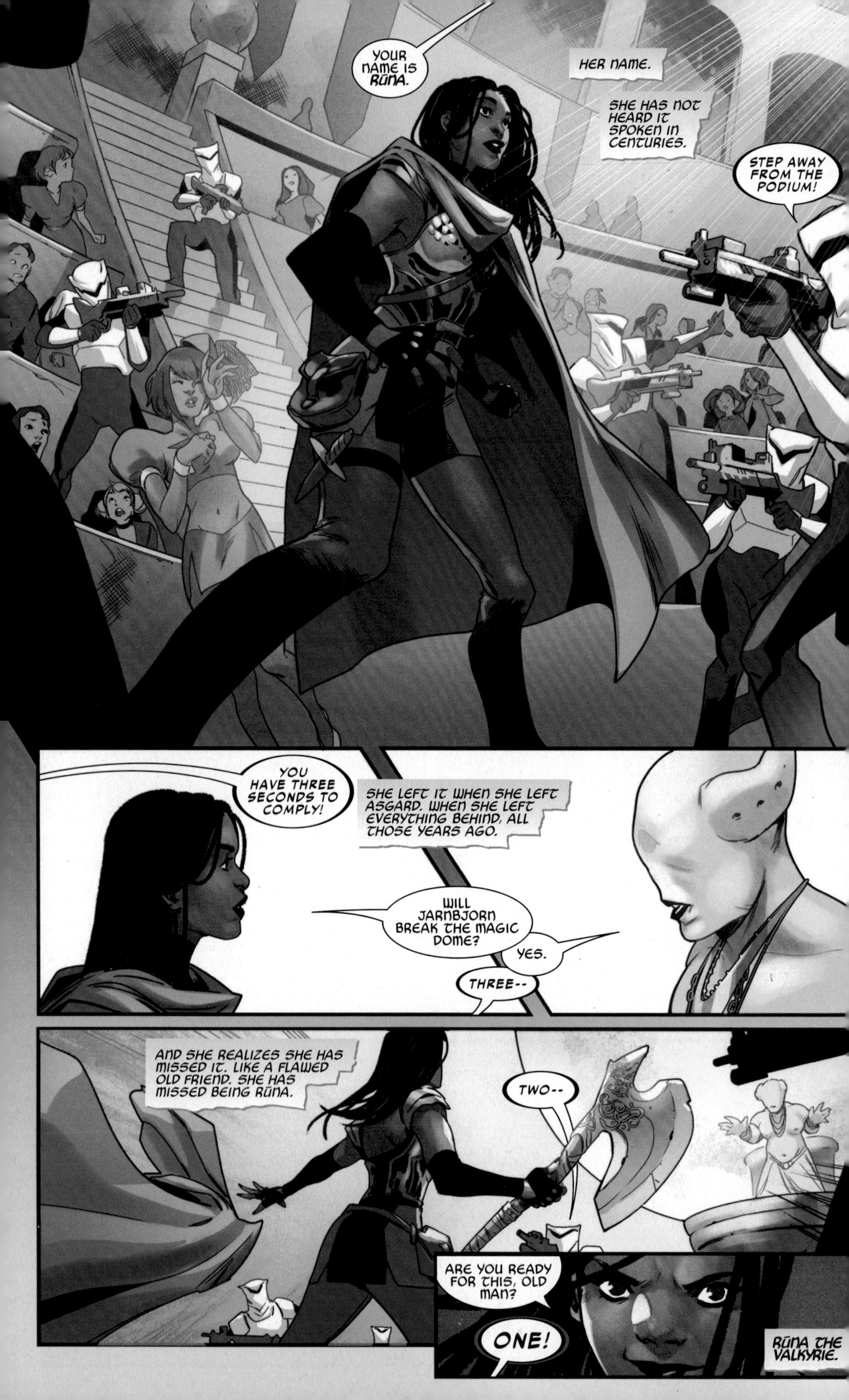
YOUR NAME IS RŪNA.
HER NAME.
SHE HAS NOT HEARD IT SPOKEN IN CENTURIES.
STEP AWAY FROM THE PODIUM!
YOU HAVE THREE SECONDS TO COMPLY!
SHE LEFT IT WHEN SHE LEFT ASGARD. WHEN SHE LEFT EVERYTHING BEHIND, ALL THOSE YEARS AGO.
WILL JARNBJORN BREAK THE MAGIC DOME?
YES.
THREE--
AND SHE REALIZES SHE HAS MISSED IT. LIKE A FLAWED OLD FRIEND. SHE HAS MISSED BEING RŪNA.
TWO--
ARE YOU READY FOR THIS, OLD MAN?
ONE!
RŪNA THE VALKYRIE.

2.

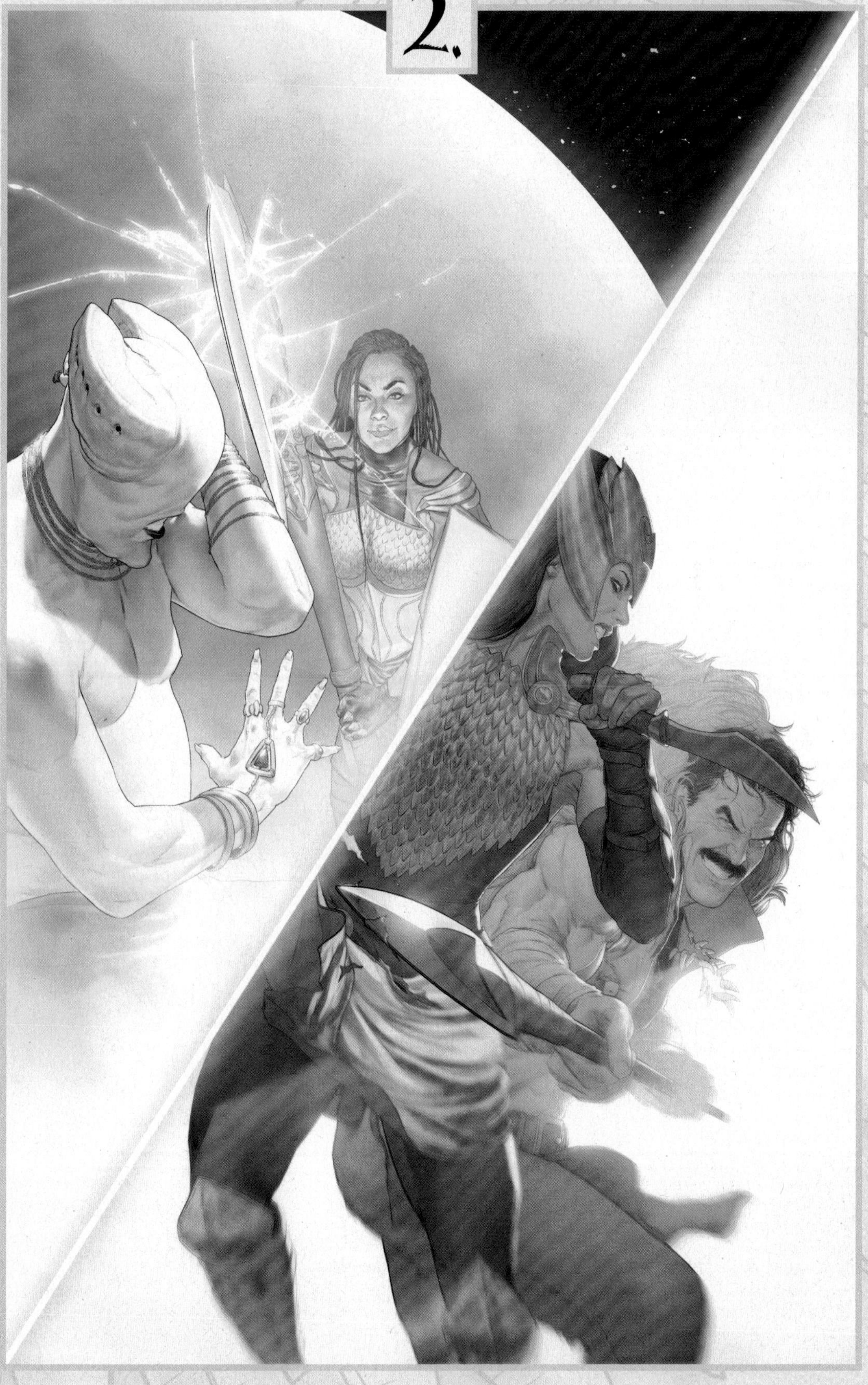

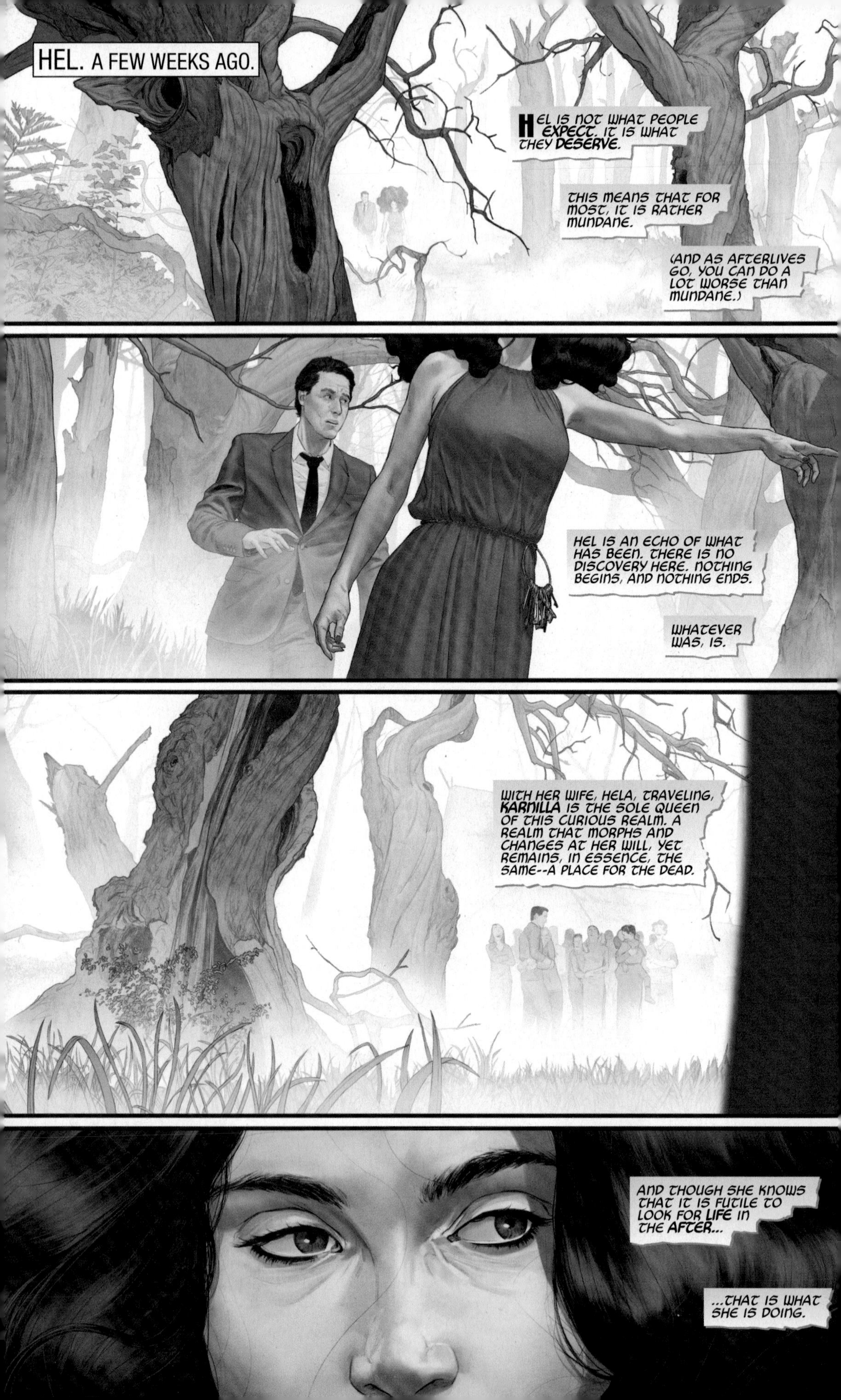
HEL. A FEW WEEKS AGO.
HEL IS NOT WHAT PEOPLE EXPECT. IT IS WHAT THEY DESERVE.
THIS MEANS THAT FOR MOST, IT IS RATHER MUNDANE.
(AND AS AFTERLIVES GO, YOU CAN DO A LOT WORSE THAN MUNDANE.)
HEL IS AN ECHO OF WHAT HAS BEEN. THERE IS NO DISCOVERY HERE. NOTHING BEGINS, AND NOTHING ENDS.
WHATEVER WAS, IS.
WITH HER WIFE, HELA, TRAVELING, KARNILLA IS THE SOLE QUEEN OF THIS CURIOUS REALM. A REALM THAT MORPHS AND CHANGES AT HER WILL, YET REMAINS, IN ESSENCE, THE SAME--A PLACE FOR THE DEAD.
AND THOUGH SHE KNOWS THAT IT IS FUTILE TO LOOK FOR LIFE IN THE AFTER...
...THAT IS WHAT SHE IS DOING.

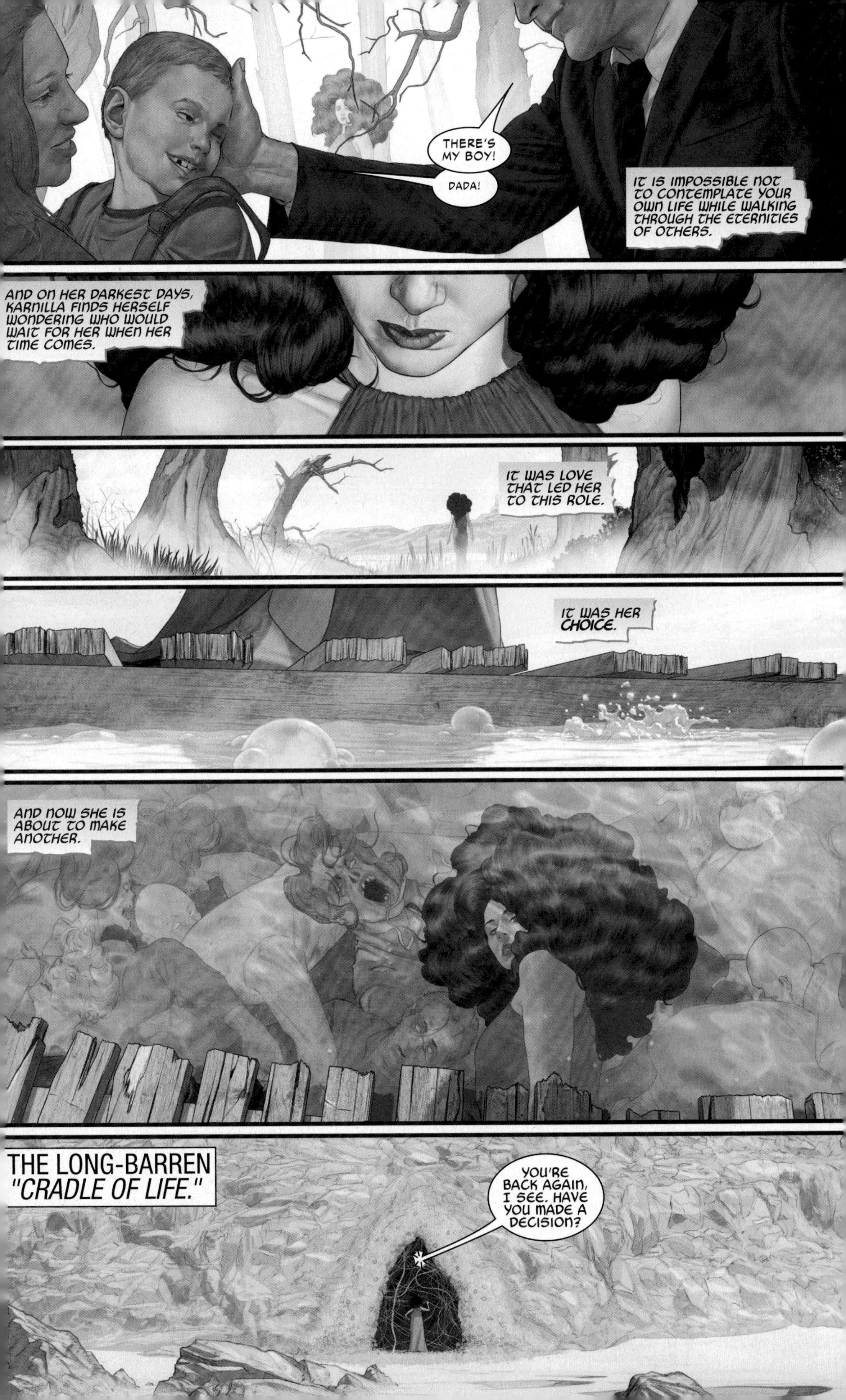
THERE'S MY BOY!
DADA!
IT IS IMPOSSIBLE NOT TO CONTEMPLATE YOUR OWN LIFE WHILE WALKING THROUGH THE ETERNITIES OF OTHERS.
AND ON HER DARKEST DAYS, KARNILLA FINDS HERSELF WONDERING WHO WOULD WAIT FOR HER WHEN HER TIME COMES.
IT WAS LOVE THAT LED HER TO THIS ROLE.
IT WAS HER CHOICE.
AND NOW SHE IS ABOUT TO MAKE ANOTHER.
THE LONG-BARREN "CRADLE OF LIFE."
YOU'RE BACK AGAIN, I SEE. HAVE YOU MADE A DECISION?

A CHOICE THAT WILL RELEASE ANOTHER LIVING CREATURE THAT HAS BEEN TRAPPED HERE IN THE REALM OF THE DEAD.

DO IT.

YOU FIRST.

AS SHE REACHES TO UNDO THE LOCK AROUND THEIR NECK, KARNILLA IS TEMPTED TO ASK FOR REASSURANCE.

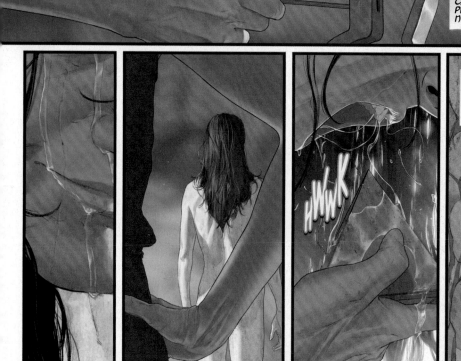

ASK THIS CREATURE THAT CALLS ITSELF MORE TO PROMISE HER SHE WILL NOT REGRET THIS.

BUT THE BARGAIN HAS BEEN MADE--MORE'S FREEDOM FOR THE WATERS OF URDARBRUNNR.

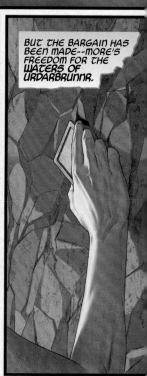

HWWWK

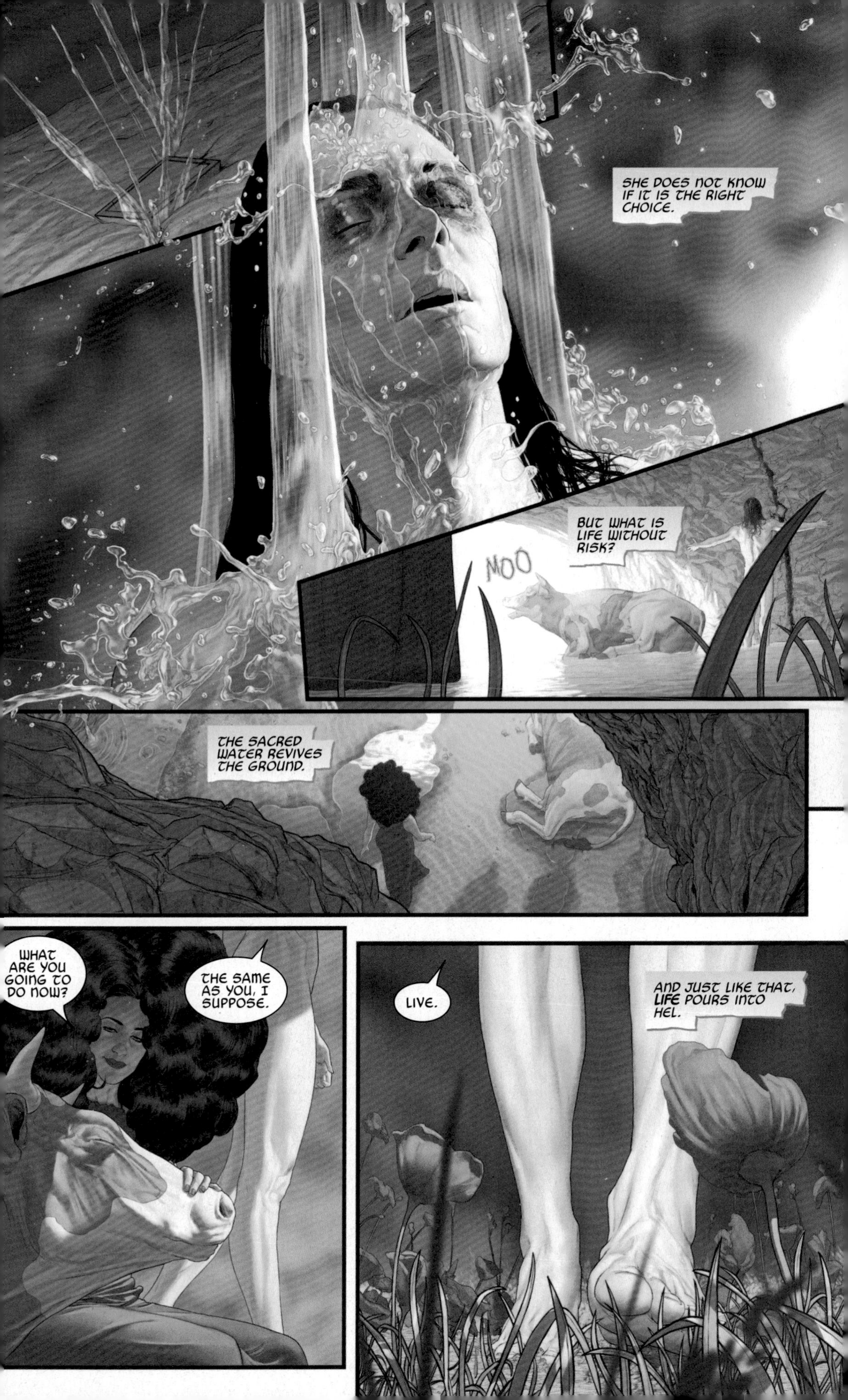
SHE DOES NOT KNOW IF IT IS THE RIGHT CHOICE.
BUT WHAT IS LIFE WITHOUT RISK?
MOO
THE SACRED WATER REVIVES THE GROUND.
WHAT ARE YOU GOING TO DO NOW?
THE SAME AS YOU, I SUPPOSE.
LIVE.
AND JUST LIKE THAT, **LIFE** POURS INTO HEL.

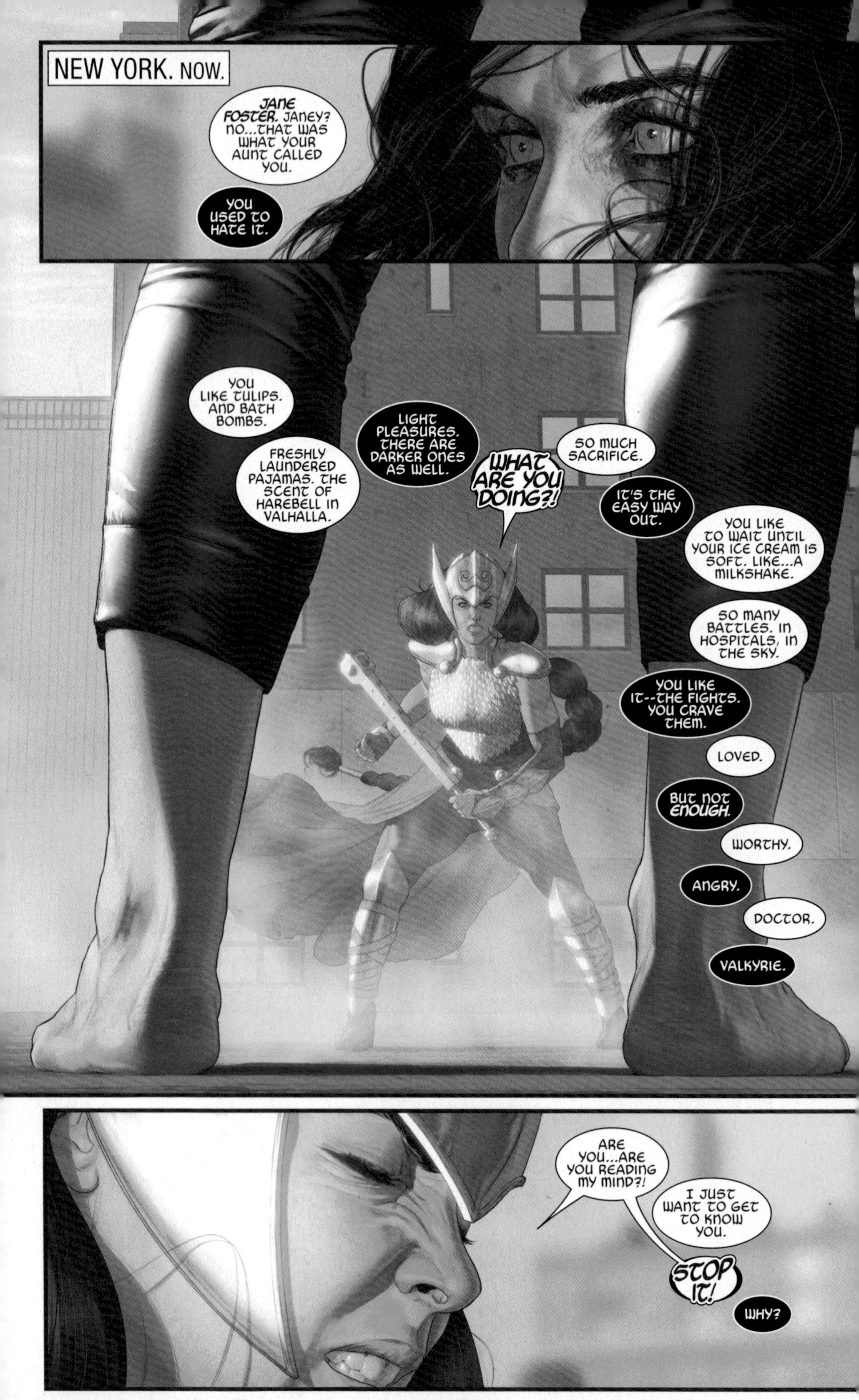
NEW YORK. NOW.
JANE FOSTER. JANEY? NO...THAT WAS WHAT YOUR AUNT CALLED YOU.
YOU USED TO HATE IT.
YOU LIKE TULIPS. AND BATH BOMBS.
FRESHLY LAUNDERED PAJAMAS. THE SCENT OF HAREBELL IN VALHALLA.
LIGHT PLEASURES. THERE ARE DARKER ONES AS WELL.
WHAT ARE YOU DOING?!
SO MUCH SACRIFICE.
IT'S THE EASY WAY OUT.
YOU LIKE TO WAIT UNTIL YOUR ICE CREAM IS SOFT. LIKE...A MILKSHAKE.
SO MANY BATTLES. IN HOSPITALS, IN THE SKY.
YOU LIKE IT--THE FIGHTS. YOU CRAVE THEM.
LOVED.
BUT NOT ENOUGH.
WORTHY.
ANGRY.
DOCTOR.
VALKYRIE.
ARE YOU...ARE YOU READING MY MIND?!
I JUST WANT TO GET TO KNOW YOU.
STOP IT!
WHY?

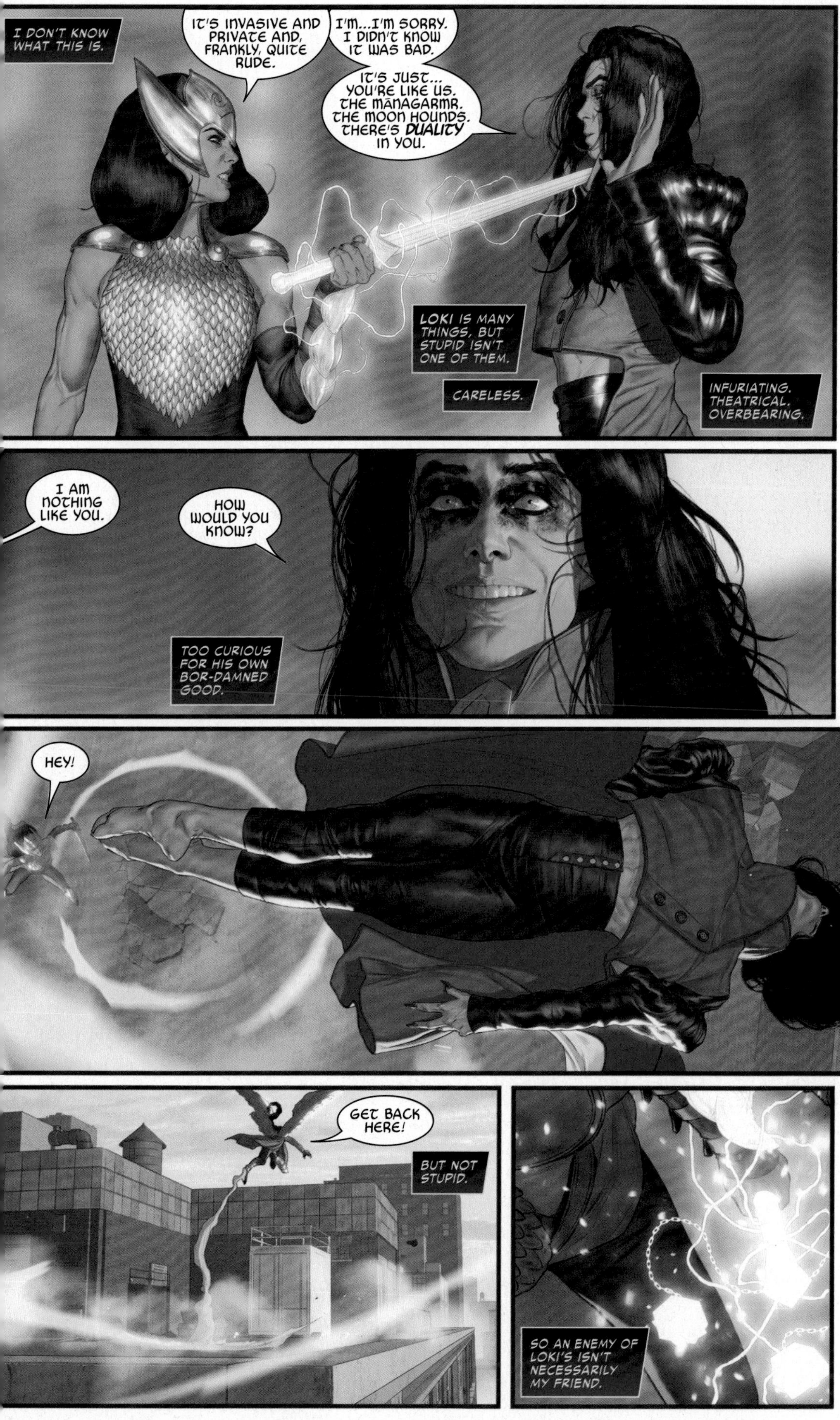
I DON'T KNOW WHAT THIS IS.
IT'S INVASIVE AND PRIVATE AND, FRANKLY, QUITE RUDE.
I'M...I'M SORRY. I DIDN'T KNOW IT WAS BAD.
IT'S JUST... YOU'RE LIKE US. THE MÁNAGARMR. THE MOON HOUNDS. THERE'S DUALITY IN YOU.
LOKI IS MANY THINGS, BUT STUPID ISN'T ONE OF THEM.
CARELESS.
INFURIATING. THEATRICAL. OVERBEARING.
I AM NOTHING LIKE YOU.
HOW WOULD YOU KNOW?
TOO CURIOUS FOR HIS OWN BOR-DAMNED GOOD.
HEY!
GET BACK HERE!
BUT NOT STUPID.
SO AN ENEMY OF LOKI'S ISN'T NECESSARILY MY FRIEND.

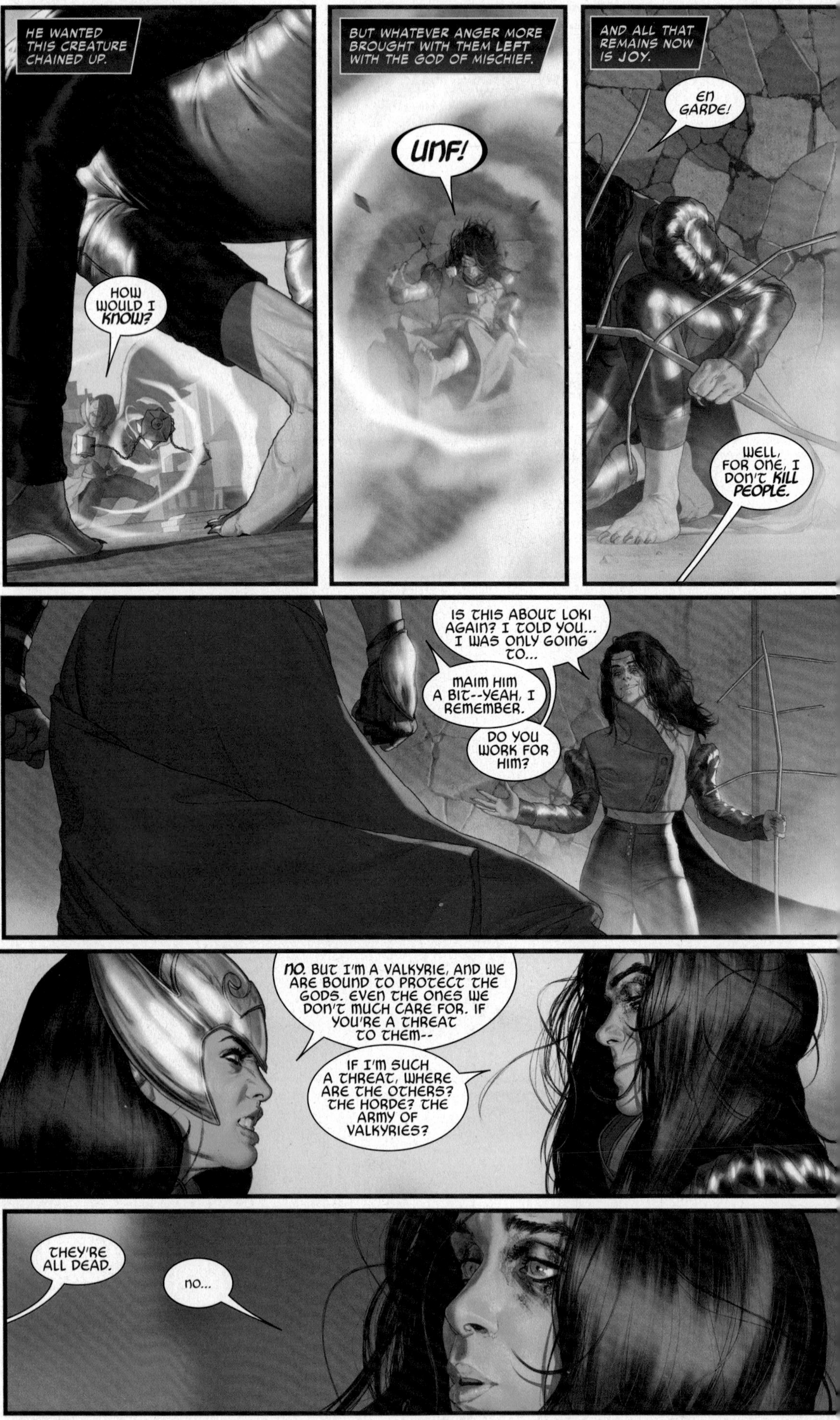
HE WANTED THIS CREATURE CHAINED UP.
HOW WOULD I KNOW?
BUT WHATEVER ANGER MORE BROUGHT WITH THEM LEFT WITH THE GOD OF MISCHIEF.
UNF!
AND ALL THAT REMAINS NOW IS JOY.
EN GARDE!
WELL, FOR ONE, I DON'T KILL PEOPLE.
IS THIS ABOUT LOKI AGAIN? I TOLD YOU... I WAS ONLY GOING TO...
MAIM HIM A BIT--YEAH, I REMEMBER.
DO YOU WORK FOR HIM?
NO. BUT I'M A VALKYRIE, AND WE ARE BOUND TO PROTECT THE GODS. EVEN THE ONES WE DON'T MUCH CARE FOR. IF YOU'RE A THREAT TO THEM--
IF I'M SUCH A THREAT, WHERE ARE THE OTHERS? THE HORDE? THE ARMY OF VALKYRIES?
THEY'RE ALL DEAD.
no...

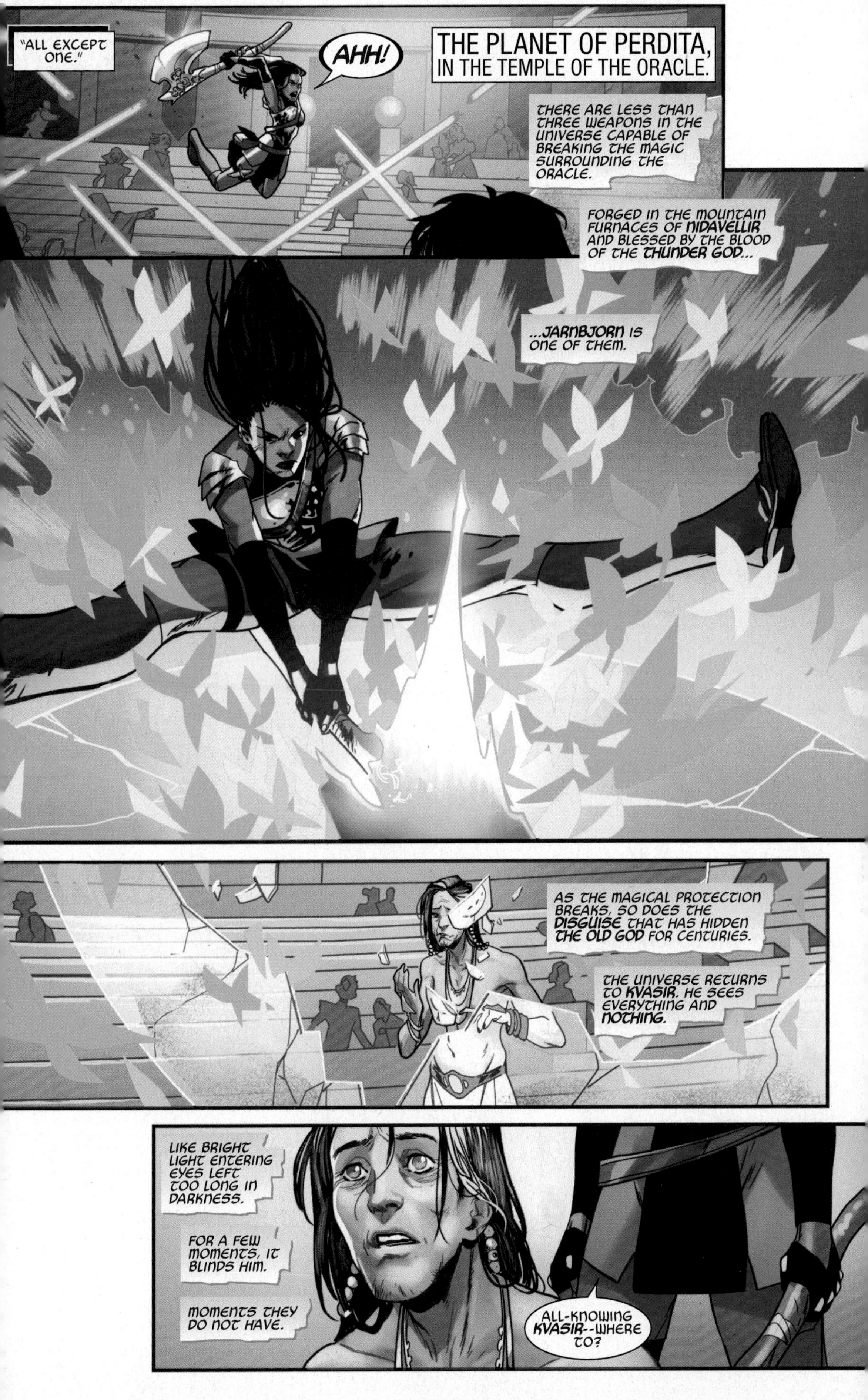

"ALL EXCEPT ONE."
AHH!
THE PLANET OF PERDITA, IN THE TEMPLE OF THE ORACLE.
THERE ARE LESS THAN THREE WEAPONS IN THE UNIVERSE CAPABLE OF BREAKING THE MAGIC SURROUNDING THE ORACLE.
FORGED IN THE MOUNTAIN FURNACES OF NIDAVELLIR AND BLESSED BY THE BLOOD OF THE THUNDER GOD...
...JARNBJORN IS ONE OF THEM.
AS THE MAGICAL PROTECTION BREAKS, SO DOES THE DISGUISE THAT HAS HIDDEN THE OLD GOD FOR CENTURIES.
THE UNIVERSE RETURNS TO KVASIR. HE SEES EVERYTHING AND NOTHING.
LIKE BRIGHT LIGHT ENTERING EYES LEFT TOO LONG IN DARKNESS.
FOR A FEW MOMENTS, IT BLINDS HIM.
MOMENTS THEY DO NOT HAVE.
ALL-KNOWING KVASIR--WHERE TO?

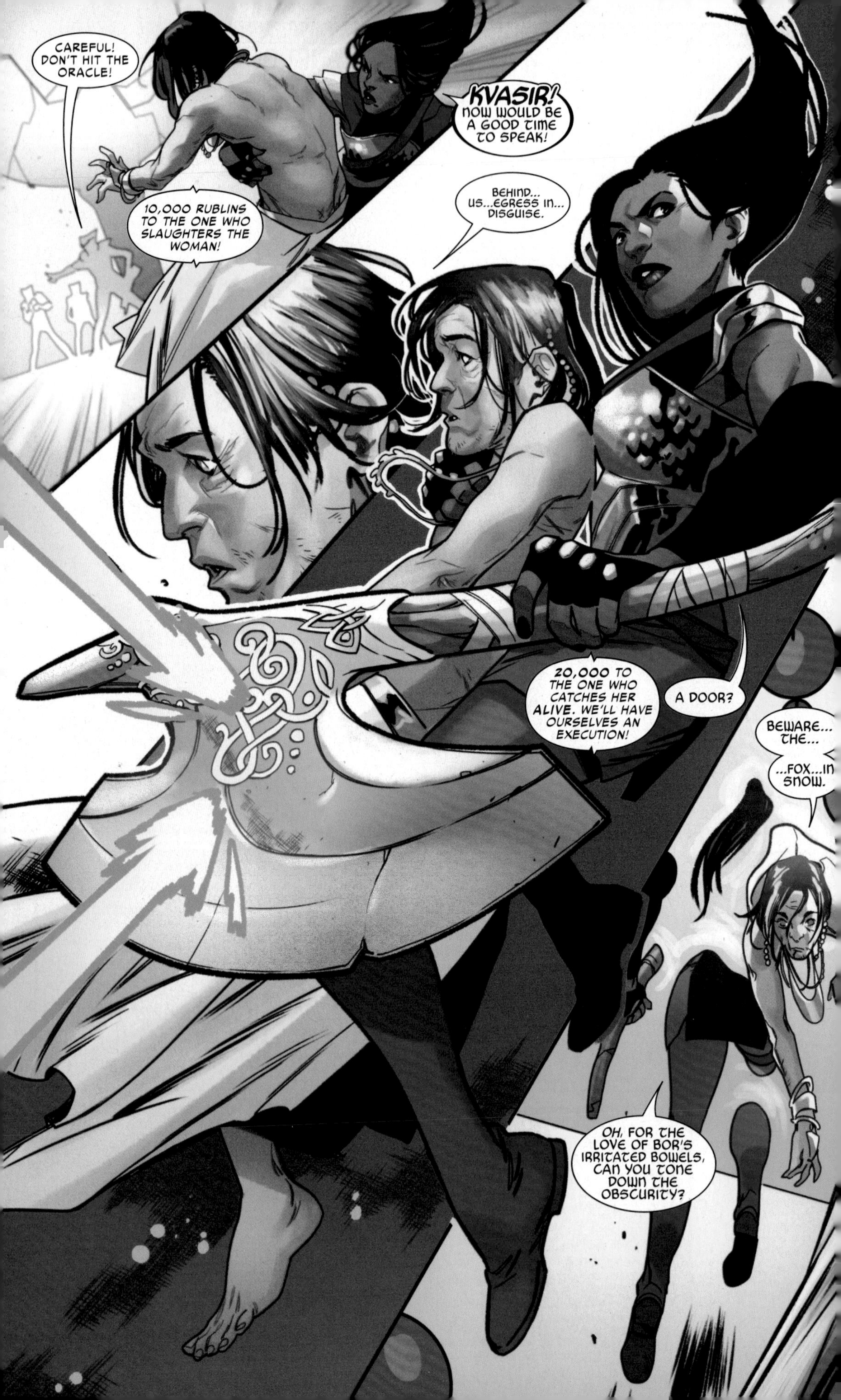

CAREFUL! DON'T HIT THE ORACLE!
10,000 RUBLINS TO THE ONE WHO SLAUGHTERS THE WOMAN!
KVASIR! NOW WOULD BE A GOOD TIME TO SPEAK!
BEHIND... US...EGRESS IN... DISGUISE.
20,000 TO THE ONE WHO CATCHES HER ALIVE. WE'LL HAVE OURSELVES AN EXECUTION!
A DOOR?
BEWARE... THE...
...FOX...IN SNOW.
OH, FOR THE LOVE OF BOR'S IRRITATED BOWELS, CAN YOU TONE DOWN THE OBSCURITY?

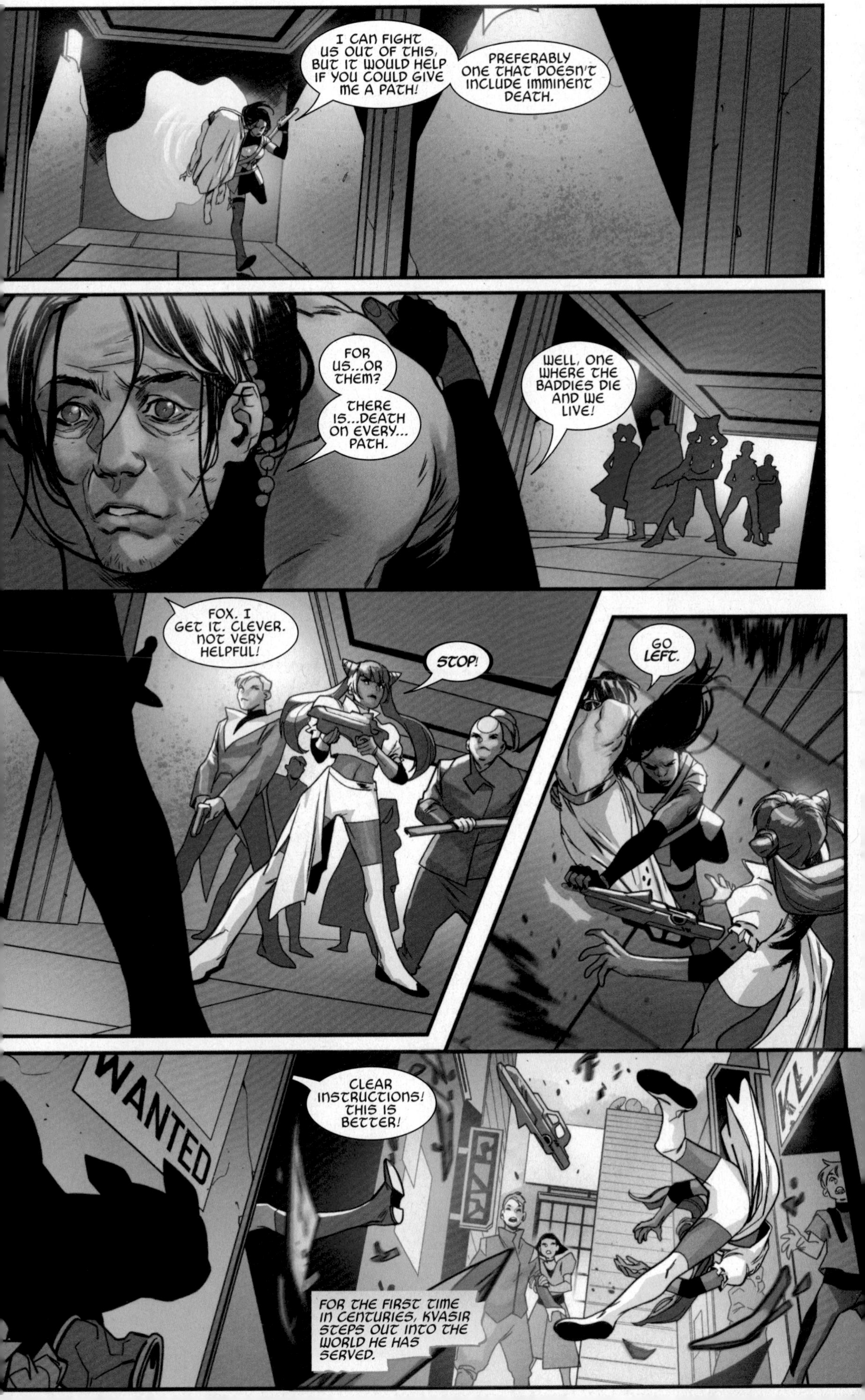
I CAN FIGHT US OUT OF THIS, BUT IT WOULD HELP IF YOU COULD GIVE ME A PATH!
PREFERABLY ONE THAT DOESN'T INCLUDE IMMINENT DEATH.
FOR US...OR THEM?
THERE IS...DEATH ON EVERY... PATH.
WELL, ONE WHERE THE BADDIES DIE AND WE LIVE!
FOX. I GET IT. CLEVER. NOT VERY HELPFUL!
STOP!
GO LEFT.
WANTED
CLEAR INSTRUCTIONS! THIS IS BETTER!
FOR THE FIRST TIME IN CENTURIES, KVASIR STEPS OUT INTO THE WORLD HE HAS SERVED.

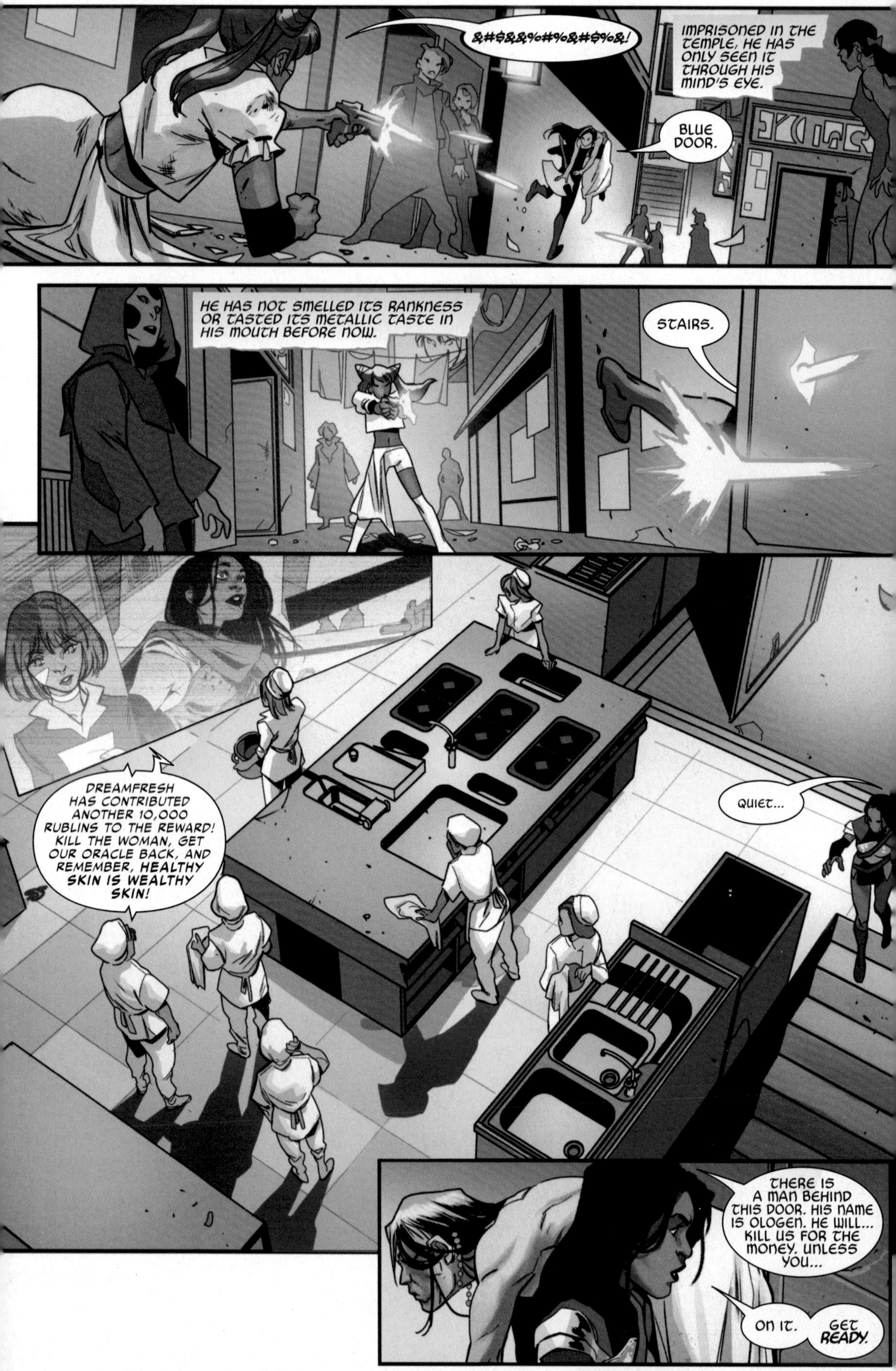
&#$&&%#%&#$%&!
IMPRISONED IN THE TEMPLE, HE HAS ONLY SEEN IT THROUGH HIS MIND'S EYE.
BLUE DOOR.
HE HAS NOT SMELLED ITS RANKNESS OR TASTED ITS METALLIC TASTE IN HIS MOUTH BEFORE NOW.
STAIRS.
DREAMFRESH HAS CONTRIBUTED ANOTHER 10,000 RUBLINS TO THE REWARD! KILL THE WOMAN, GET OUR ORACLE BACK, AND REMEMBER, **HEALTHY SKIN IS WEALTHY SKIN!**
QUIET...
THERE IS A MAN BEHIND THIS DOOR. HIS NAME IS OLOGEN. HE WILL... KILL US FOR THE MONEY. UNLESS YOU...
ON IT.
GET ***READY.***

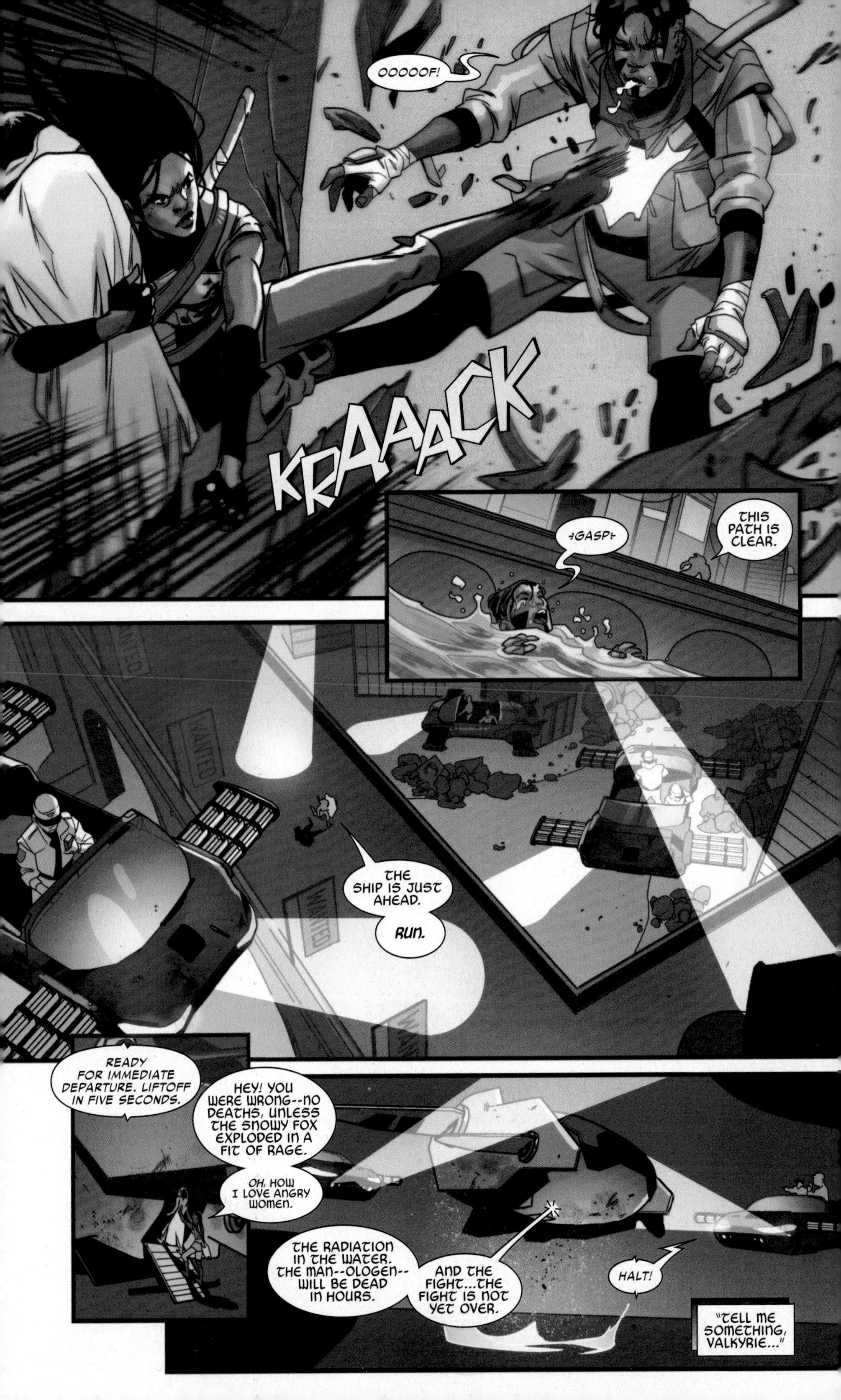
OOOOOF!
KRAAAACK
-GASP-
THIS PATH IS CLEAR.
THE SHIP IS JUST AHEAD.
RUN.
READY FOR IMMEDIATE DEPARTURE. LIFTOFF IN FIVE SECONDS.
HEY! YOU WERE WRONG--NO DEATHS, UNLESS THE SNOWY FOX EXPLODED IN A FIT OF RAGE.
OH, HOW I LOVE ANGRY WOMEN.
THE RADIATION IN THE WATER. THE MAN--OLOGEN--WILL BE DEAD IN HOURS.
AND THE FIGHT...THE FIGHT IS NOT YET OVER.
HALT!
"TELL ME SOMETHING, VALKYRIE..."

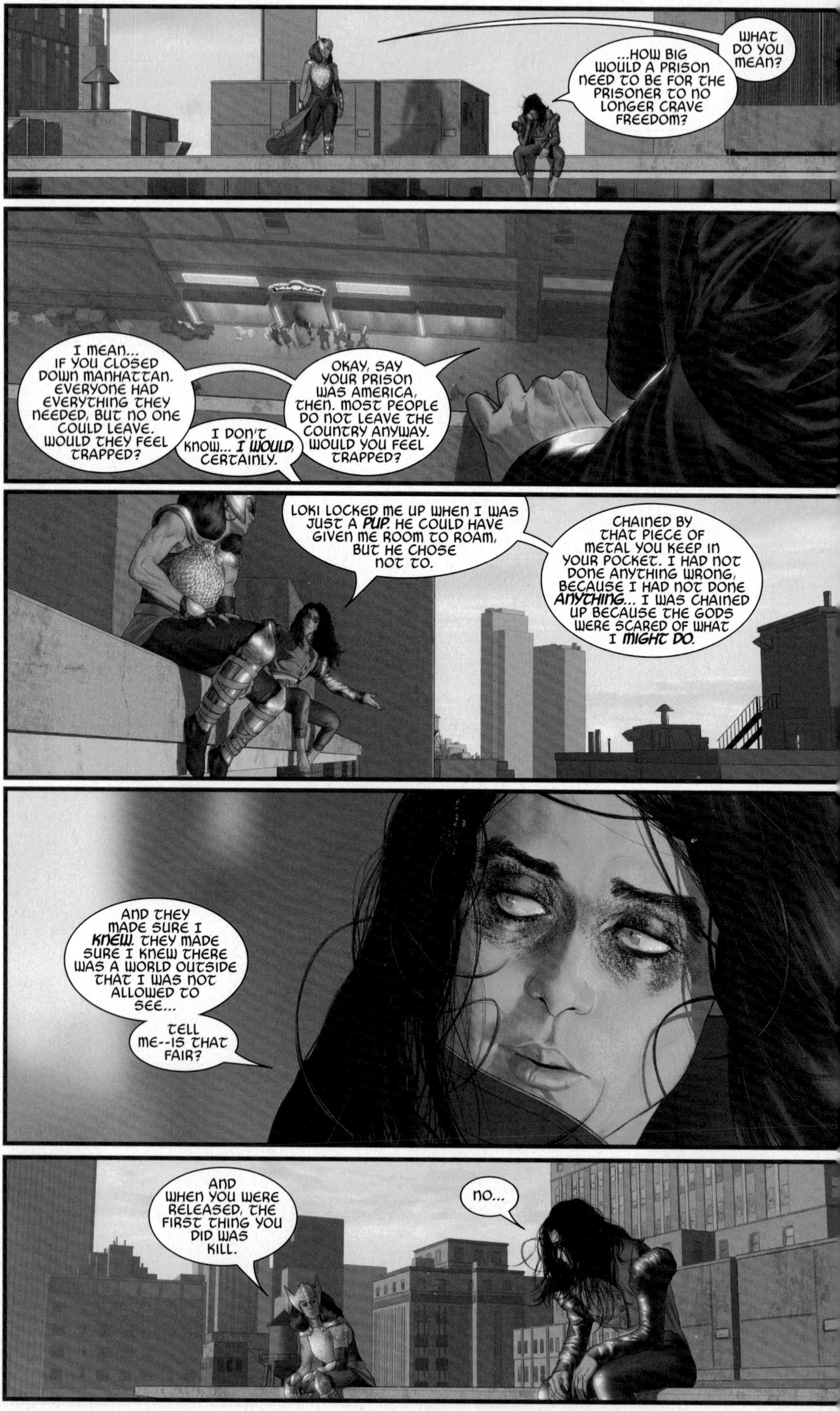
...HOW BIG WOULD A PRISON NEED TO BE FOR THE PRISONER TO NO LONGER CRAVE FREEDOM?
WHAT DO YOU MEAN?
I MEAN... IF YOU CLOSED DOWN MANHATTAN. EVERYONE HAD EVERYTHING THEY NEEDED, BUT NO ONE COULD LEAVE. WOULD THEY FEEL TRAPPED?
I DON'T KNOW... I WOULD, CERTAINLY.
OKAY, SAY YOUR PRISON WAS AMERICA, THEN. MOST PEOPLE DO NOT LEAVE THE COUNTRY ANYWAY. WOULD YOU FEEL TRAPPED?
LOKI LOCKED ME UP WHEN I WAS JUST A PUP. HE COULD HAVE GIVEN ME ROOM TO ROAM, BUT HE CHOSE NOT TO.
CHAINED BY THAT PIECE OF METAL YOU KEEP IN YOUR POCKET. I HAD NOT DONE ANYTHING WRONG, BECAUSE I HAD NOT DONE ANYTHING... I WAS CHAINED UP BECAUSE THE GODS WERE SCARED OF WHAT I MIGHT DO.
AND THEY MADE SURE I KNEW. THEY MADE SURE I KNEW THERE WAS A WORLD OUTSIDE THAT I WAS NOT ALLOWED TO SEE...
TELL ME--IS THAT FAIR?
AND WHEN YOU WERE RELEASED, THE FIRST THING YOU DID WAS KILL.
NO...

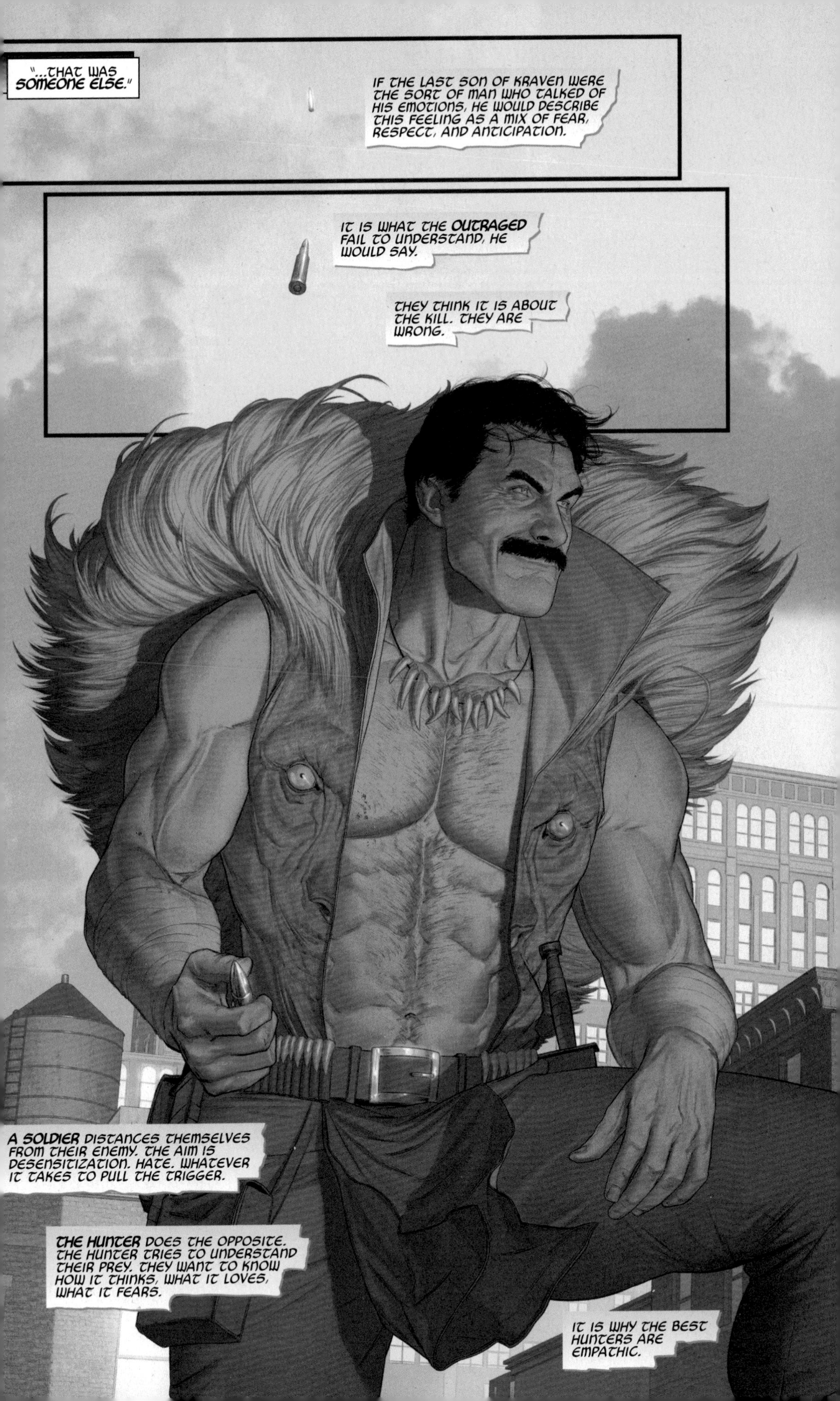

"...THAT WAS SOMEONE ELSE."
IF THE LAST SON OF KRAVEN WERE THE SORT OF MAN WHO TALKED OF HIS EMOTIONS, HE WOULD DESCRIBE THIS FEELING AS A MIX OF FEAR, RESPECT, AND ANTICIPATION.
IT IS WHAT THE OUTRAGED FAIL TO UNDERSTAND, HE WOULD SAY.
THEY THINK IT IS ABOUT THE KILL. THEY ARE WRONG.
A SOLDIER DISTANCES THEMSELVES FROM THEIR ENEMY. THE AIM IS DESENSITIZATION. HATE. WHATEVER IT TAKES TO PULL THE TRIGGER.
THE HUNTER DOES THE OPPOSITE. THE HUNTER TRIES TO UNDERSTAND THEIR PREY. THEY WANT TO KNOW HOW IT THINKS, WHAT IT LOVES, WHAT IT FEARS.
IT IS WHY THE BEST HUNTERS ARE EMPATHIC.

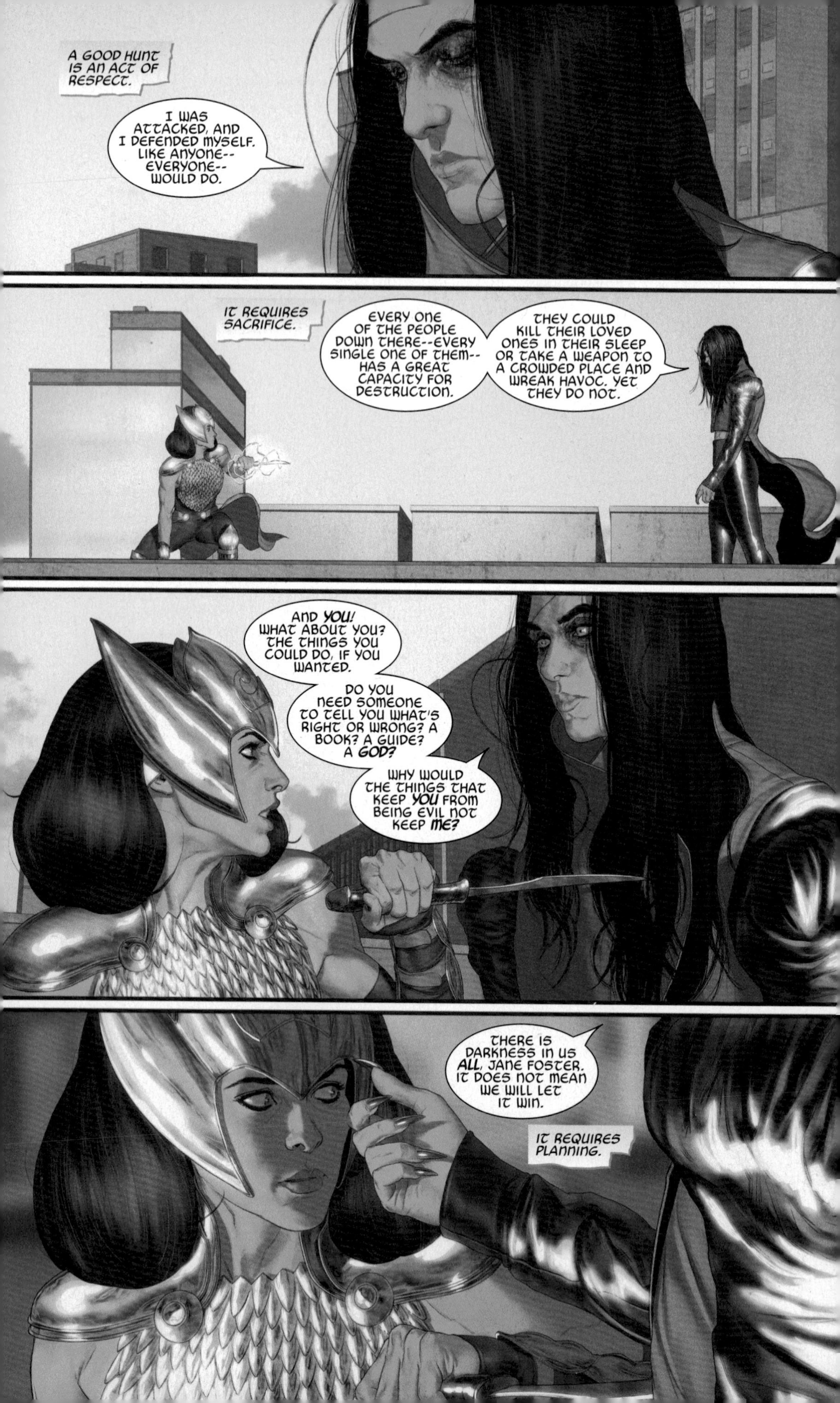
A GOOD HUNT IS AN ACT OF RESPECT.
I WAS ATTACKED, AND I DEFENDED MYSELF. LIKE ANYONE-- EVERYONE-- WOULD DO.
IT REQUIRES SACRIFICE.
EVERY ONE OF THE PEOPLE DOWN THERE--EVERY SINGLE ONE OF THEM-- HAS A GREAT CAPACITY FOR DESTRUCTION.
THEY COULD KILL THEIR LOVED ONES IN THEIR SLEEP OR TAKE A WEAPON TO A CROWDED PLACE AND WREAK HAVOC. YET THEY DO NOT.
AND YOU! WHAT ABOUT YOU? THE THINGS YOU COULD DO, IF YOU WANTED.
DO YOU NEED SOMEONE TO TELL YOU WHAT'S RIGHT OR WRONG? A BOOK? A GUIDE? A GOD?
WHY WOULD THE THINGS THAT KEEP YOU FROM BEING EVIL NOT KEEP ME?
THERE IS DARKNESS IN US ALL, JANE FOSTER. IT DOES NOT MEAN WE WILL LET IT WIN.
IT REQUIRES PLANNING.

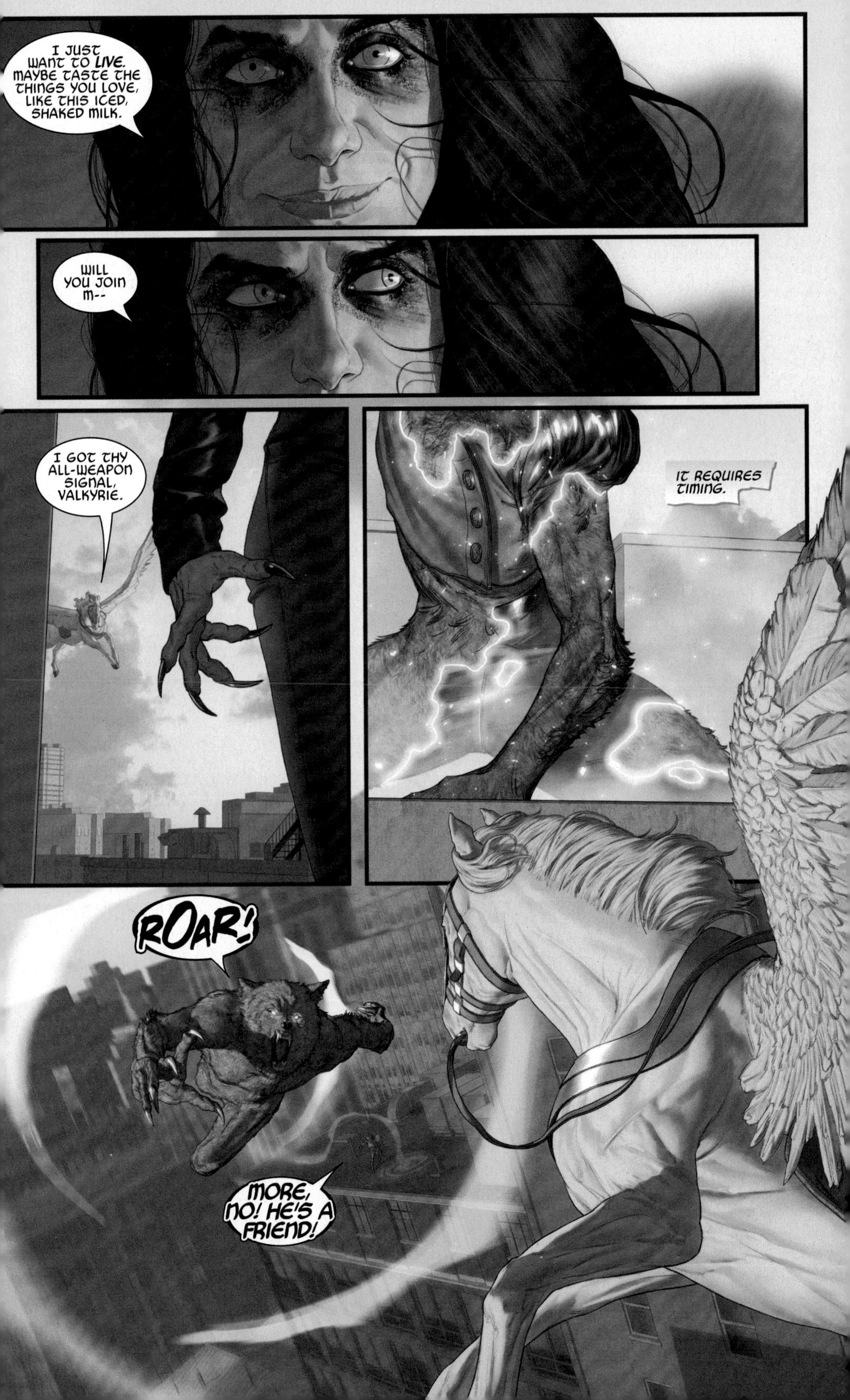
I JUST WANT TO LIVE. MAYBE TASTE THE THINGS YOU LOVE, LIKE THIS ICED, SHAKED MILK.
WILL YOU JOIN M--
I GOT THY ALL-WEAPON SIGNAL, VALKYRIE.
IT REQUIRES TIMING.
ROAR!
MORE, NO! HE'S A FRIEND!

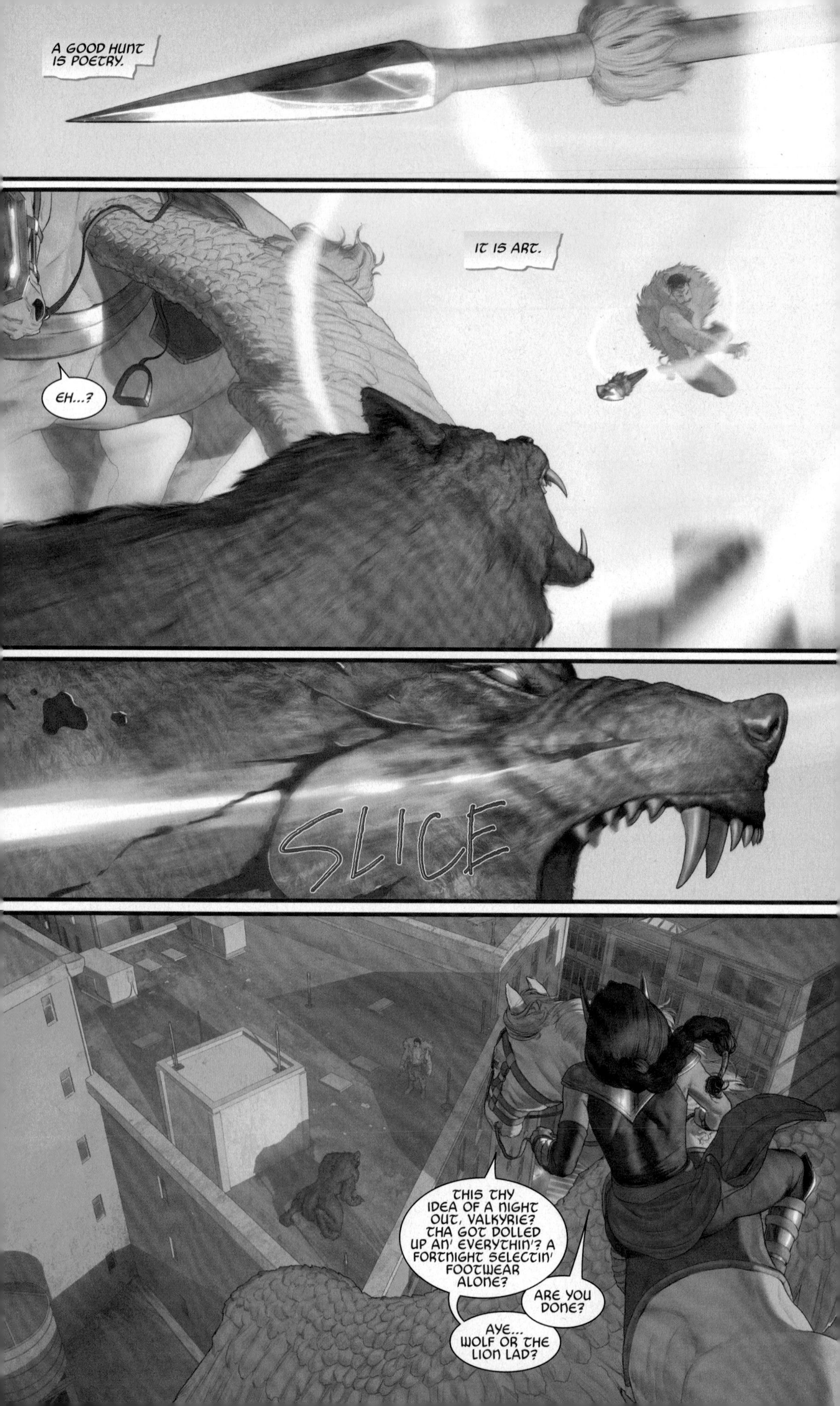
A GOOD HUNT IS POETRY.
IT IS ART.
EH...?
SLICE
THIS THY IDEA OF A NIGHT OUT, VALKYRIE? THA GOT DOLLED UP AN' EVERYTHIN'? A FORTNIGHT SELECTIN' FOOTWEAR ALONE?
ARE YOU DONE?
AYE... WOLF OR THE LION LAD?

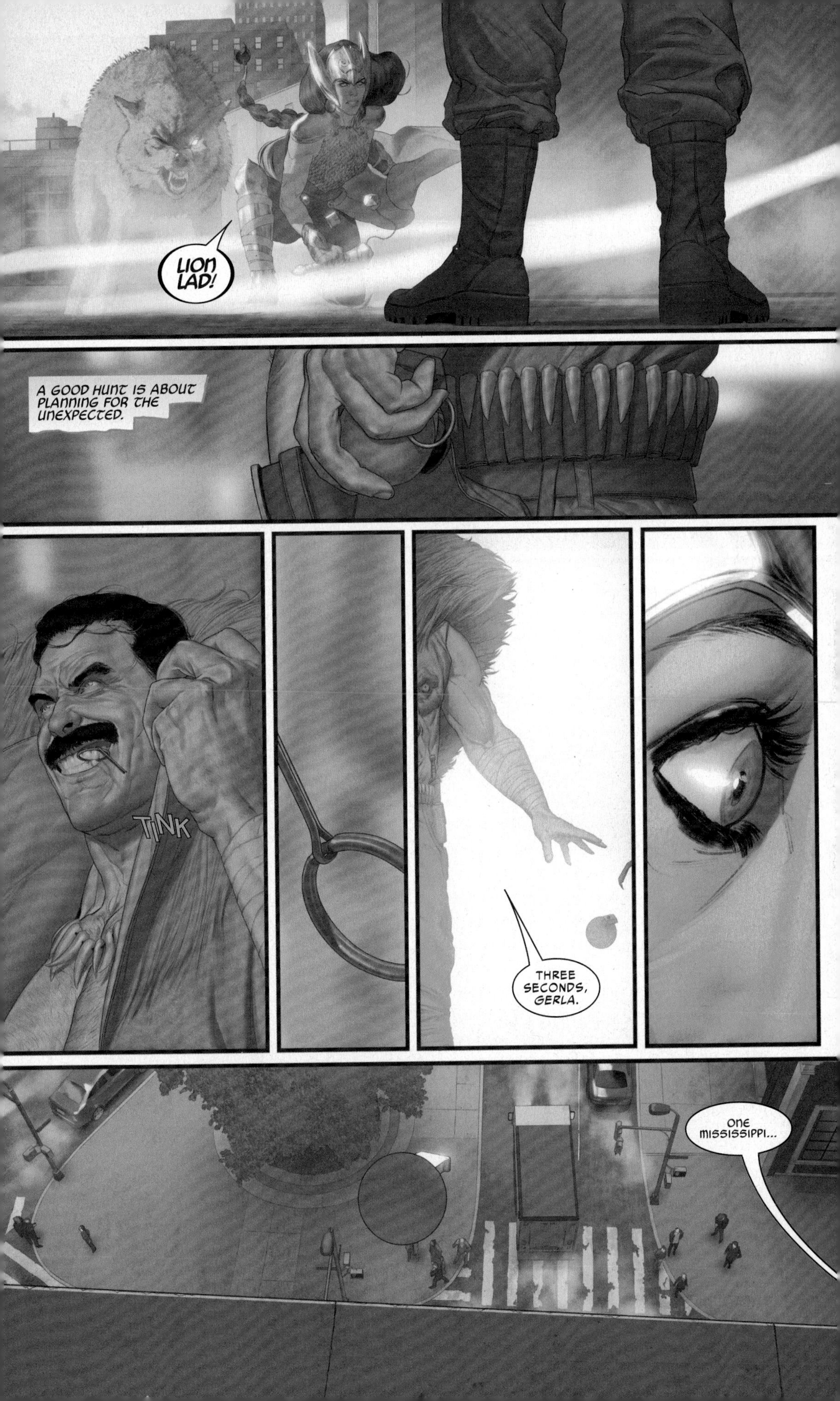
LION LAD!
A GOOD HUNT IS ABOUT PLANNING FOR THE UNEXPECTED.
TINK
THREE SECONDS, GERLA.
ONE MISSISSIPPI...

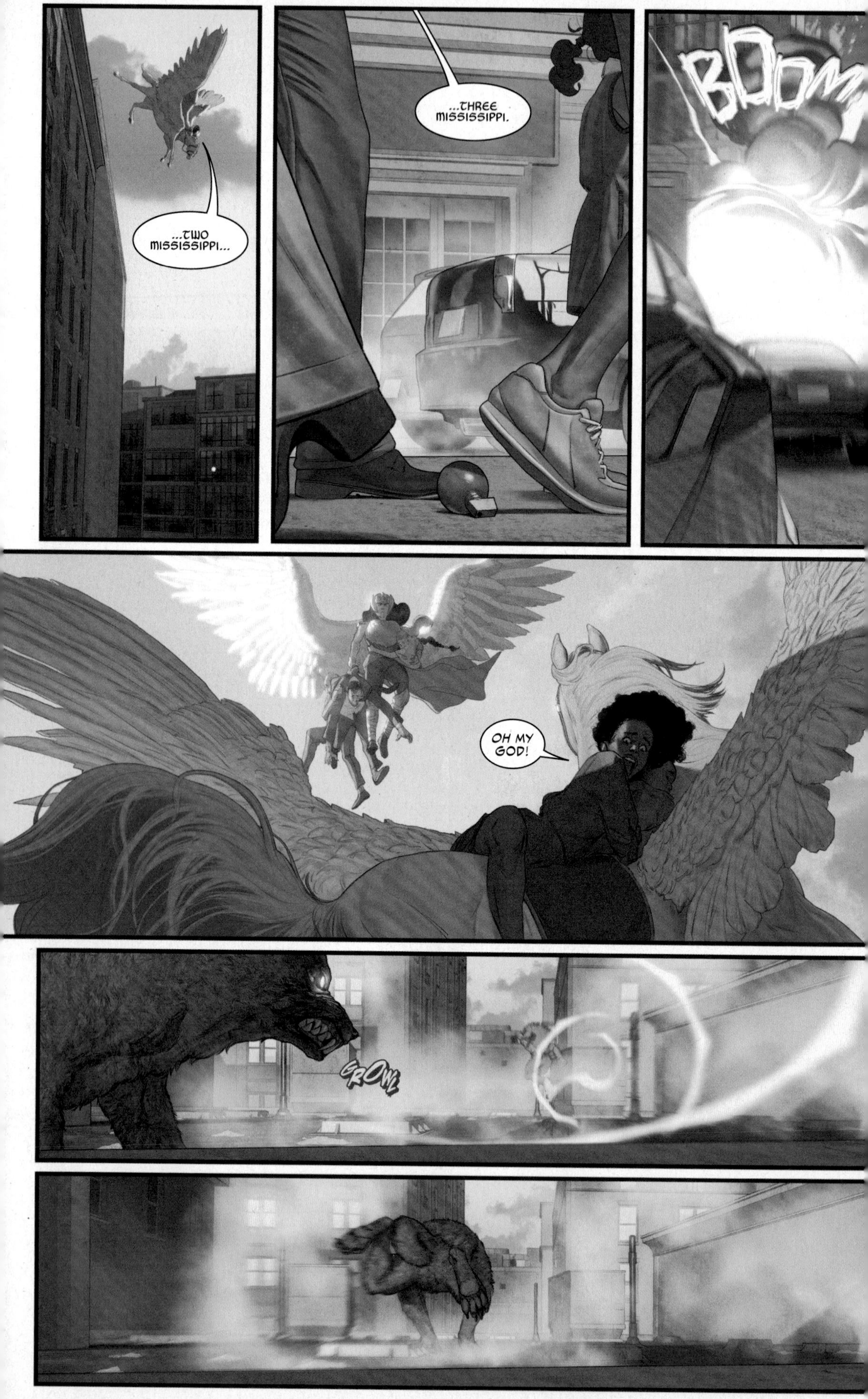
...TWO MISSISSIPPI...
...THREE MISSISSIPPI.
BOOM
OH MY GOD!
GROWL

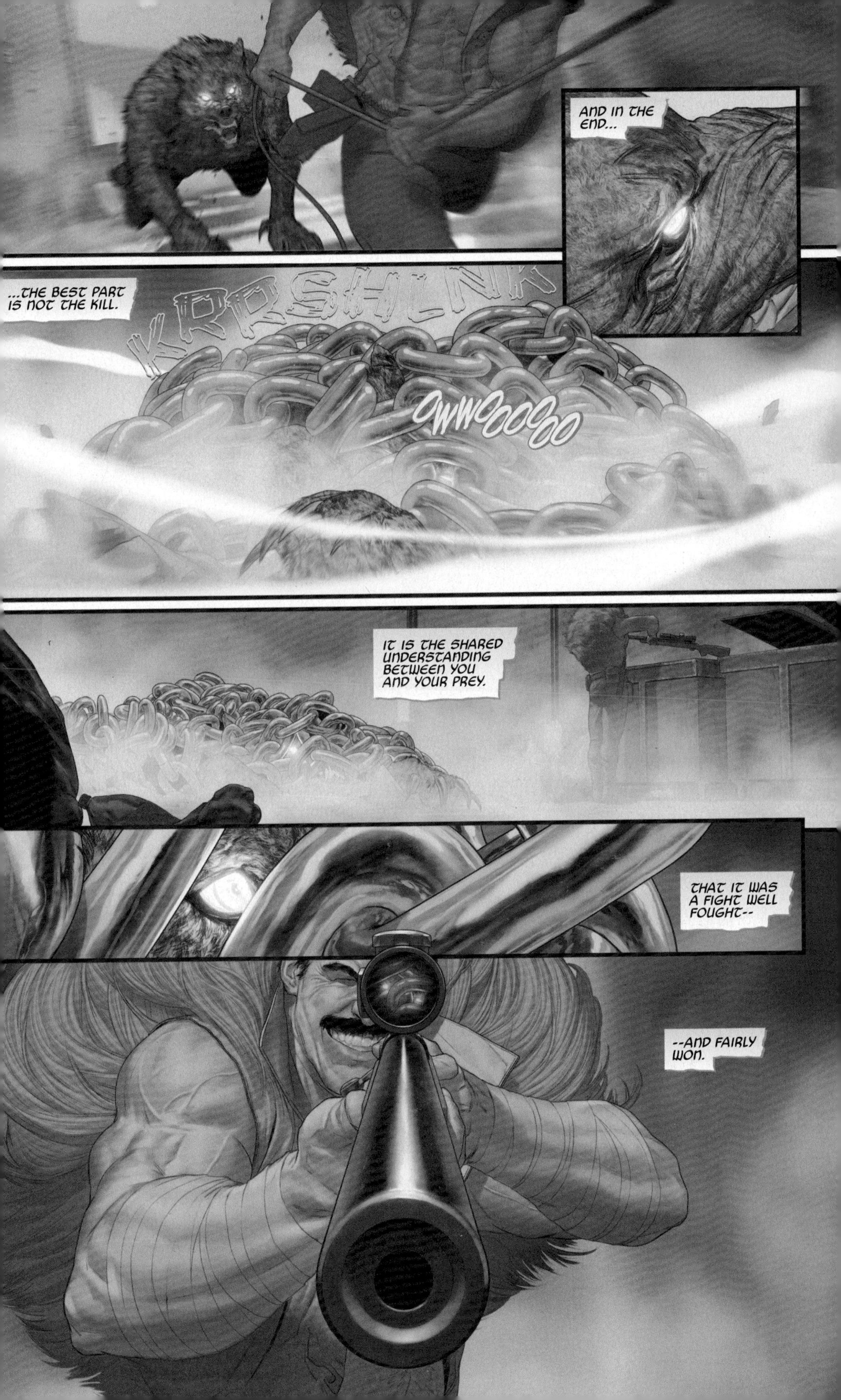
AND IN THE END...
...THE BEST PART IS NOT THE KILL.
KRRSHLNK
OWWOOOOOO
IT IS THE SHARED UNDERSTANDING BETWEEN YOU AND YOUR PREY.
THAT IT WAS A FIGHT WELL FOUGHT--
--AND FAIRLY WON.

3.

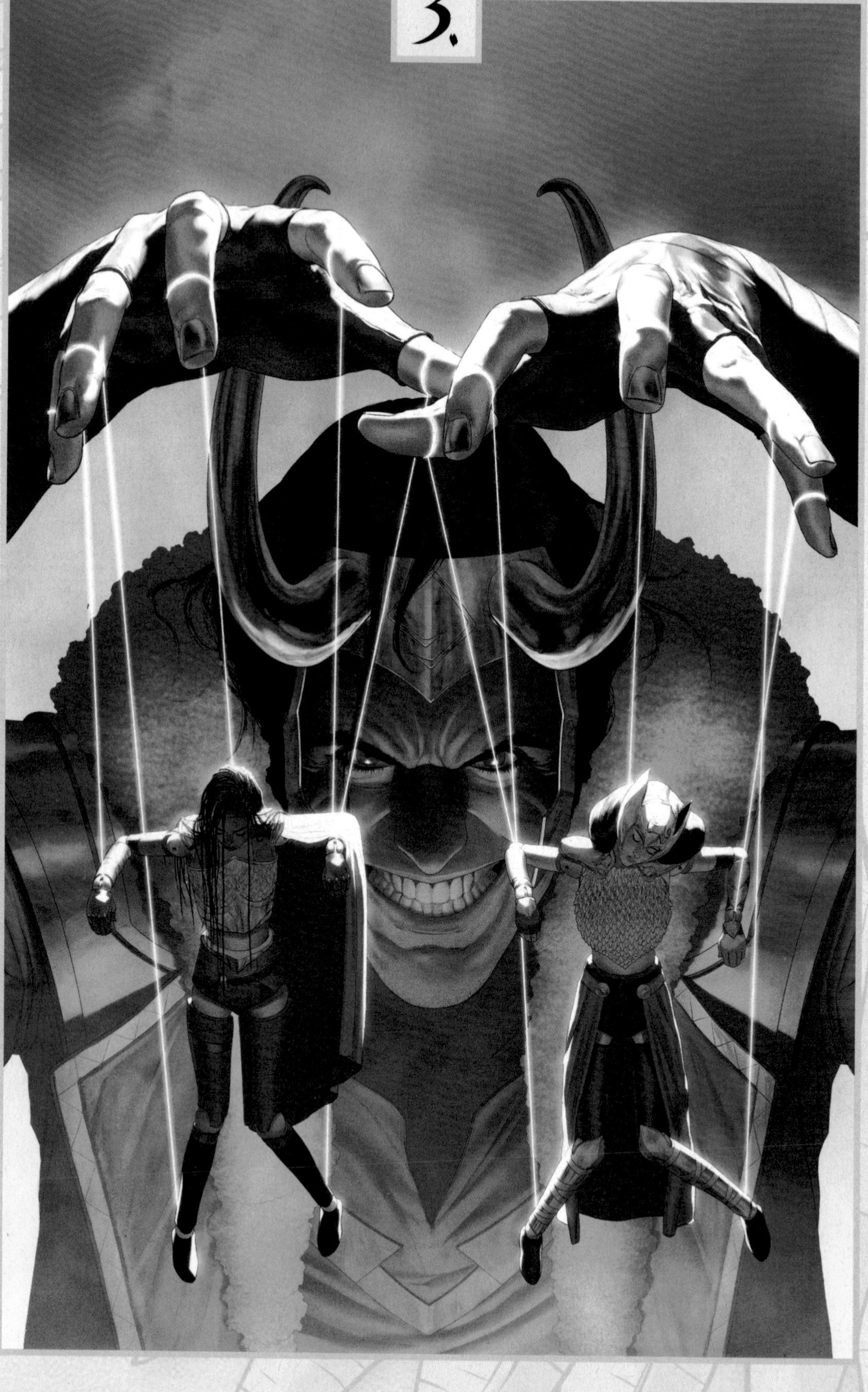

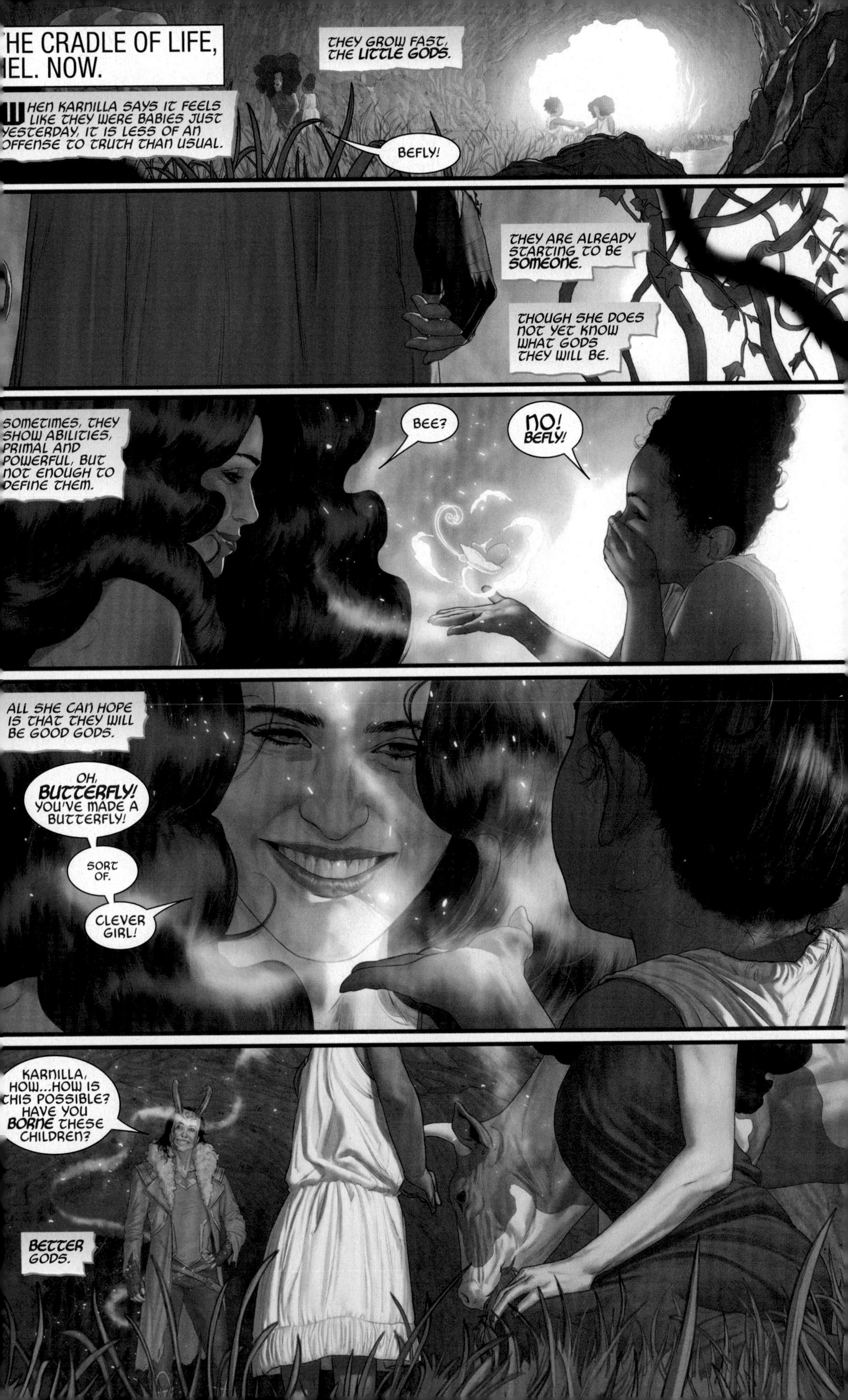

THE CRADLE OF LIFE,
HEL. NOW.
WHEN KARNILLA SAYS IT FEELS LIKE THEY WERE BABIES JUST YESTERDAY, IT IS LESS OF AN OFFENSE TO TRUTH THAN USUAL.
THEY GROW FAST, THE LITTLE GODS.
BEFLY!
THEY ARE ALREADY STARTING TO BE SOMEONE.
THOUGH SHE DOES NOT YET KNOW WHAT GODS THEY WILL BE.
SOMETIMES, THEY SHOW ABILITIES, PRIMAL AND POWERFUL, BUT NOT ENOUGH TO DEFINE THEM.
BEE?
NO! BEFLY!
ALL SHE CAN HOPE IS THAT THEY WILL BE GOOD GODS.
OH, BUTTERFLY! YOU'VE MADE A BUTTERFLY!
SORT OF.
CLEVER GIRL!
KARNILLA, HOW...HOW IS THIS POSSIBLE? HAVE YOU BORNE THESE CHILDREN?
BETTER GODS.

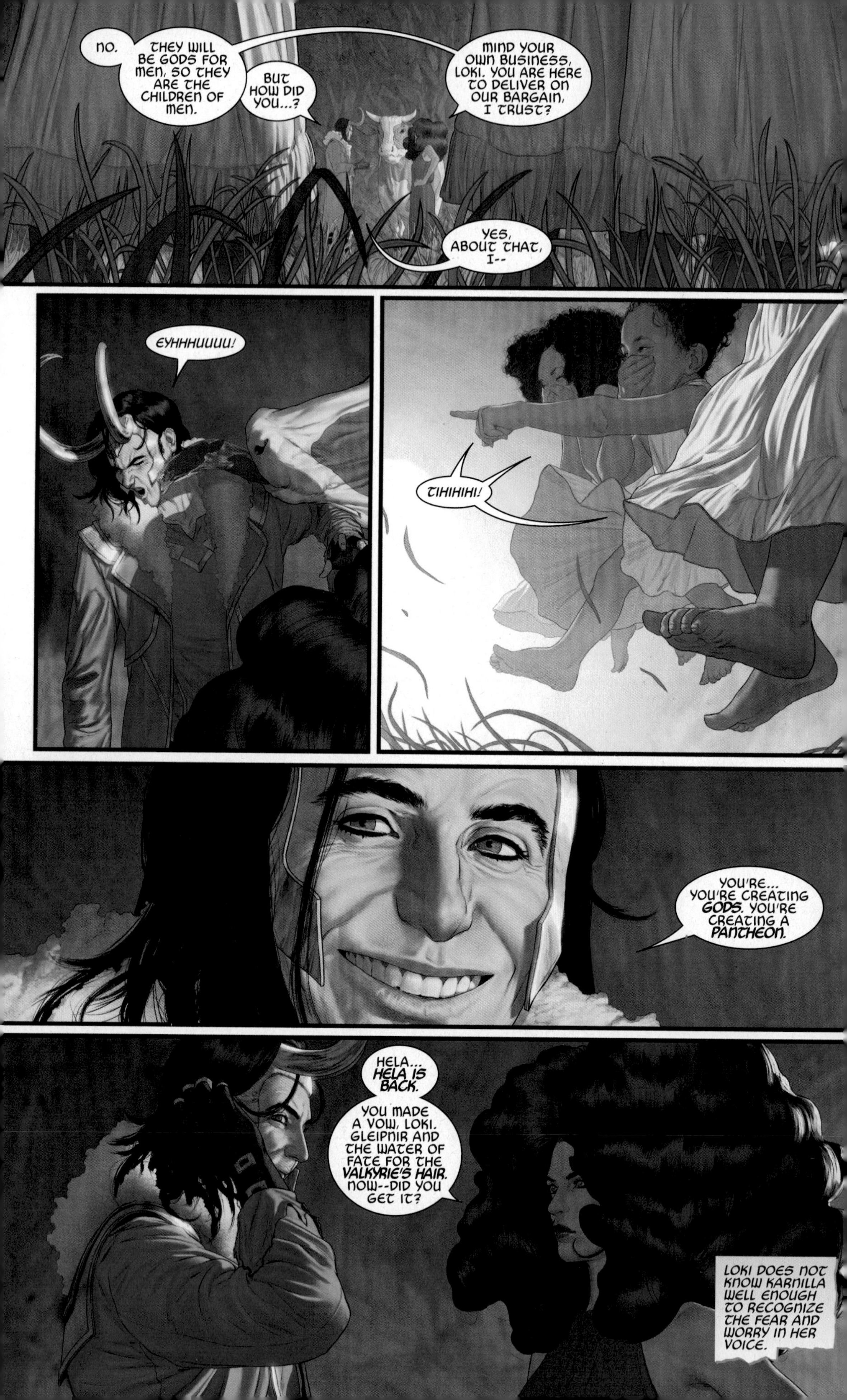
NO.
THEY WILL BE GODS FOR MEN, SO THEY ARE THE CHILDREN OF MEN.
BUT HOW DID YOU...?
MIND YOUR OWN BUSINESS, LOKI. YOU ARE HERE TO DELIVER ON OUR BARGAIN, I TRUST?
YES, ABOUT THAT, I--
EYHHHUUUU!
TIHIHIHI!
YOU'RE... YOU'RE CREATING GODS. YOU'RE CREATING A PANTHEON.
HELA... HELA IS BACK.
YOU MADE A VOW, LOKI. GLEIPNIR AND THE WATER OF FATE FOR THE VALKYRIE'S HAIR. NOW--DID YOU GET IT?
LOKI DOES NOT KNOW KARNILLA WELL ENOUGH TO RECOGNIZE THE FEAR AND WORRY IN HER VOICE.

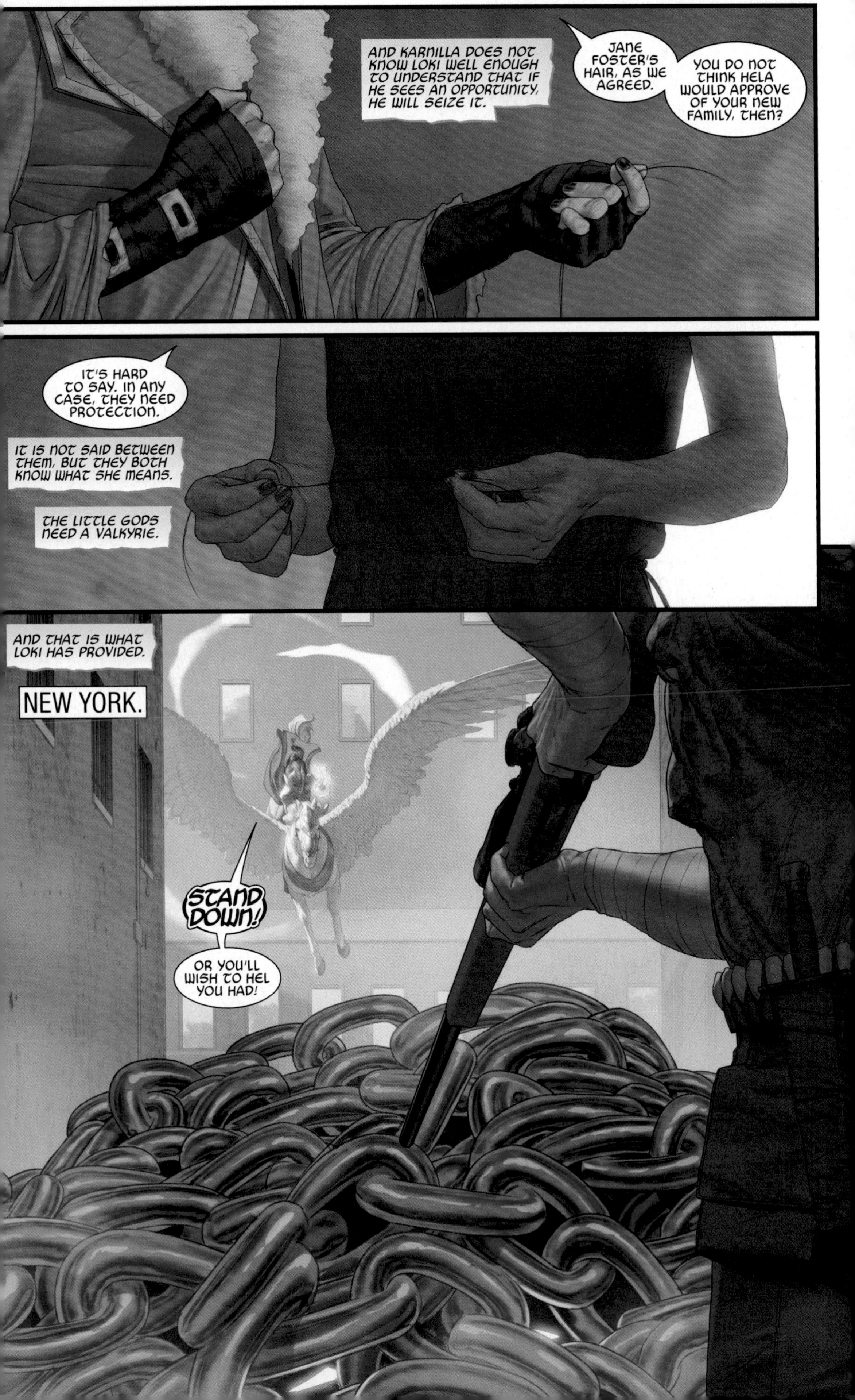
AND KARNILLA DOES NOT KNOW LOKI WELL ENOUGH TO UNDERSTAND THAT IF HE SEES AN OPPORTUNITY, HE WILL SEIZE IT.
JANE FOSTER'S HAIR, AS WE AGREED.
YOU DO NOT THINK HELA WOULD APPROVE OF YOUR NEW FAMILY, THEN?
IT'S HARD TO SAY. IN ANY CASE, THEY NEED PROTECTION.
IT IS NOT SAID BETWEEN THEM, BUT THEY BOTH KNOW WHAT SHE MEANS.
THE LITTLE GODS NEED A VALKYRIE.
AND THAT IS WHAT LOKI HAS PROVIDED.
NEW YORK.
STAND DOWN!
OR YOU'LL WISH TO HEL YOU HAD!

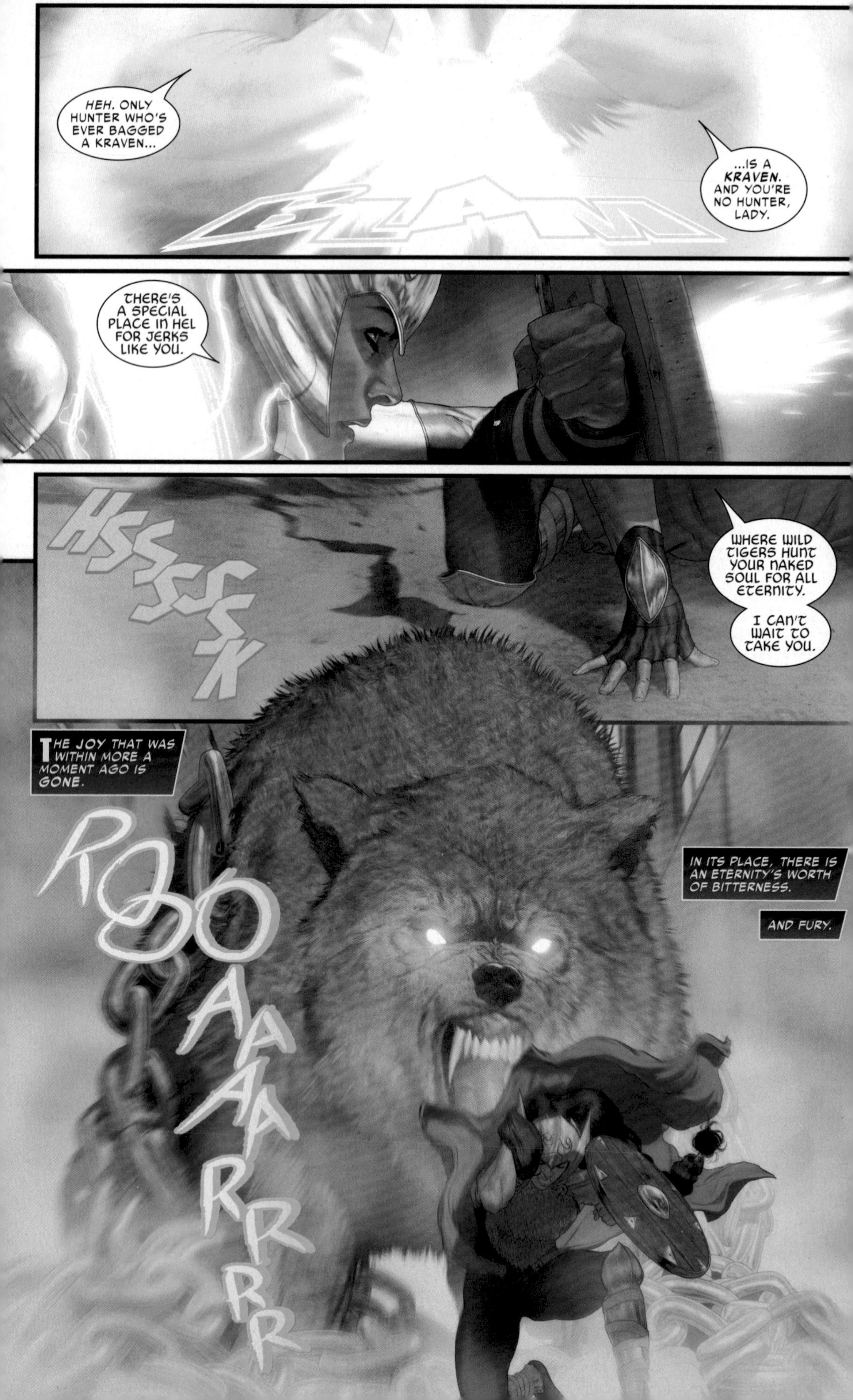

HEH. ONLY HUNTER WHO'S EVER BAGGED A KRAVEN...
...IS A KRAVEN. AND YOU'RE NO HUNTER, LADY.
BLAM
THERE'S A SPECIAL PLACE IN HEL FOR JERKS LIKE YOU.
HSSSSSK
WHERE WILD TIGERS HUNT YOUR NAKED SOUL FOR ALL ETERNITY.
I CAN'T WAIT TO TAKE YOU.
THE JOY THAT WAS WITHIN MORE A MOMENT AGO IS GONE.
IN ITS PLACE, THERE IS AN ETERNITY'S WORTH OF BITTERNESS.
AND FURY.
ROOOAAAARRRR

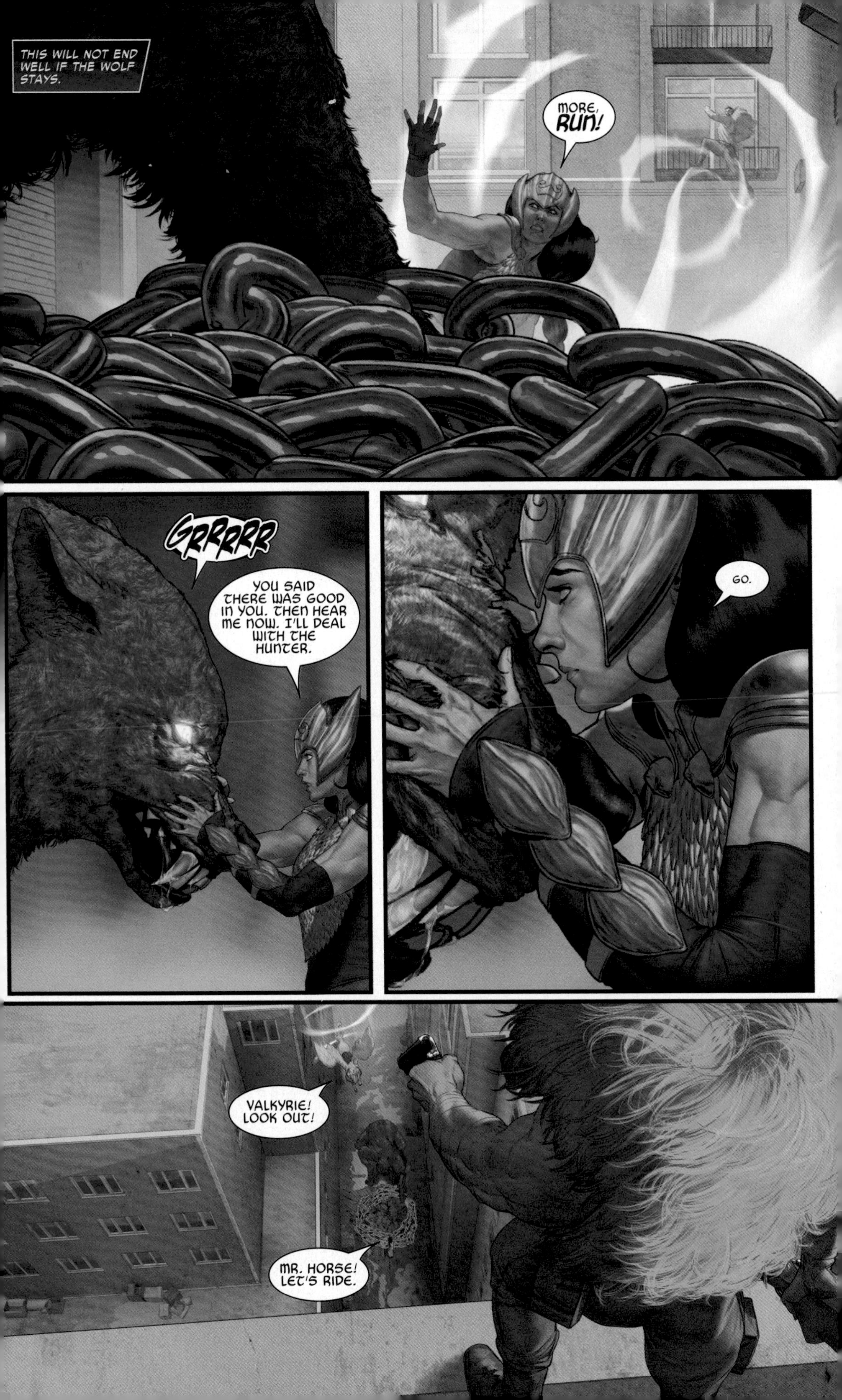
THIS WILL NOT END WELL IF THE WOLF STAYS.
MORE, RUN!
GRRRRR
YOU SAID THERE WAS GOOD IN YOU. THEN HEAR ME NOW. I'LL DEAL WITH THE HUNTER.
GO.
VALKYRIE! LOOK OUT!
MR. HORSE! LET'S RIDE.

THE BIGGER THE BULLETS, THE SMALLER THE MAN.

TINK TINK

WHO ARE YOU? WHO SENT YOU?

MAGNIFICENT!

I KNOW I AM, BUT ANSWER THE QUESTION!

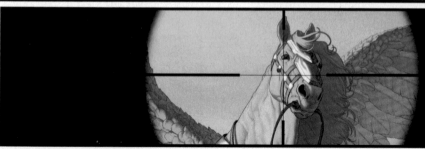

I WAS TALKING ABOUT THE HORSE.

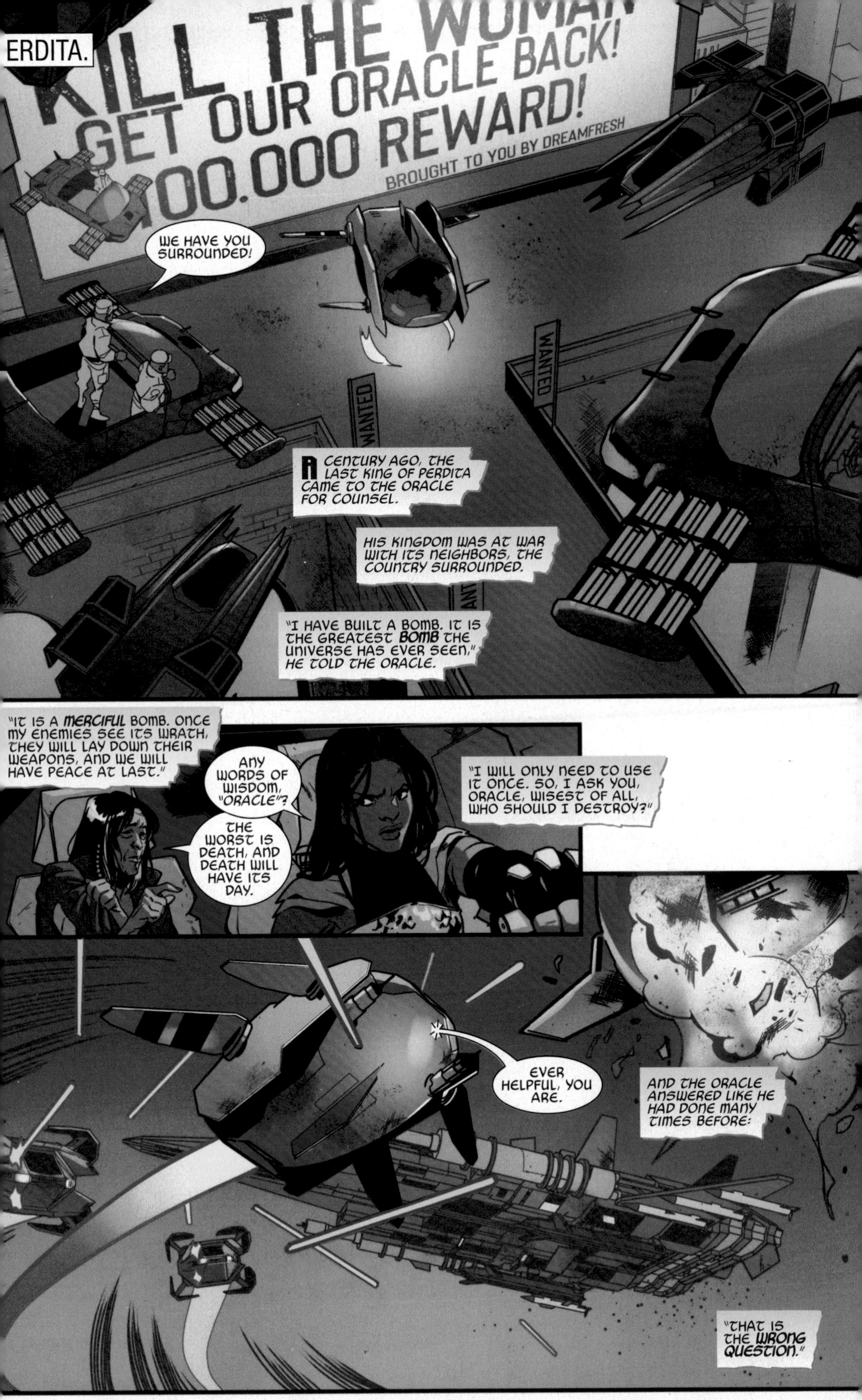
ERDITA.
KILL THE WOMAN
GET OUR ORACLE BACK!
100.000 REWARD!
BROUGHT TO YOU BY DREAMFRESH
WE HAVE YOU SURROUNDED!
WANTED
WANTED
A CENTURY AGO, THE LAST KING OF PERDITA CAME TO THE ORACLE FOR COUNSEL.
HIS KINGDOM WAS AT WAR WITH ITS NEIGHBORS, THE COUNTRY SURROUNDED.
"I HAVE BUILT A BOMB. IT IS THE GREATEST BOMB THE UNIVERSE HAS EVER SEEN," HE TOLD THE ORACLE.
"IT IS A MERCIFUL BOMB. ONCE MY ENEMIES SEE ITS WRATH, THEY WILL LAY DOWN THEIR WEAPONS, AND WE WILL HAVE PEACE AT LAST."
ANY WORDS OF WISDOM, "ORACLE"?
THE WORST IS DEATH, AND DEATH WILL HAVE ITS DAY.
"I WILL ONLY NEED TO USE IT ONCE. SO, I ASK YOU, ORACLE, WISEST OF ALL, WHO SHOULD I DESTROY?"
EVER HELPFUL, YOU ARE.
AND THE ORACLE ANSWERED LIKE HE HAD DONE MANY TIMES BEFORE:
"THAT IS THE WRONG QUESTION."

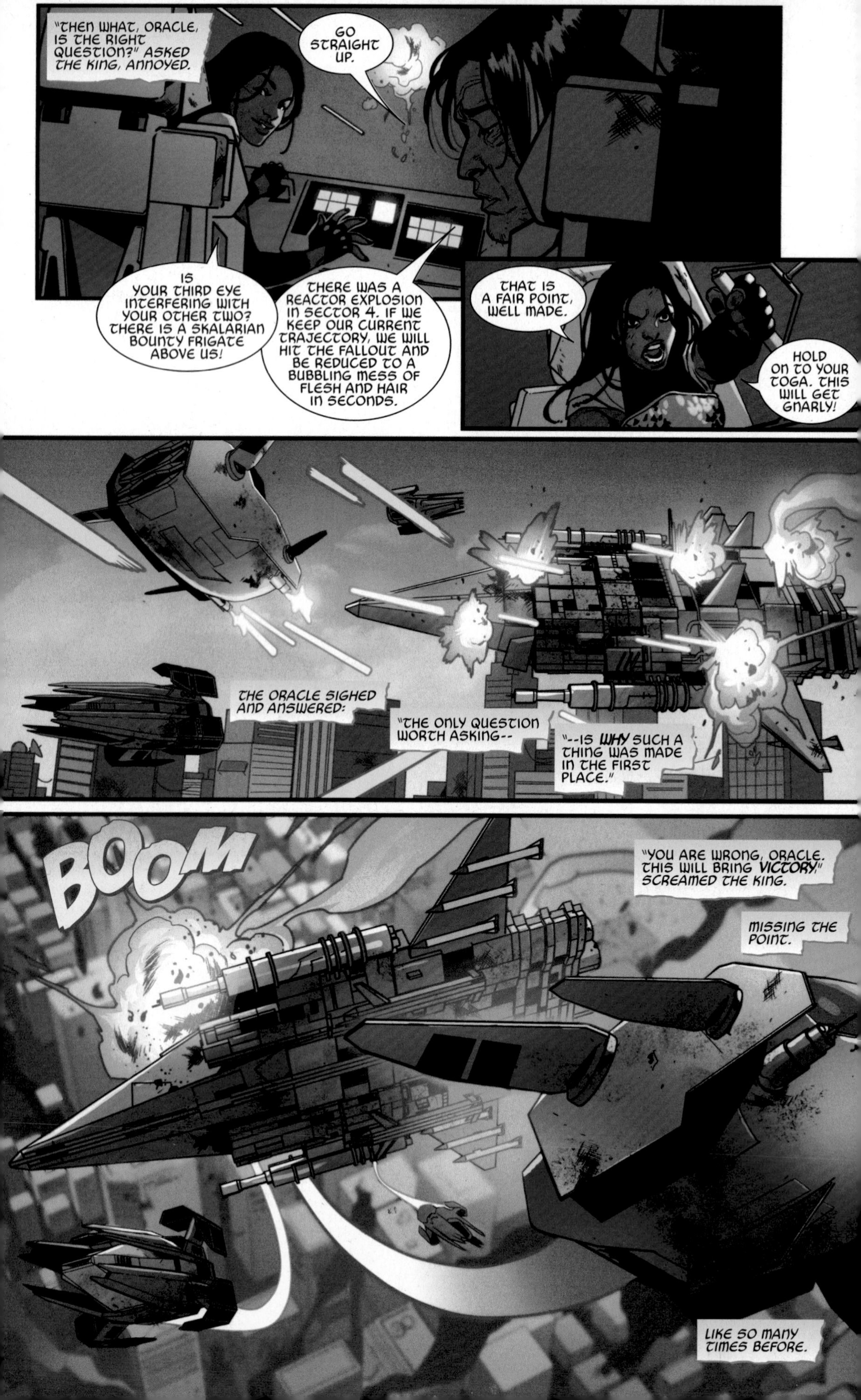
"THEN WHAT, ORACLE, IS THE RIGHT QUESTION?" ASKED THE KING, ANNOYED.
GO STRAIGHT UP.
IS YOUR THIRD EYE INTERFERING WITH YOUR OTHER TWO? THERE IS A SKALARIAN BOUNTY FRIGATE ABOVE US!
THERE WAS A REACTOR EXPLOSION IN SECTOR 4. IF WE KEEP OUR CURRENT TRAJECTORY, WE WILL HIT THE FALLOUT AND BE REDUCED TO A BUBBLING MESS OF FLESH AND HAIR IN SECONDS.
THAT IS A FAIR POINT, WELL MADE.
HOLD ON TO YOUR TOGA. THIS WILL GET GNARLY!
THE ORACLE SIGHED AND ANSWERED:
"THE ONLY QUESTION WORTH ASKING--
"--IS WHY SUCH A THING WAS MADE IN THE FIRST PLACE."
BOOM
"YOU ARE WRONG, ORACLE. THIS WILL BRING VICTORY!" SCREAMED THE KING.
MISSING THE POINT.
LIKE SO MANY TIMES BEFORE.

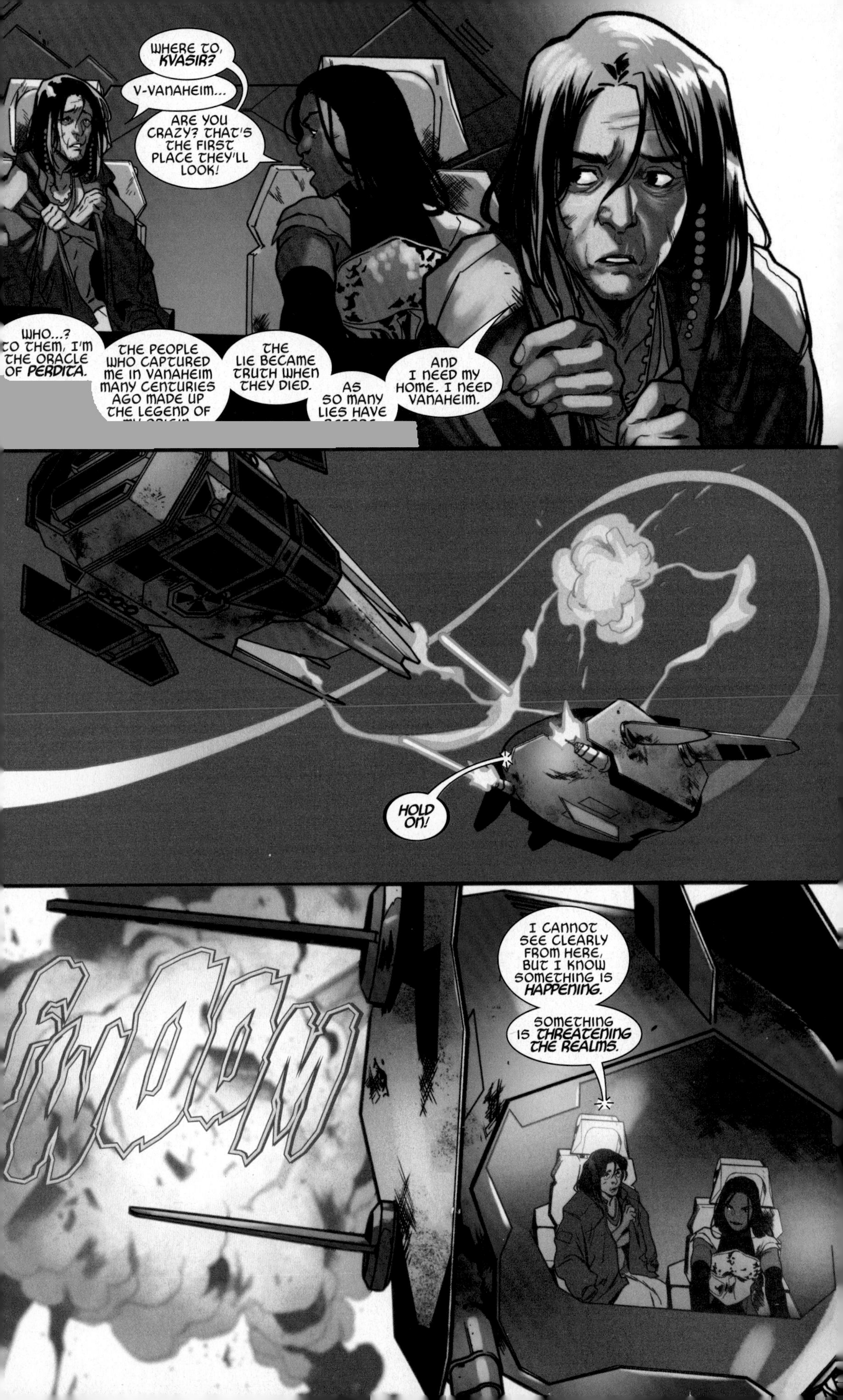
WHERE TO, **KVASIR?**
V-VANAHEIM...
ARE YOU CRAZY? THAT'S THE FIRST PLACE THEY'LL LOOK!
WHO...? TO THEM, I'M THE ORACLE OF **PERDITA.**
THE PEOPLE WHO CAPTURED ME IN VANAHEIM MANY CENTURIES AGO MADE UP THE LEGEND OF
THE LIE BECAME TRUTH WHEN THEY DIED.
AS SO MANY LIES HAVE
AND I NEED MY HOME. I NEED VANAHEIM.
HOLD ON!
FWOOM
I CANNOT SEE CLEARLY FROM HERE, BUT I KNOW SOMETHING IS ***HAPPENING.***
SOMETHING IS ***THREATENING THE REALMS.***

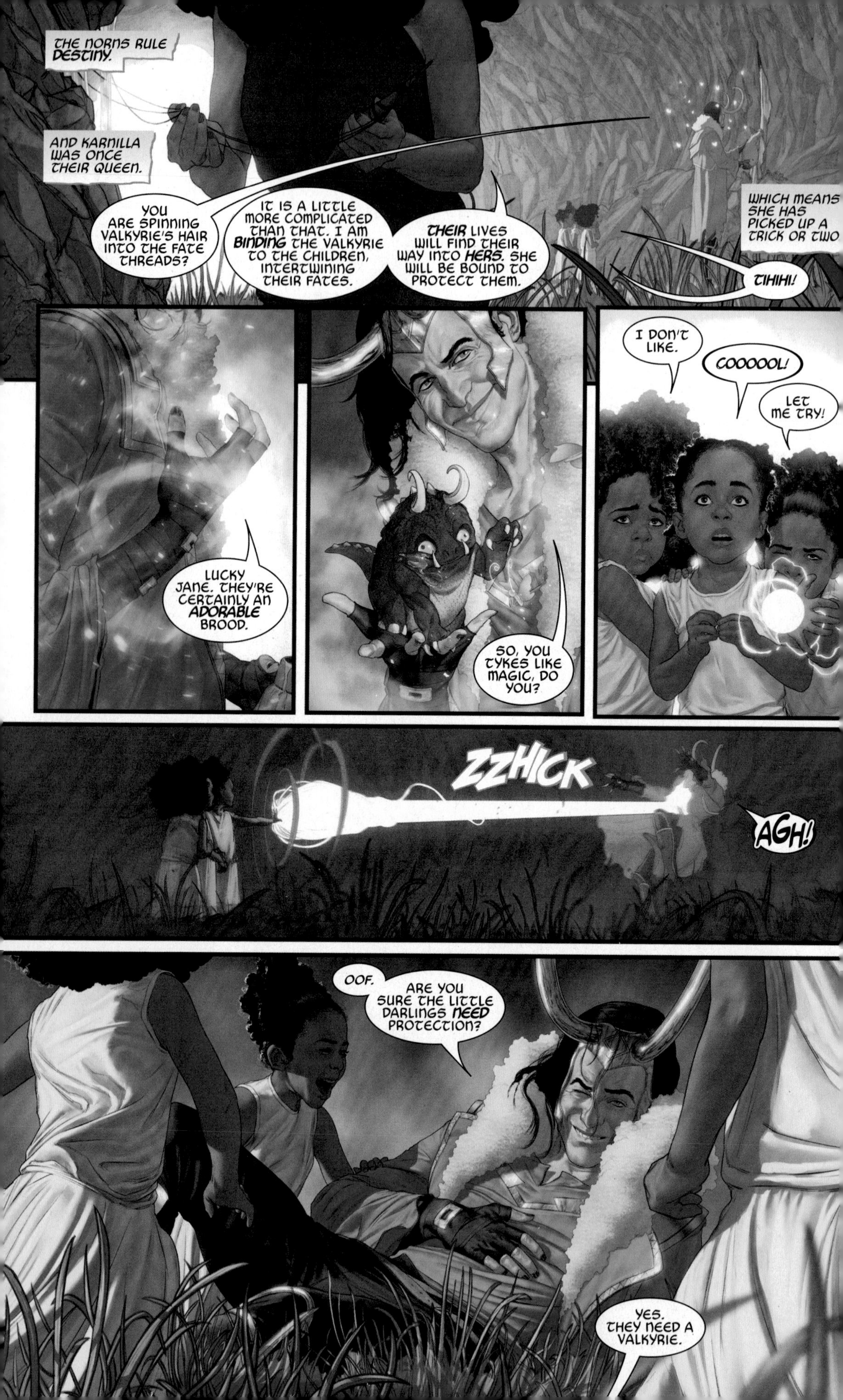

THE NORNS RULE DESTINY.
AND KARNILLA WAS ONCE THEIR QUEEN.
YOU ARE SPINNING VALKYRIE'S HAIR INTO THE FATE THREADS?
IT IS A LITTLE MORE COMPLICATED THAN THAT. I AM BINDING THE VALKYRIE TO THE CHILDREN, INTERTWINING THEIR FATES.
THEIR LIVES WILL FIND THEIR WAY INTO HERS. SHE WILL BE BOUND TO PROTECT THEM.
WHICH MEANS SHE HAS PICKED UP A TRICK OR TWO
TIHIHI!
LUCKY JANE. THEY'RE CERTAINLY AN ADORABLE BROOD.
SO, YOU TYKES LIKE MAGIC, DO YOU?
I DON'T LIKE.
COOOOOL!
LET ME TRY!
ZZHICK
AGH!
OOF.
ARE YOU SURE THE LITTLE DARLINGS NEED PROTECTION?
YES. THEY NEED A VALKYRIE.

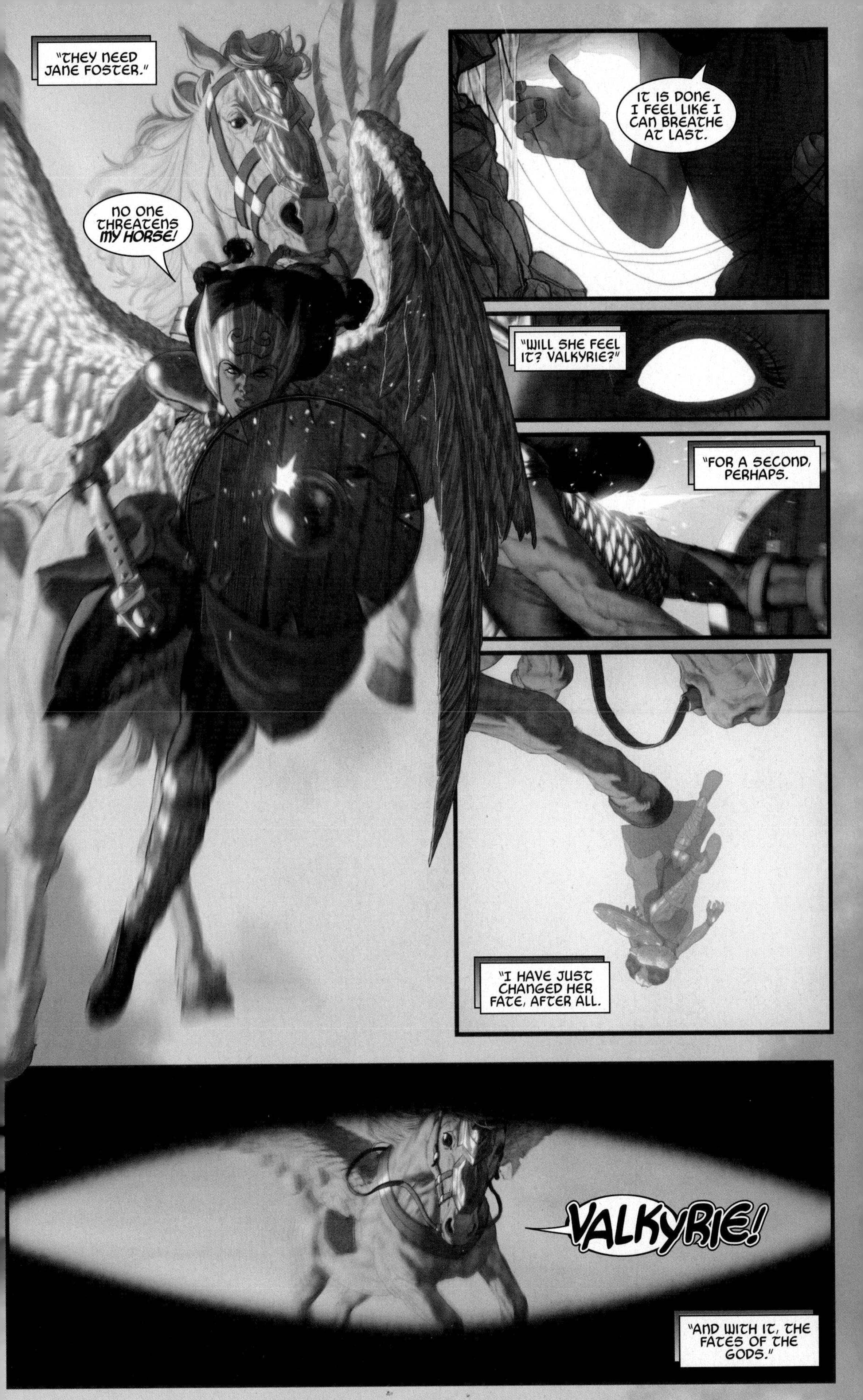
"THEY NEED JANE FOSTER."
NO ONE THREATENS MY HORSE!
IT IS DONE. I FEEL LIKE I CAN BREATHE AT LAST.
"WILL SHE FEEL IT? VALKYRIE?"
"FOR A SECOND, PERHAPS.
"I HAVE JUST CHANGED HER FATE, AFTER ALL.
VALKYRIE!
"AND WITH IT, THE FATES OF THE GODS."

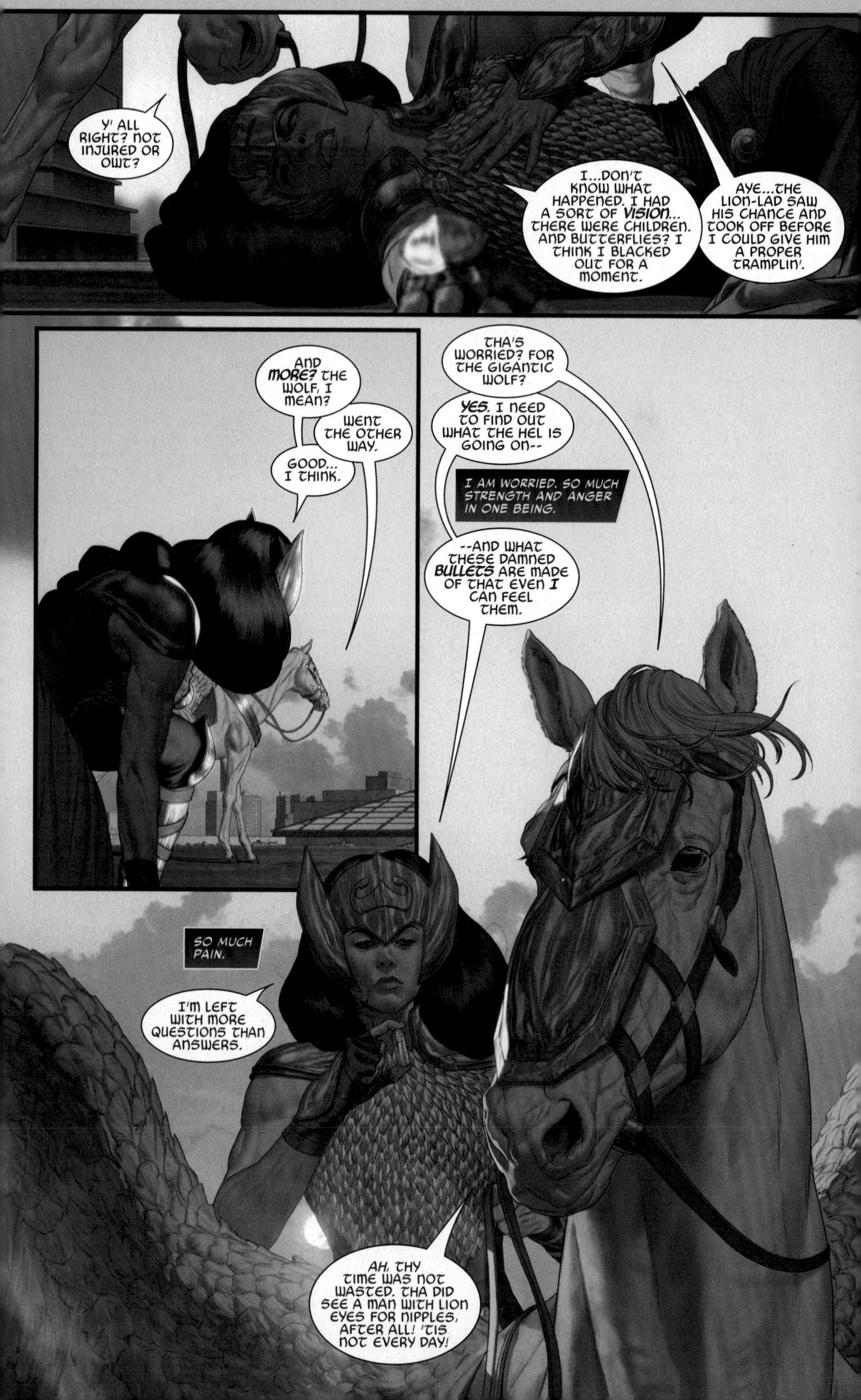
Y' ALL RIGHT? NOT INJURED OR OWT?
I...DON'T KNOW WHAT HAPPENED. I HAD A SORT OF VISION... THERE WERE CHILDREN. AND BUTTERFLIES? I THINK I BLACKED OUT FOR A MOMENT.
AYE...THE LION-LAD SAW HIS CHANCE AND TOOK OFF BEFORE I COULD GIVE HIM A PROPER TRAMPLIN'.
AND MORE? THE WOLF, I MEAN?
WENT THE OTHER WAY.
GOOD... I THINK.
THA'S WORRIED? FOR THE GIGANTIC WOLF?
YES. I NEED TO FIND OUT WHAT THE HEL IS GOING ON--
I AM WORRIED. SO MUCH STRENGTH AND ANGER IN ONE BEING.
--AND WHAT THESE DAMNED BULLETS ARE MADE OF THAT EVEN I CAN FEEL THEM.
SO MUCH PAIN.
I'M LEFT WITH MORE QUESTIONS THAN ANSWERS.
AH, THY TIME WAS NOT WASTED. THA DID SEE A MAN WITH LION EYES FOR NIPPLES, AFTER ALL! 'TIS NOT EVERY DAY!

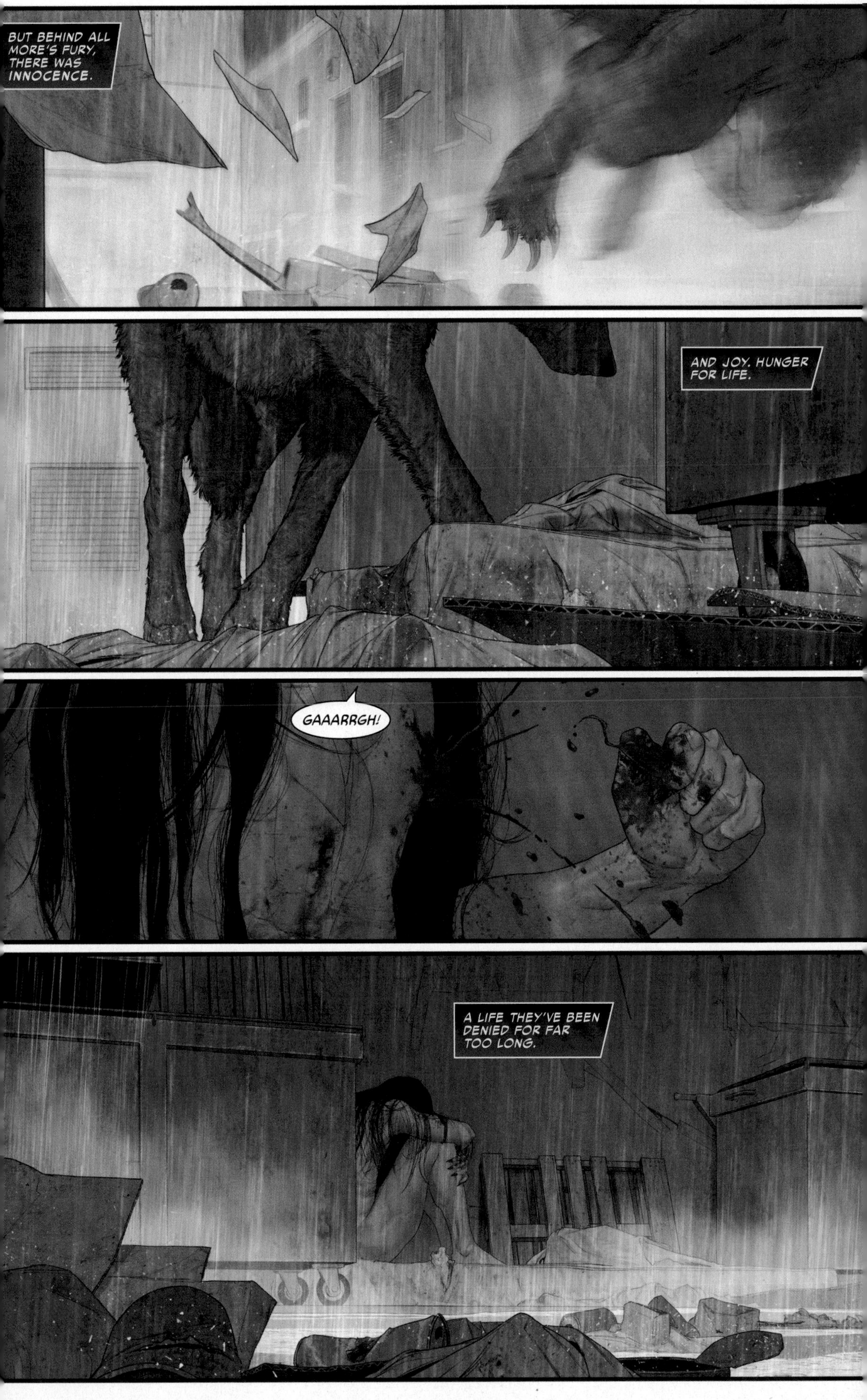

BUT BEHIND ALL MORE'S FURY, THERE WAS INNOCENCE.
AND JOY. HUNGER FOR LIFE.
GAAARRGH!
A LIFE THEY'VE BEEN DENIED FOR FAR TOO LONG.

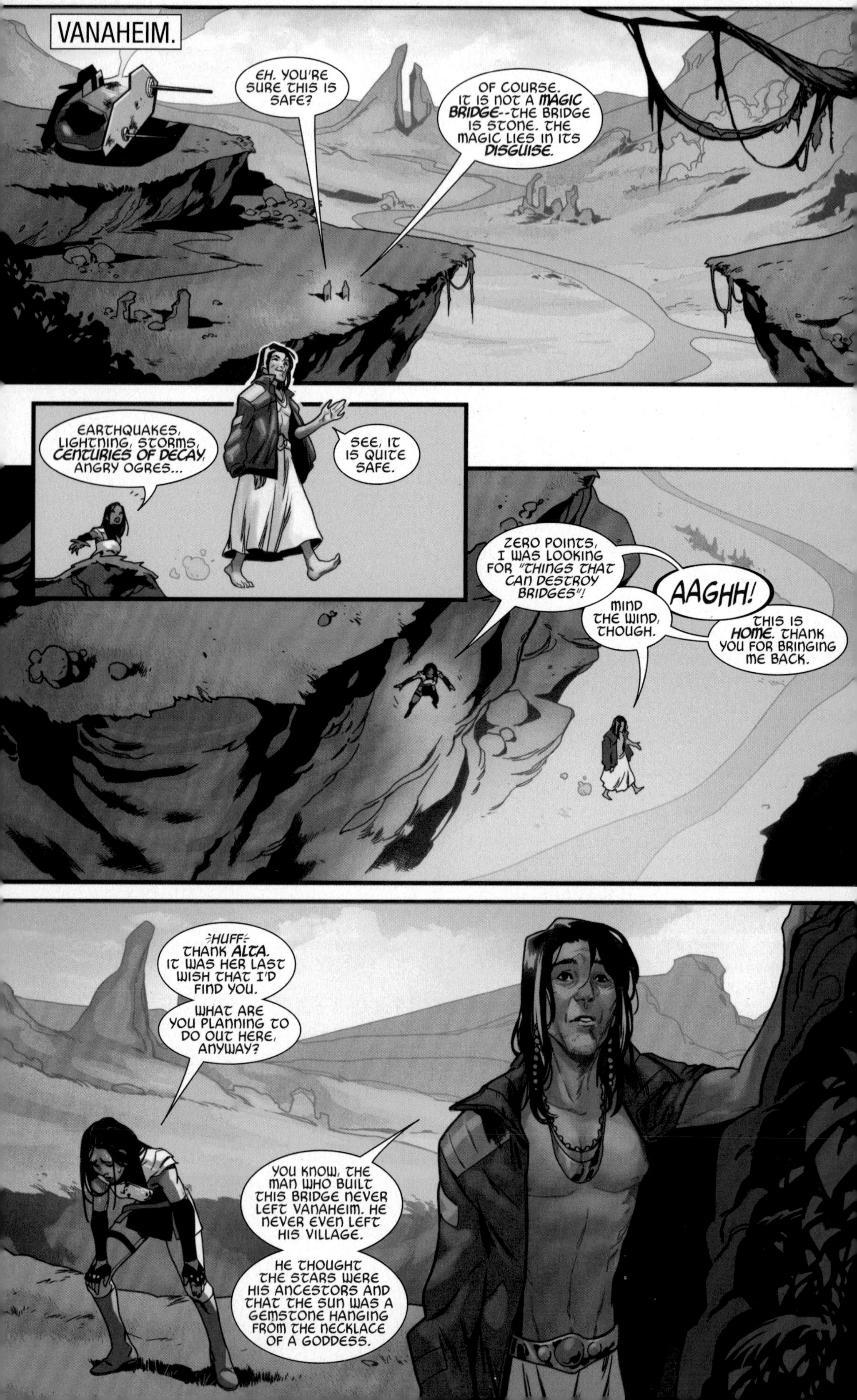
VANAHEIM.
EH. YOU'RE SURE THIS IS SAFE?
OF COURSE. IT IS NOT A MAGIC BRIDGE--THE BRIDGE IS STONE. THE MAGIC LIES IN ITS DISGUISE.
EARTHQUAKES, LIGHTNING, STORMS, CENTURIES OF DECAY, ANGRY OGRES...
SEE, IT IS QUITE SAFE.
ZERO POINTS, I WAS LOOKING FOR "THINGS THAT CAN DESTROY BRIDGES"!
AAGHH!
MIND THE WIND, THOUGH.
THIS IS HOME. THANK YOU FOR BRINGING ME BACK.
HUFF THANK ALTA. IT WAS HER LAST WISH THAT I'D FIND YOU.
WHAT ARE YOU PLANNING TO DO OUT HERE, ANYWAY?
YOU KNOW, THE MAN WHO BUILT THIS BRIDGE NEVER LEFT VANAHEIM. HE NEVER EVEN LEFT HIS VILLAGE.
HE THOUGHT THE STARS WERE HIS ANCESTORS AND THAT THE SUN WAS A GEMSTONE HANGING FROM THE NECKLACE OF A GODDESS.

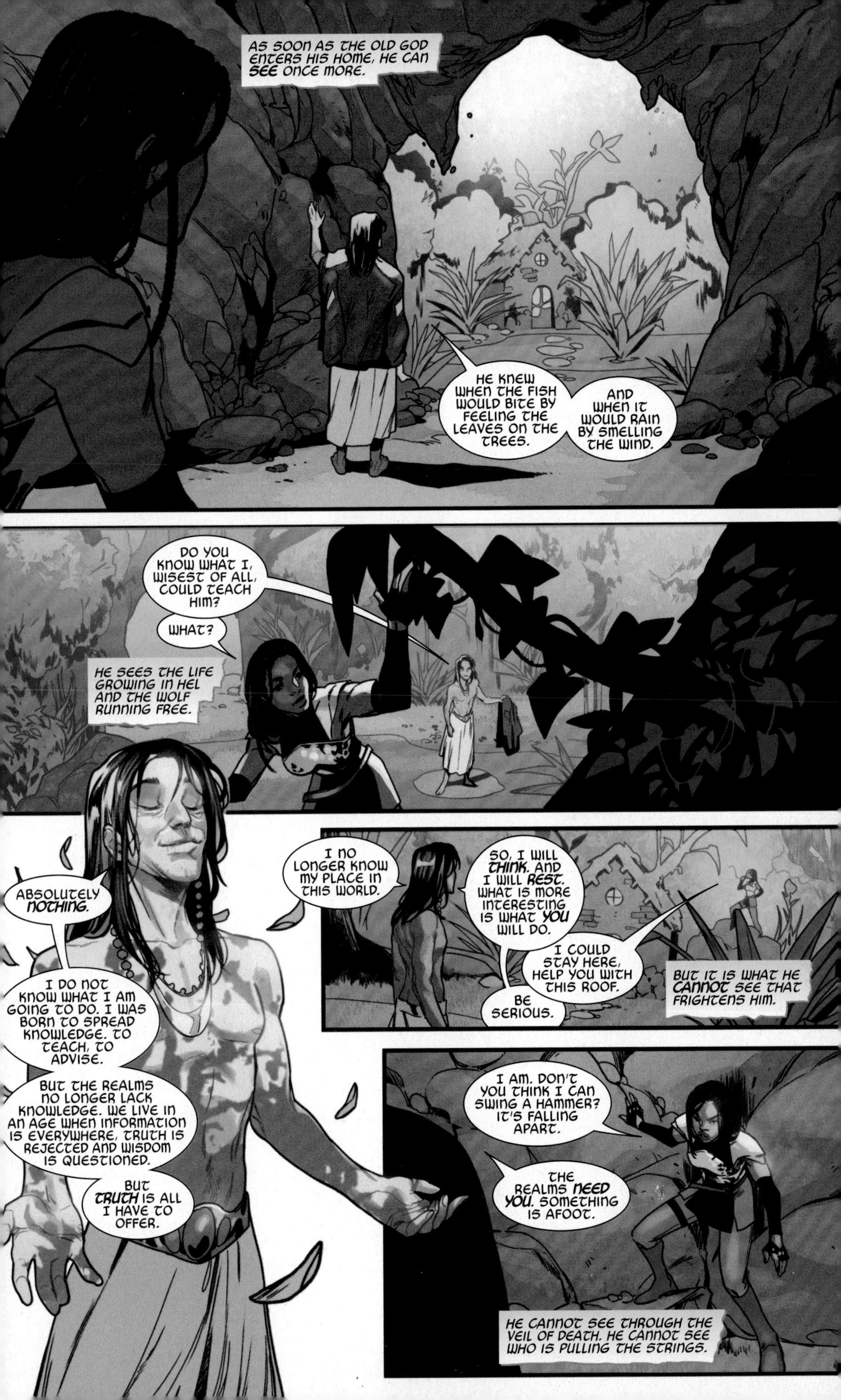
AS SOON AS THE OLD GOD ENTERS HIS HOME, HE CAN SEE ONCE MORE.
HE KNEW WHEN THE FISH WOULD BITE BY FEELING THE LEAVES ON THE TREES.
AND WHEN IT WOULD RAIN BY SMELLING THE WIND.
DO YOU KNOW WHAT I, WISEST OF ALL, COULD TEACH HIM?
WHAT?
HE SEES THE LIFE GROWING IN HEL AND THE WOLF RUNNING FREE.
ABSOLUTELY NOTHING.
I DO NOT KNOW WHAT I AM GOING TO DO. I WAS BORN TO SPREAD KNOWLEDGE. TO TEACH, TO ADVISE.
BUT THE REALMS NO LONGER LACK KNOWLEDGE. WE LIVE IN AN AGE WHEN INFORMATION IS EVERYWHERE, TRUTH IS REJECTED AND WISDOM IS QUESTIONED.
BUT TRUTH IS ALL I HAVE TO OFFER.
I NO LONGER KNOW MY PLACE IN THIS WORLD.
SO, I WILL THINK. AND I WILL REST. WHAT IS MORE INTERESTING IS WHAT YOU WILL DO.
I COULD STAY HERE, HELP YOU WITH THIS ROOF.
BE SERIOUS.
BUT IT IS WHAT HE CANNOT SEE THAT FRIGHTENS HIM.
I AM. DON'T YOU THINK I CAN SWING A HAMMER? IT'S FALLING APART.
THE REALMS NEED YOU. SOMETHING IS AFOOT.
HE CANNOT SEE THROUGH THE VEIL OF DEATH. HE CANNOT SEE WHO IS PULLING THE STRINGS.

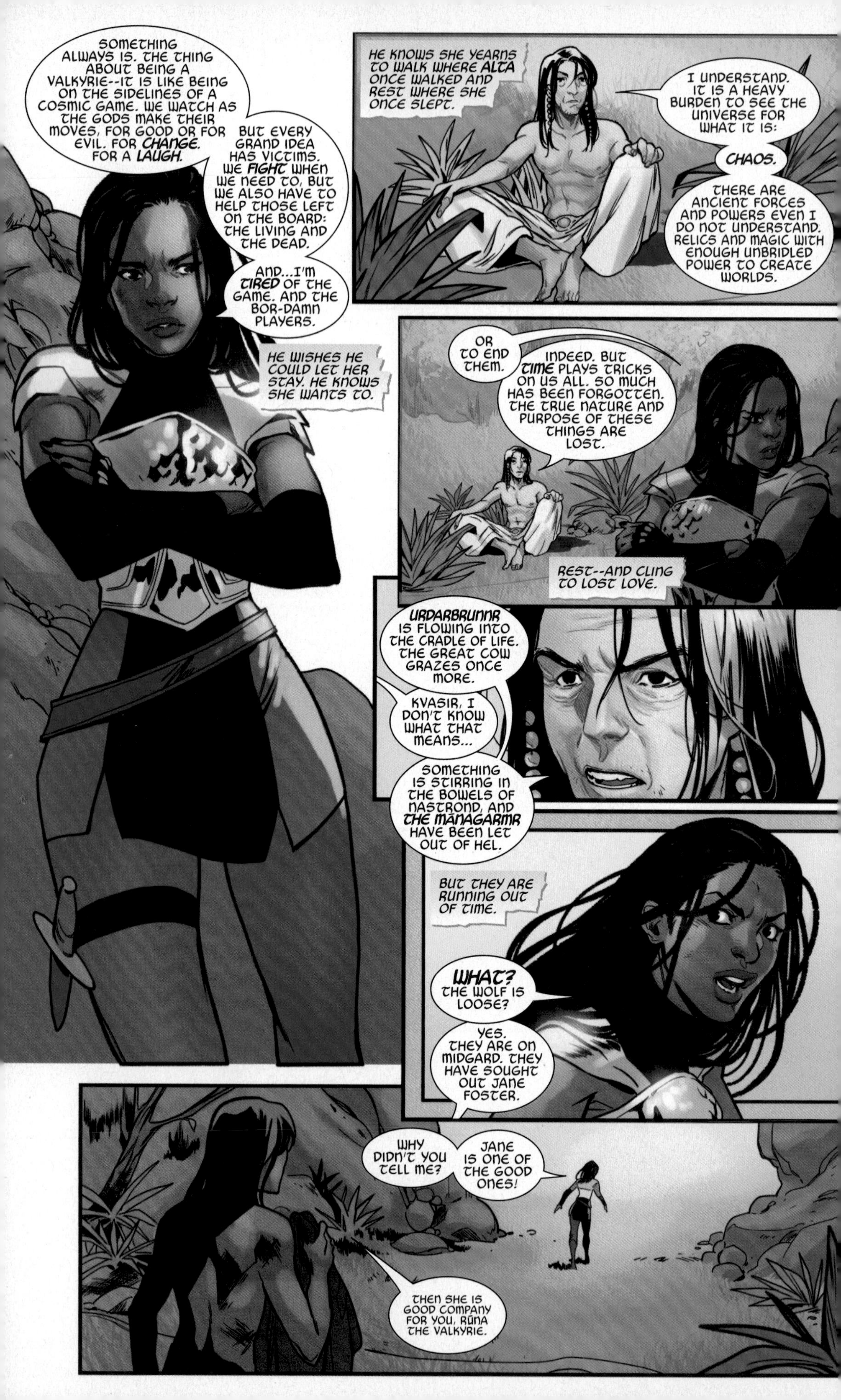
SOMETHING ALWAYS IS. THE THING ABOUT BEING A VALKYRIE--IT IS LIKE BEING ON THE SIDELINES OF A COSMIC GAME. WE WATCH AS THE GODS MAKE THEIR MOVES, FOR GOOD OR FOR EVIL. FOR CHANGE. FOR A LAUGH.
BUT EVERY GRAND IDEA HAS VICTIMS. WE FIGHT WHEN WE NEED TO, BUT WE ALSO HAVE TO HELP THOSE LEFT ON THE BOARD: THE LIVING AND THE DEAD.
AND...I'M TIRED OF THE GAME. AND THE BOR-DAMN PLAYERS.
HE WISHES HE COULD LET HER STAY. HE KNOWS SHE WANTS TO.
HE KNOWS SHE YEARNS TO WALK WHERE ALTA ONCE WALKED AND REST WHERE SHE ONCE SLEPT.
I UNDERSTAND. IT IS A HEAVY BURDEN TO SEE THE UNIVERSE FOR WHAT IT IS:
CHAOS.
THERE ARE ANCIENT FORCES AND POWERS EVEN I DO NOT UNDERSTAND. RELICS AND MAGIC WITH ENOUGH UNBRIDLED POWER TO CREATE WORLDS.
OR TO END THEM.
INDEED. BUT TIME PLAYS TRICKS ON US ALL. SO MUCH HAS BEEN FORGOTTEN. THE TRUE NATURE AND PURPOSE OF THESE THINGS ARE LOST.
REST--AND CLING TO LOST LOVE.
URDARBRUNNR IS FLOWING INTO THE CRADLE OF LIFE. THE GREAT COW GRAZES ONCE MORE.
KVASIR, I DON'T KNOW WHAT THAT MEANS...
SOMETHING IS STIRRING IN THE BOWELS OF NASTROND, AND THE MÄNAGARMR HAVE BEEN LET OUT OF HEL.
BUT THEY ARE RUNNING OUT OF TIME.
WHAT? THE WOLF IS LOOSE?
YES. THEY ARE ON MIDGARD. THEY HAVE SOUGHT OUT JANE FOSTER.
WHY DIDN'T YOU TELL ME?
JANE IS ONE OF THE GOOD ONES!
THEN SHE IS GOOD COMPANY FOR YOU, RÚNA THE VALKYRIE.

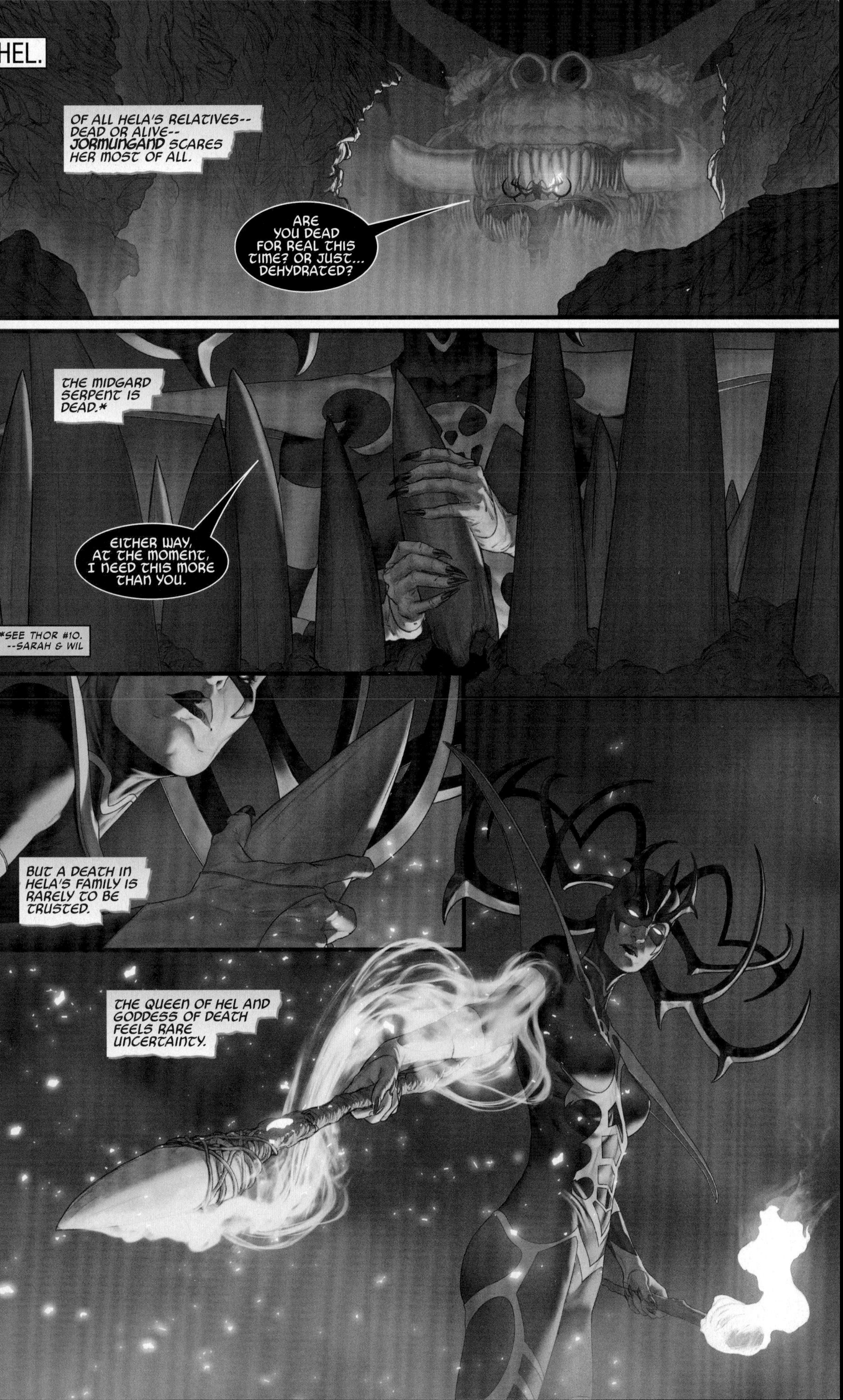

HEL.
OF ALL HELA'S RELATIVES-- DEAD OR ALIVE-- JORMUNGAND SCARES HER MOST OF ALL.
ARE YOU DEAD FOR REAL THIS TIME? OR JUST... DEHYDRATED?
THE MIDGARD SERPENT IS DEAD.*
EITHER WAY, AT THE MOMENT, I NEED THIS MORE THAN YOU.
*SEE THOR #10. --SARAH & WIL
BUT A DEATH IN HELA'S FAMILY IS RARELY TO BE TRUSTED.
THE QUEEN OF HEL AND GODDESS OF DEATH FEELS RARE UNCERTAINTY.

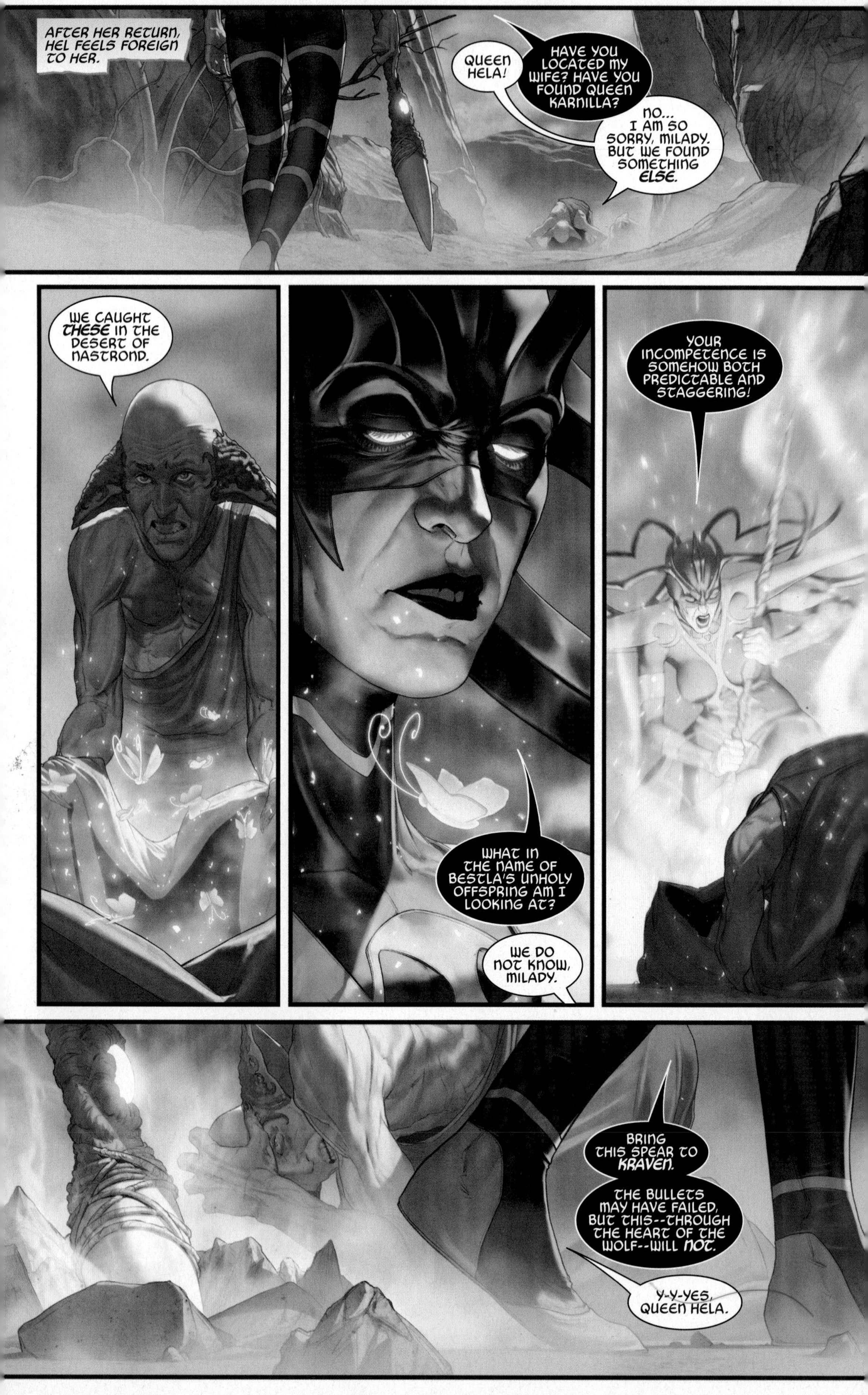
AFTER HER RETURN, HEL FEELS FOREIGN TO HER.
QUEEN HELA!
HAVE YOU LOCATED MY WIFE? HAVE YOU FOUND QUEEN KARNILLA?
NO... I AM SO SORRY, MILADY. BUT WE FOUND SOMETHING ELSE.
WE CAUGHT THESE IN THE DESERT OF NASTROND.
WHAT IN THE NAME OF BESTLA'S UNHOLY OFFSPRING AM I LOOKING AT?
WE DO NOT KNOW, MILADY.
YOUR INCOMPETENCE IS SOMEHOW BOTH PREDICTABLE AND STAGGERING!
BRING THIS SPEAR TO KRAVEN.
THE BULLETS MAY HAVE FAILED, BUT THIS--THROUGH THE HEART OF THE WOLF--WILL NOT.
Y-Y-YES, QUEEN HELA.

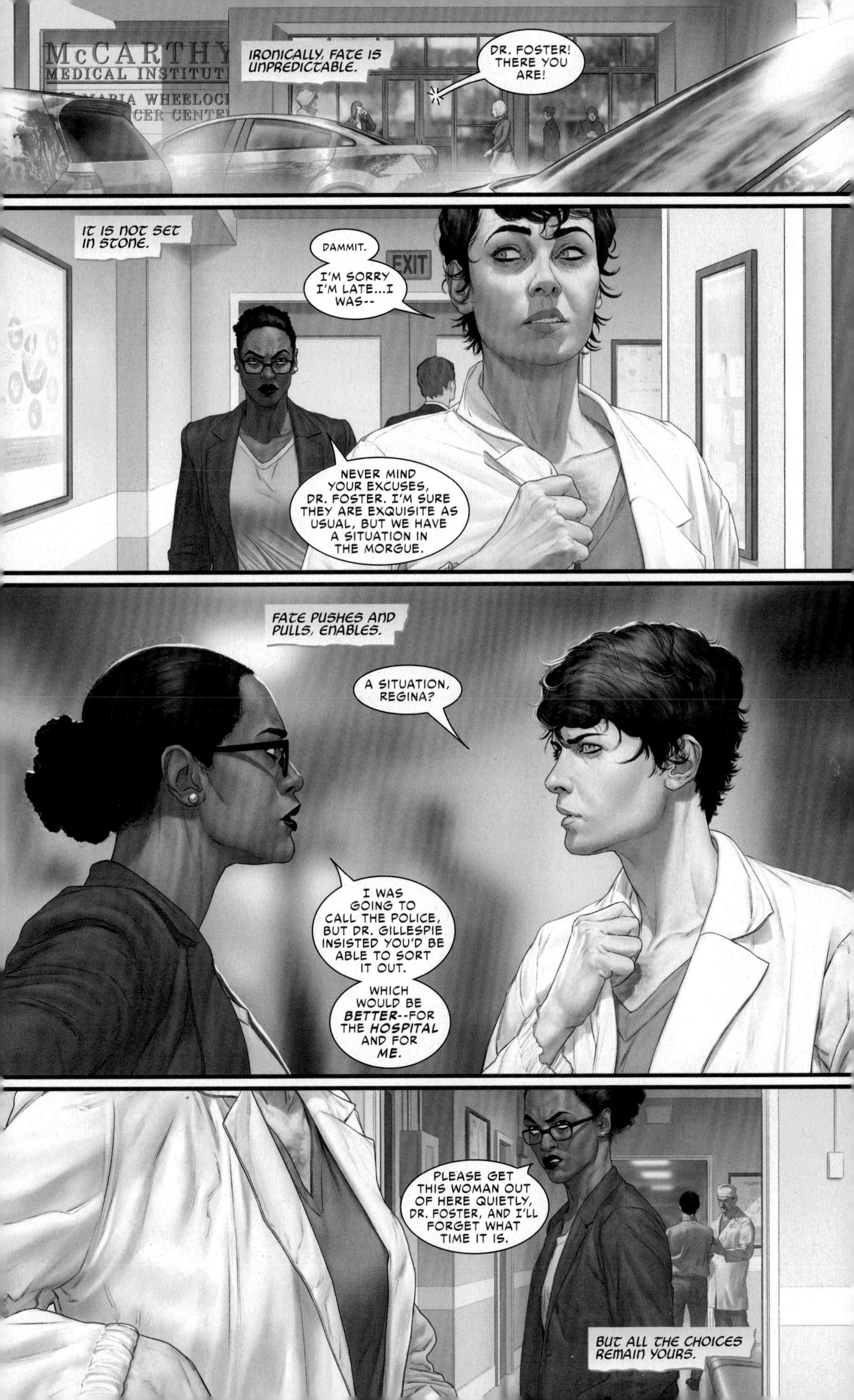
McCARTHY
MEDICAL INSTITUTE
IRONICALLY, FATE IS UNPREDICTABLE.
DR. FOSTER! THERE YOU ARE!
IT IS NOT SET IN STONE.
DAMMIT.
I'M SORRY I'M LATE...I WAS--
EXIT
NEVER MIND YOUR EXCUSES, DR. FOSTER. I'M SURE THEY ARE EXQUISITE AS USUAL, BUT WE HAVE A SITUATION IN THE MORGUE.
FATE PUSHES AND PULLS, ENABLES.
A SITUATION, REGINA?
I WAS GOING TO CALL THE POLICE, BUT DR. GILLESPIE INSISTED YOU'D BE ABLE TO SORT IT OUT.
WHICH WOULD BE *BETTER*--FOR THE *HOSPITAL* AND FOR *ME.*
PLEASE GET THIS WOMAN OUT OF HERE QUIETLY, DR. FOSTER, AND I'LL FORGET WHAT TIME IT IS.
BUT ALL THE CHOICES REMAIN YOURS.

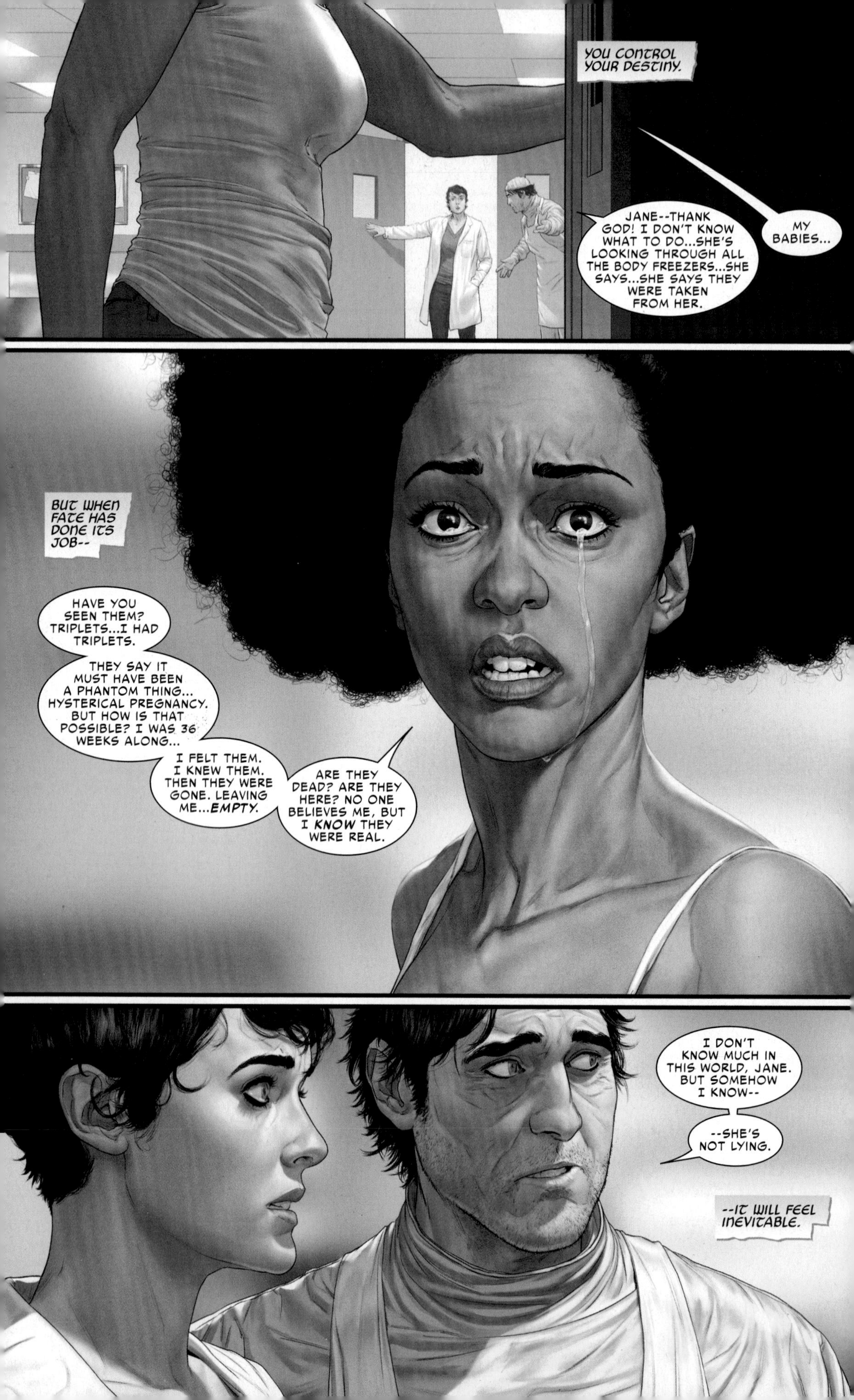
YOU CONTROL YOUR DESTINY.
JANE--THANK GOD! I DON'T KNOW WHAT TO DO...SHE'S LOOKING THROUGH ALL THE BODY FREEZERS...SHE SAYS...SHE SAYS THEY WERE TAKEN FROM HER.
MY BABIES...
BUT WHEN FATE HAS DONE ITS JOB--
HAVE YOU SEEN THEM? TRIPLETS...I HAD TRIPLETS.
THEY SAY IT MUST HAVE BEEN A PHANTOM THING... HYSTERICAL PREGNANCY. BUT HOW IS THAT POSSIBLE? I WAS 36 WEEKS ALONG...
I FELT THEM. I KNEW THEM. THEN THEY WERE GONE. LEAVING ME...*EMPTY*.
ARE THEY DEAD? ARE THEY HERE? NO ONE BELIEVES ME, BUT I *KNOW* THEY WERE REAL.
I DON'T KNOW MUCH IN THIS WORLD, JANE. BUT SOMEHOW I KNOW--
--SHE'S NOT LYING.
--IT WILL FEEL INEVITABLE.

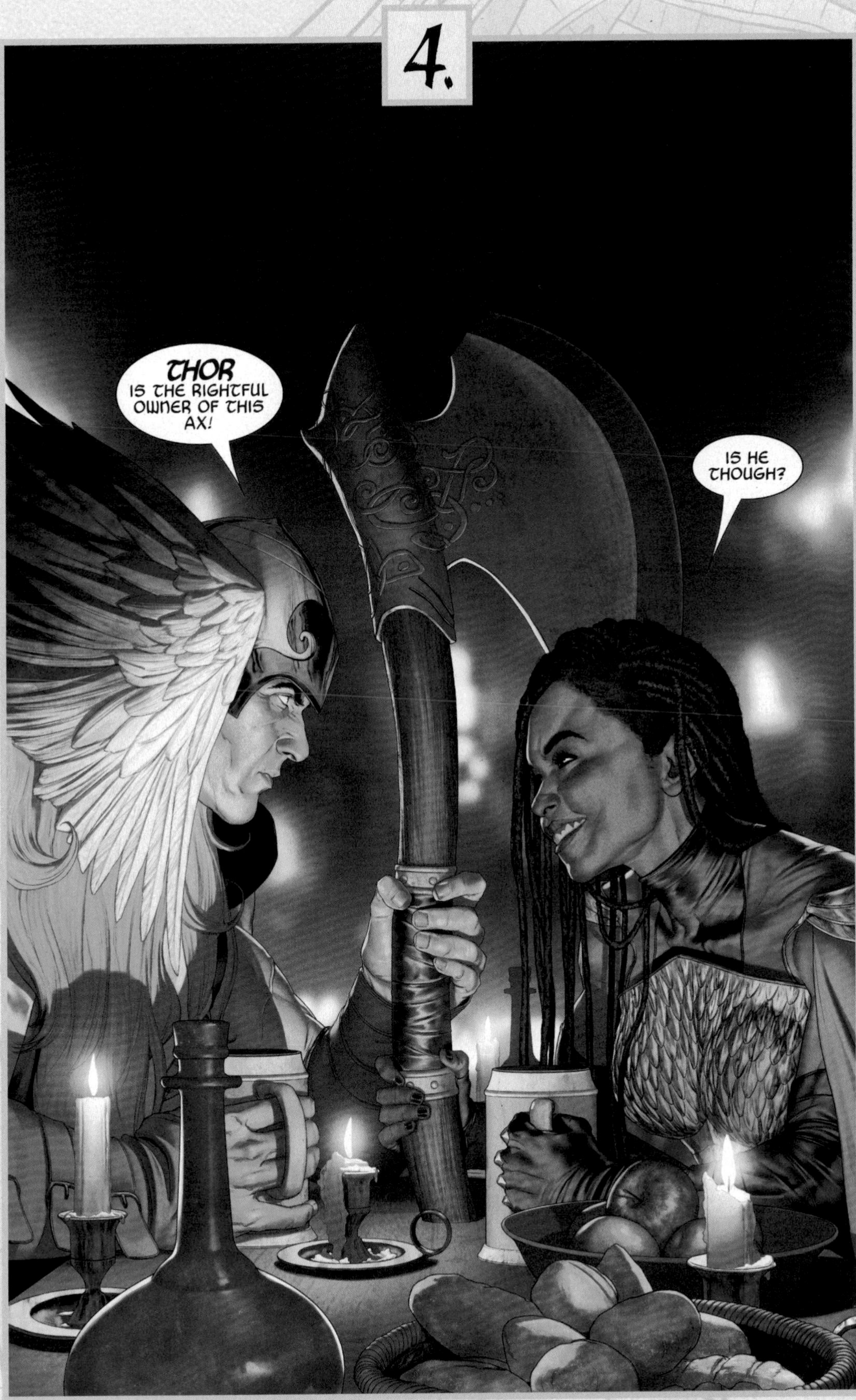
4.
THOR IS THE RIGHTFUL OWNER OF THIS AX!
IS HE THOUGH?

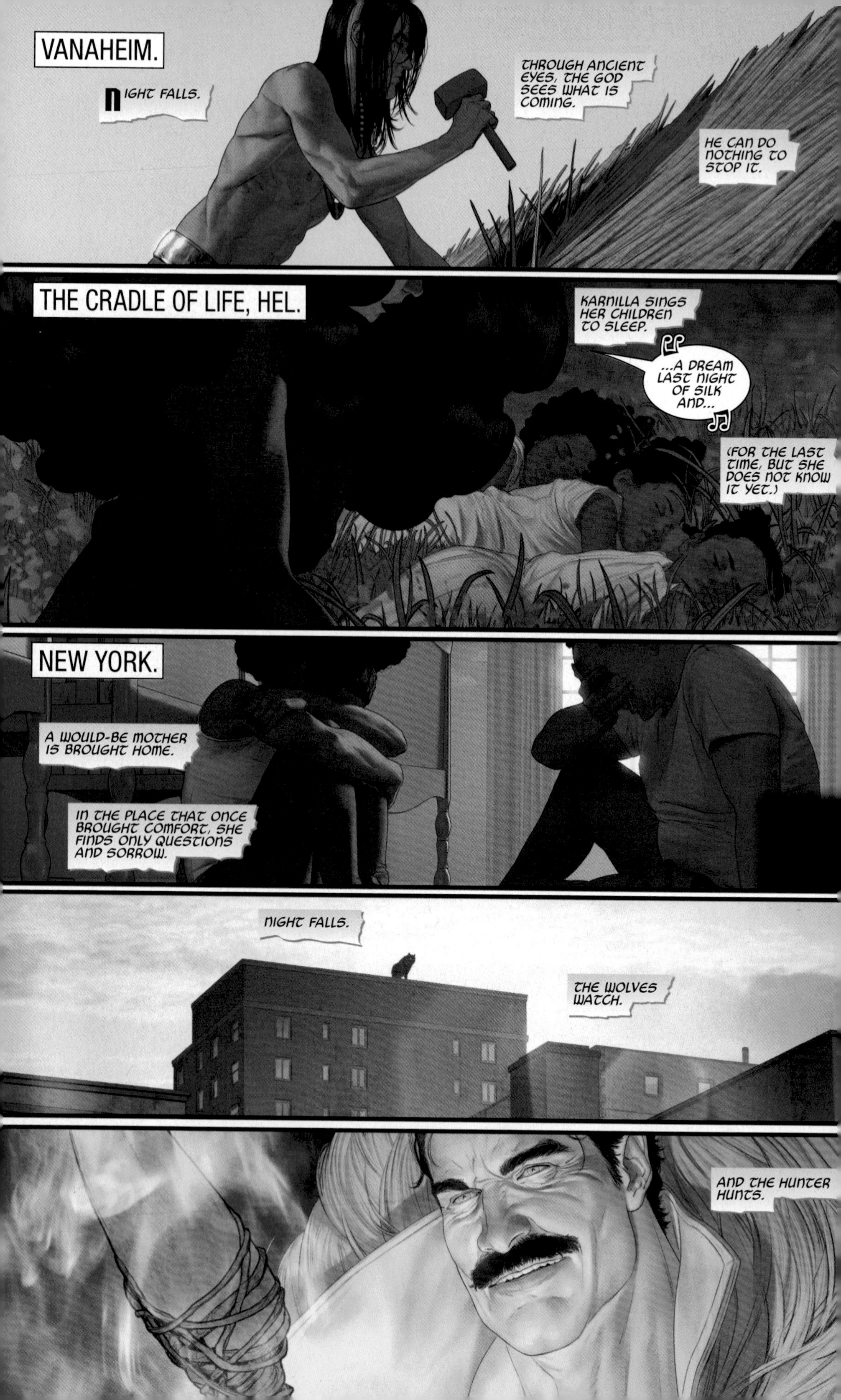

VANAHEIM.
NIGHT FALLS.
THROUGH ANCIENT EYES, THE GOD SEES WHAT IS COMING.
HE CAN DO NOTHING TO STOP IT.
THE CRADLE OF LIFE, HEL.
KARNILLA SINGS HER CHILDREN TO SLEEP.
...A DREAM LAST NIGHT OF SILK AND...
(FOR THE LAST TIME, BUT SHE DOES NOT KNOW IT YET.)
NEW YORK.
A WOULD-BE MOTHER IS BROUGHT HOME.
IN THE PLACE THAT ONCE BROUGHT COMFORT, SHE FINDS ONLY QUESTIONS AND SORROW.
NIGHT FALLS.
THE WOLVES WATCH.
AND THE HUNTER HUNTS.

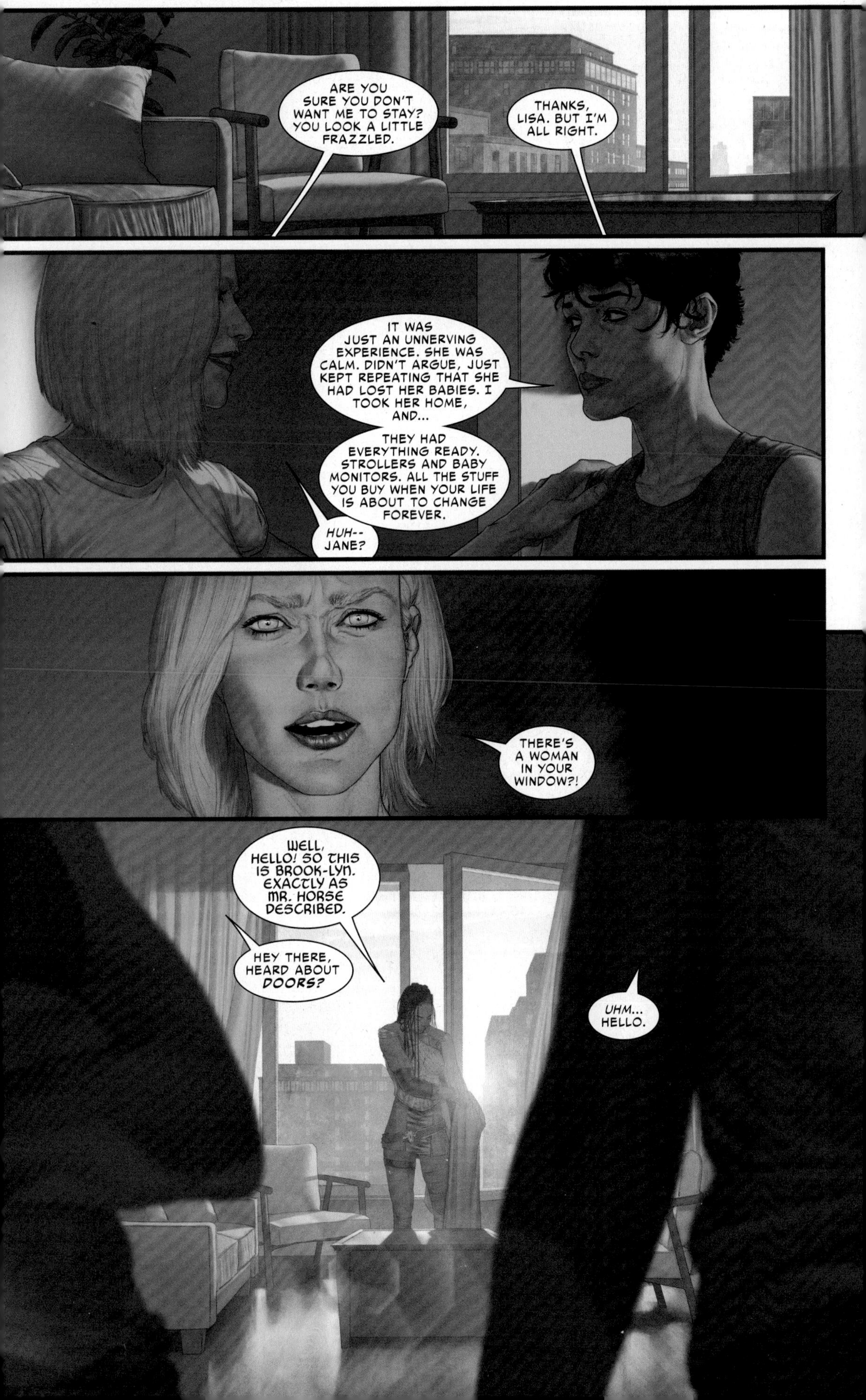
ARE YOU SURE YOU DON'T WANT ME TO STAY? YOU LOOK A LITTLE FRAZZLED.
THANKS, LISA. BUT I'M ALL RIGHT.
IT WAS JUST AN UNNERVING EXPERIENCE. SHE WAS CALM. DIDN'T ARGUE, JUST KEPT REPEATING THAT SHE HAD LOST HER BABIES. I TOOK HER HOME, AND...
THEY HAD EVERYTHING READY. STROLLERS AND BABY MONITORS. ALL THE STUFF YOU BUY WHEN YOUR LIFE IS ABOUT TO CHANGE FOREVER.
HUH-- JANE?
THERE'S A WOMAN IN YOUR WINDOW?!
WELL, HELLO! SO THIS IS BROOK-LYN. EXACTLY AS MR. HORSE DESCRIBED.
HEY THERE, HEARD ABOUT DOORS?
UHM... HELLO.

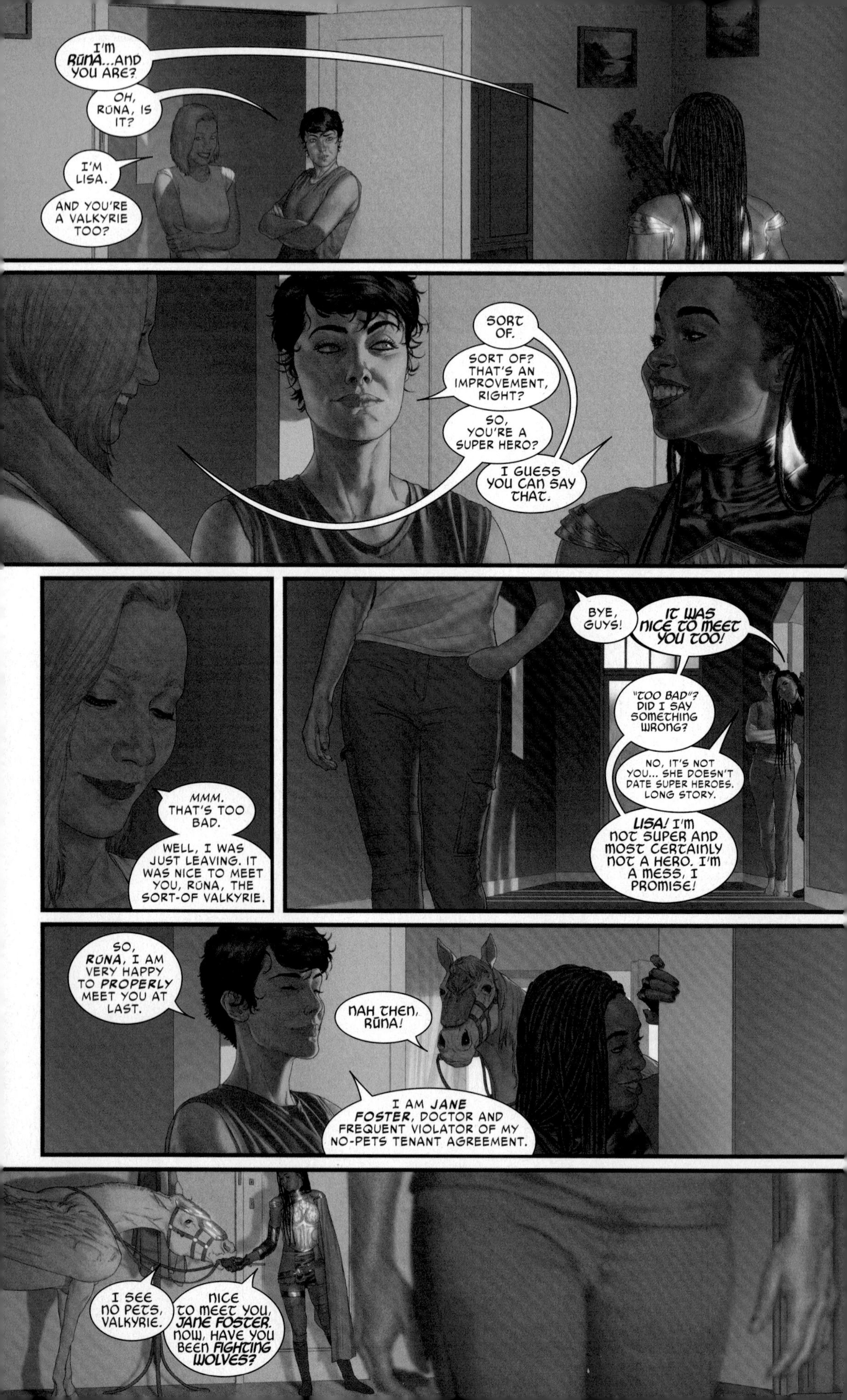
I'M RŪNA...AND YOU ARE?
OH, RŪNA, IS IT?
I'M LISA.
AND YOU'RE A VALKYRIE TOO?
SORT OF.
SORT OF? THAT'S AN IMPROVEMENT, RIGHT?
SO, YOU'RE A SUPER HERO?
I GUESS YOU CAN SAY THAT.
MMM. THAT'S TOO BAD.
WELL, I WAS JUST LEAVING. IT WAS NICE TO MEET YOU, RŪNA, THE SORT-OF VALKYRIE.
BYE, GUYS!
IT WAS NICE TO MEET YOU TOO!
"TOO BAD"? DID I SAY SOMETHING WRONG?
NO, IT'S NOT YOU... SHE DOESN'T DATE SUPER HEROES. LONG STORY.
LISA! I'M NOT SUPER AND MOST CERTAINLY NOT A HERO. I'M A MESS, I PROMISE!
SO, RŪNA, I AM VERY HAPPY TO PROPERLY MEET YOU AT LAST.
NAH THEN, RŪNA!
I AM JANE FOSTER, DOCTOR AND FREQUENT VIOLATOR OF MY NO-PETS TENANT AGREEMENT.
I SEE NO PETS, VALKYRIE.
NICE TO MEET YOU, JANE FOSTER. NOW, HAVE YOU BEEN FIGHTING WOLVES?

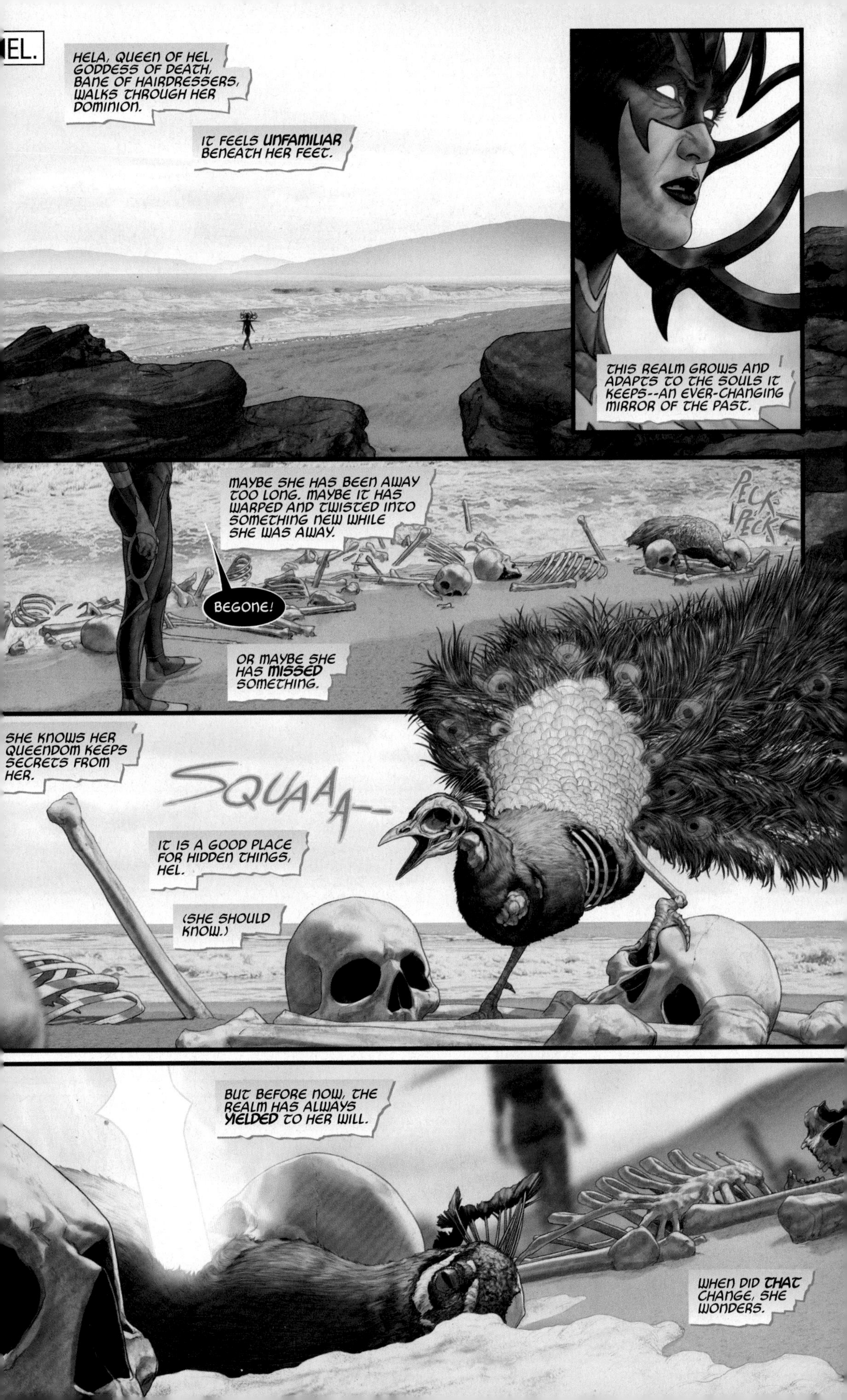
EL.
HELA, QUEEN OF HEL, GODDESS OF DEATH, BANE OF HAIRDRESSERS, WALKS THROUGH HER DOMINION.
IT FEELS UNFAMILIAR BENEATH HER FEET.
THIS REALM GROWS AND ADAPTS TO THE SOULS IT KEEPS--AN EVER-CHANGING MIRROR OF THE PAST.
MAYBE SHE HAS BEEN AWAY TOO LONG. MAYBE IT HAS WARPED AND TWISTED INTO SOMETHING NEW WHILE SHE WAS AWAY.
PECK PECK
BEGONE!
OR MAYBE SHE HAS MISSED SOMETHING.
SHE KNOWS HER QUEENDOM KEEPS SECRETS FROM HER.
SQUAAA--
IT IS A GOOD PLACE FOR HIDDEN THINGS, HEL.
(SHE SHOULD KNOW.)
BUT BEFORE NOW, THE REALM HAS ALWAYS YIELDED TO HER WILL.
WHEN DID THAT CHANGE, SHE WONDERS.

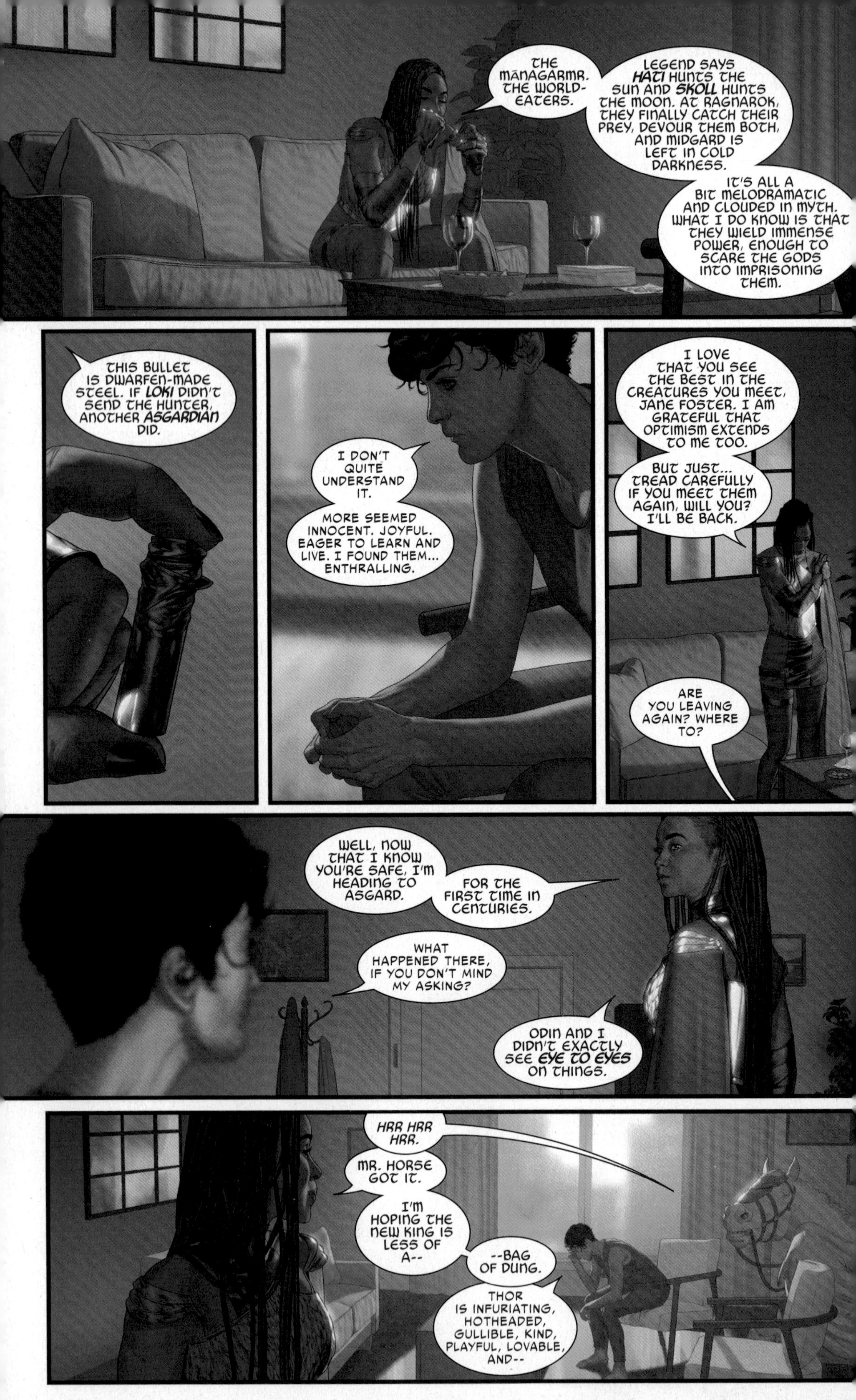
THE MĀNAGARMR. THE WORLD-EATERS.
LEGEND SAYS *HATI* HUNTS THE SUN AND *SKOLL* HUNTS THE MOON. AT RAGNAROK, THEY FINALLY CATCH THEIR PREY, DEVOUR THEM BOTH, AND MIDGARD IS LEFT IN COLD DARKNESS.
IT'S ALL A BIT MELODRAMATIC AND CLOUDED IN MYTH. WHAT I DO KNOW IS THAT THEY WIELD IMMENSE POWER, ENOUGH TO SCARE THE GODS INTO IMPRISONING THEM.
THIS BULLET IS DWARFEN-MADE STEEL. IF *LOKI* DIDN'T SEND THE HUNTER, ANOTHER *ASGARDIAN* DID.
I DON'T QUITE UNDERSTAND IT.
MORE SEEMED INNOCENT. JOYFUL. EAGER TO LEARN AND LIVE. I FOUND THEM... ENTHRALLING.
I LOVE THAT YOU SEE THE BEST IN THE CREATURES YOU MEET, JANE FOSTER. I AM GRATEFUL THAT OPTIMISM EXTENDS TO ME TOO.
BUT JUST... TREAD CAREFULLY IF YOU MEET THEM AGAIN, WILL YOU? I'LL BE BACK.
ARE YOU LEAVING AGAIN? WHERE TO?
WELL, NOW THAT I KNOW YOU'RE SAFE, I'M HEADING TO ASGARD.
FOR THE FIRST TIME IN CENTURIES.
WHAT HAPPENED THERE, IF YOU DON'T MIND MY ASKING?
ODIN AND I DIDN'T EXACTLY SEE *EYE TO EYES* ON THINGS.
HRR HRR HRR.
MR. HORSE GOT IT.
I'M HOPING THE NEW KING IS LESS OF A--
--BAG OF DUNG.
THOR IS INFURIATING, HOTHEADED, GULLIBLE, KIND, PLAYFUL, LOVABLE, AND--

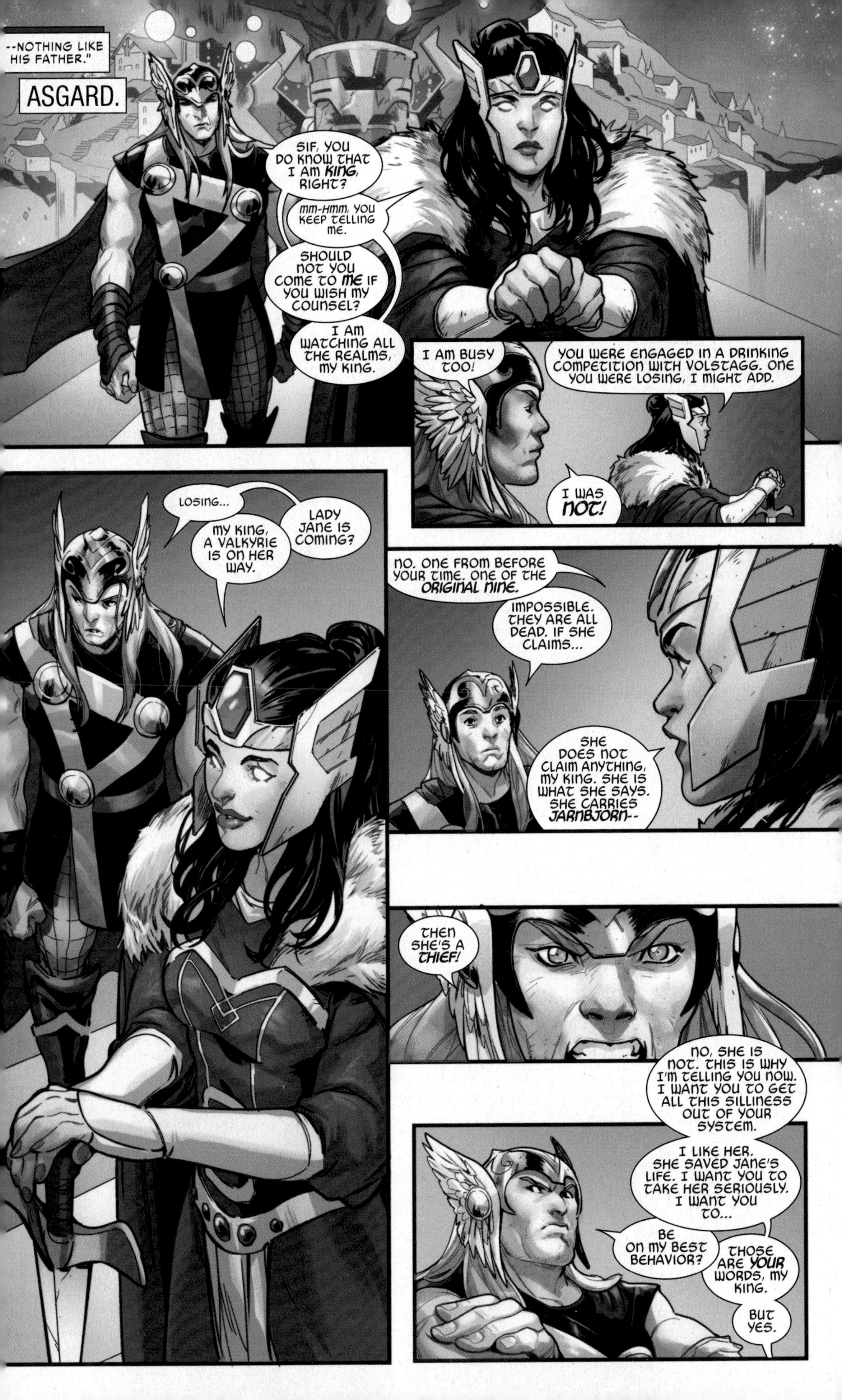

--NOTHING LIKE HIS FATHER."
ASGARD.
SIF, YOU DO KNOW THAT I AM KING, RIGHT?
MM-HMM, YOU KEEP TELLING ME.
SHOULD NOT YOU COME TO ME IF YOU WISH MY COUNSEL?
I AM WATCHING ALL THE REALMS, MY KING.
I AM BUSY TOO!
YOU WERE ENGAGED IN A DRINKING COMPETITION WITH VOLSTAGG. ONE YOU WERE LOSING, I MIGHT ADD.
I WAS NOT!
LOSING...
MY KING, A VALKYRIE IS ON HER WAY.
LADY JANE IS COMING?
NO. ONE FROM BEFORE YOUR TIME. ONE OF THE ORIGINAL NINE.
IMPOSSIBLE. THEY ARE ALL DEAD. IF SHE CLAIMS...
SHE DOES NOT CLAIM ANYTHING, MY KING. SHE IS WHAT SHE SAYS. SHE CARRIES JARNBJORN--
THEN SHE'S A THIEF!
NO, SHE IS NOT. THIS IS WHY I'M TELLING YOU NOW. I WANT YOU TO GET ALL THIS SILLINESS OUT OF YOUR SYSTEM.
I LIKE HER. SHE SAVED JANE'S LIFE. I WANT YOU TO TAKE HER SERIOUSLY. I WANT YOU TO...
BE ON MY BEST BEHAVIOR?
THOSE ARE YOUR WORDS, MY KING.
BUT YES.

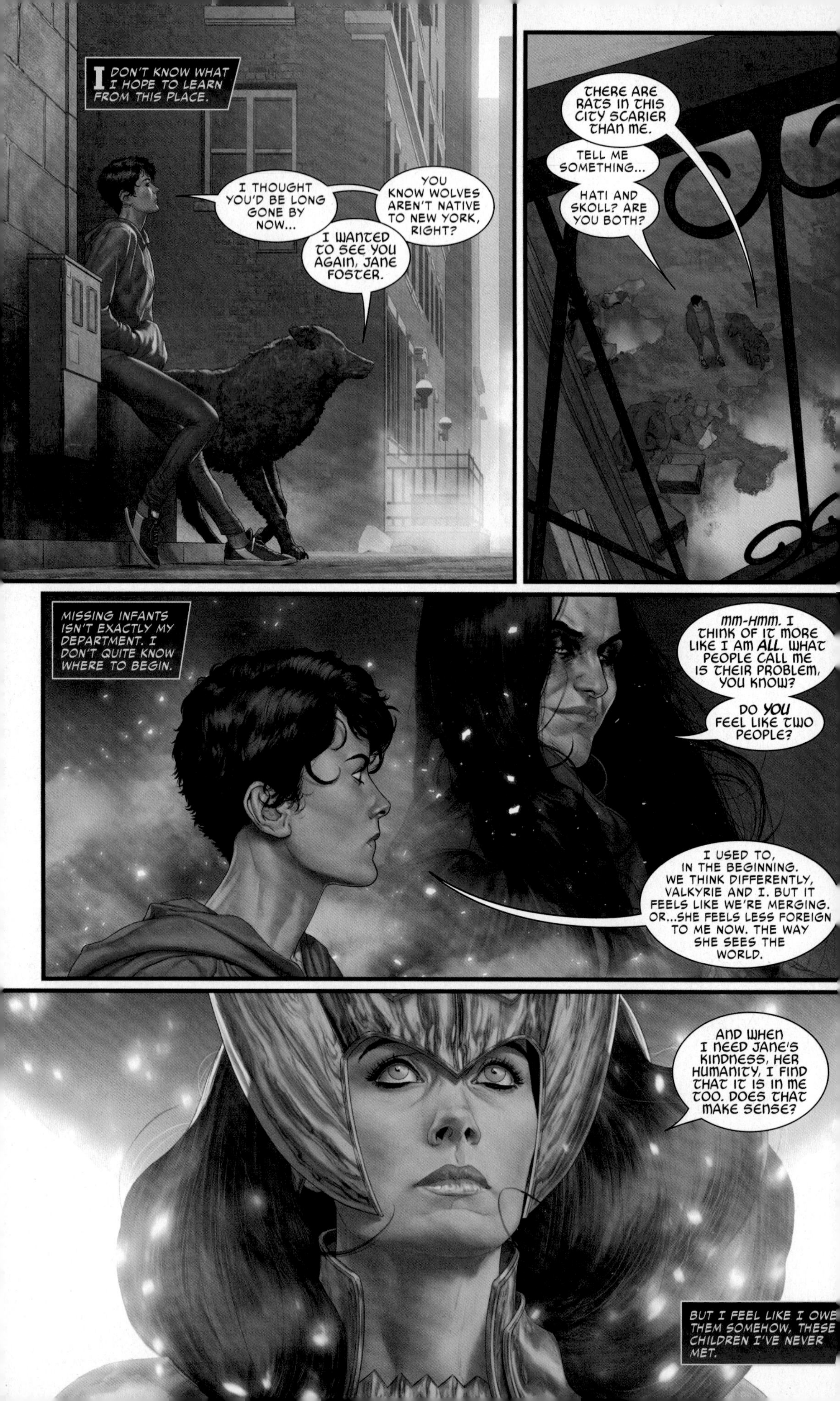
I DON'T KNOW WHAT I HOPE TO LEARN FROM THIS PLACE.
I THOUGHT YOU'D BE LONG GONE BY NOW...
YOU KNOW WOLVES AREN'T NATIVE TO NEW YORK, RIGHT?
I WANTED TO SEE YOU AGAIN, JANE FOSTER.
THERE ARE RATS IN THIS CITY SCARIER THAN ME.
TELL ME SOMETHING...
HATI AND SKOLL? ARE YOU BOTH?
MISSING INFANTS ISN'T EXACTLY MY DEPARTMENT. I DON'T QUITE KNOW WHERE TO BEGIN.
MM-HMM. I THINK OF IT MORE LIKE I AM ALL. WHAT PEOPLE CALL ME IS THEIR PROBLEM, YOU KNOW?
DO YOU FEEL LIKE TWO PEOPLE?
I USED TO, IN THE BEGINNING. WE THINK DIFFERENTLY, VALKYRIE AND I. BUT IT FEELS LIKE WE'RE MERGING. OR...SHE FEELS LESS FOREIGN TO ME NOW. THE WAY SHE SEES THE WORLD.
AND WHEN I NEED JANE'S KINDNESS, HER HUMANITY, I FIND THAT IT IS IN ME TOO. DOES THAT MAKE SENSE?
BUT I FEEL LIKE I OWE THEM SOMEHOW, THESE CHILDREN I'VE NEVER MET.

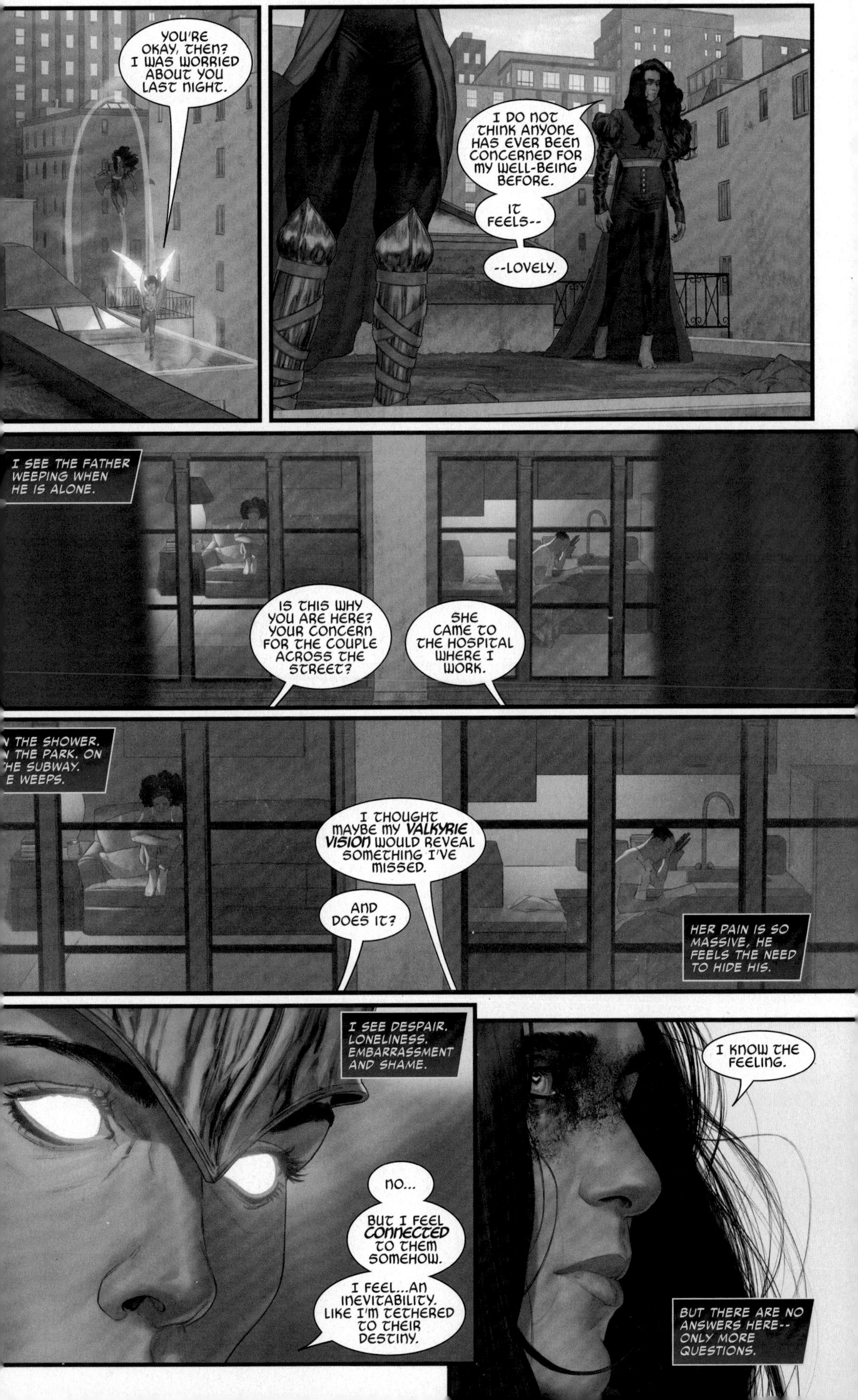

YOU'RE OKAY, THEN? I WAS WORRIED ABOUT YOU LAST NIGHT.
I DO NOT THINK ANYONE HAS EVER BEEN CONCERNED FOR MY WELL-BEING BEFORE.
IT FEELS--
--LOVELY.
I SEE THE FATHER WEEPING WHEN HE IS ALONE.
IS THIS WHY YOU ARE HERE? YOUR CONCERN FOR THE COUPLE ACROSS THE STREET?
SHE CAME TO THE HOSPITAL WHERE I WORK.
N THE SHOWER. N THE PARK. ON HE SUBWAY. E WEEPS.
I THOUGHT MAYBE MY VALKYRIE VISION WOULD REVEAL SOMETHING I'VE MISSED.
AND DOES IT?
HER PAIN IS SO MASSIVE, HE FEELS THE NEED TO HIDE HIS.
I SEE DESPAIR. LONELINESS. EMBARRASSMENT AND SHAME.
I KNOW THE FEELING.
NO...
BUT I FEEL CONNECTED TO THEM SOMEHOW.
I FEEL...AN INEVITABILITY. LIKE I'M TETHERED TO THEIR DESTINY.
BUT THERE ARE NO ANSWERS HERE-- ONLY MORE QUESTIONS.

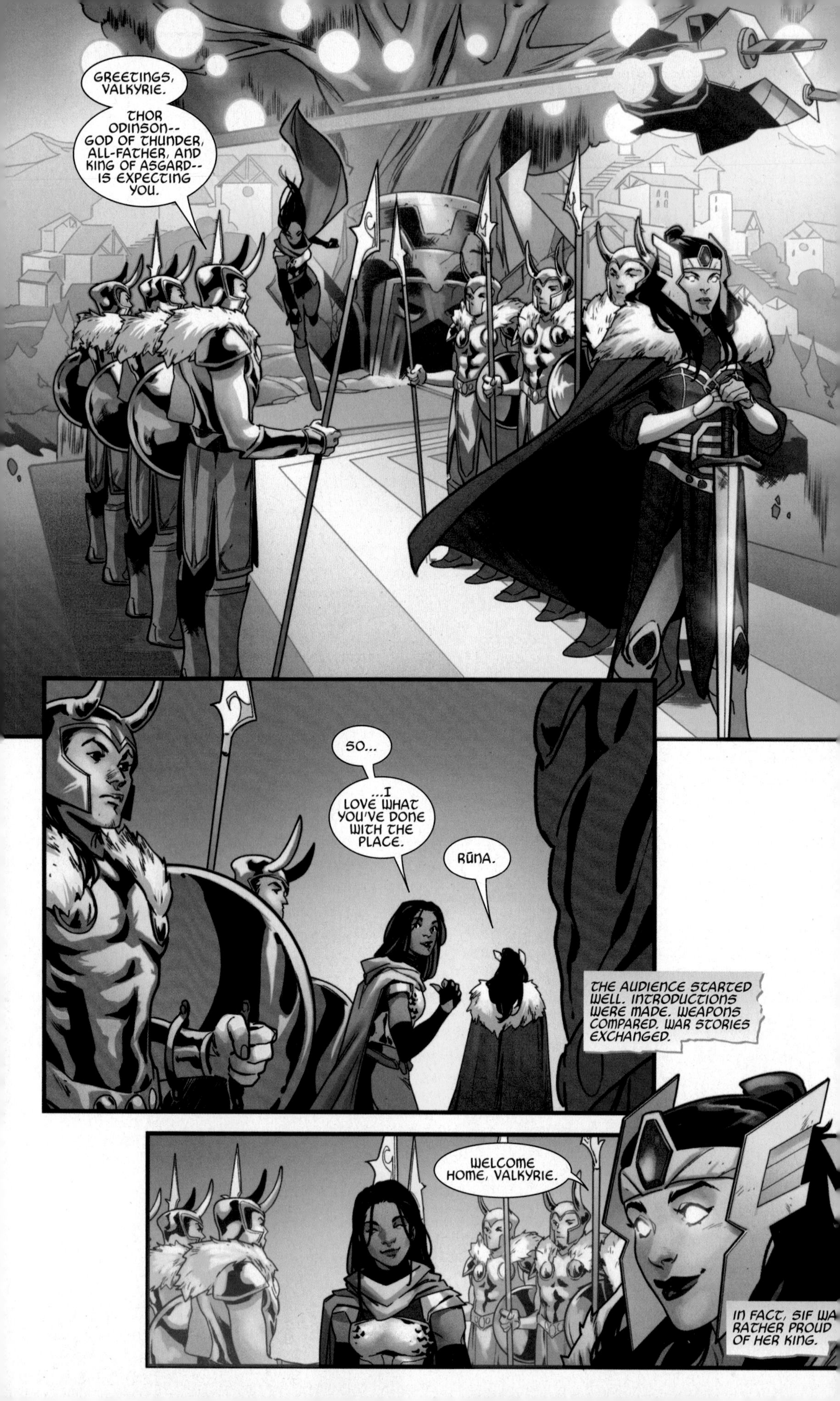

GREETINGS, VALKYRIE.
THOR ODINSON-- GOD OF THUNDER, ALL-FATHER, AND KING OF ASGARD-- IS EXPECTING YOU.
SO...
...I LOVE WHAT YOU'VE DONE WITH THE PLACE.
RŪNA.
THE AUDIENCE STARTED WELL. INTRODUCTIONS WERE MADE. WEAPONS COMPARED. WAR STORIES EXCHANGED.
WELCOME HOME, VALKYRIE.
IN FACT, SIF WA RATHER PROUD OF HER KING.

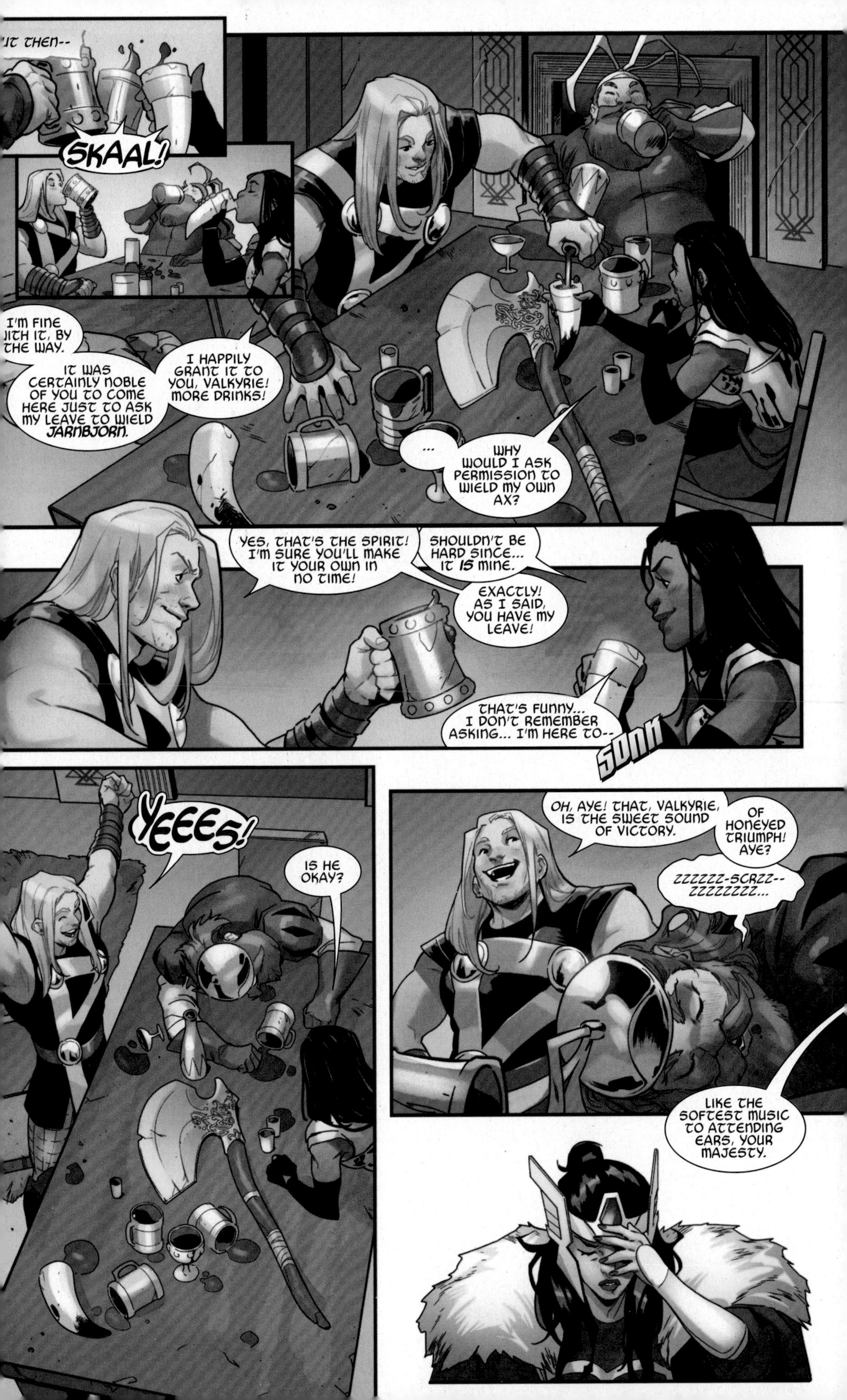

'UT THEN--
SKAAL!
I'M FINE WITH IT, BY THE WAY.
IT WAS CERTAINLY NOBLE OF YOU TO COME HERE JUST TO ASK MY LEAVE TO WIELD JARNBJORN.
I HAPPILY GRANT IT TO YOU, VALKYRIE! MORE DRINKS!
...
WHY WOULD I ASK PERMISSION TO WIELD MY OWN AX?
YES, THAT'S THE SPIRIT! I'M SURE YOU'LL MAKE IT YOUR OWN IN NO TIME!
SHOULDN'T BE HARD SINCE... IT IS MINE.
EXACTLY! AS I SAID, YOU HAVE MY LEAVE!
THAT'S FUNNY... I DON'T REMEMBER ASKING... I'M HERE TO--
SONK
YEEES!
IS HE OKAY?
OH, AYE! THAT, VALKYRIE, IS THE SWEET SOUND OF VICTORY.
OF HONEYED TRIUMPH! AYE?
ZZZZZZ-SCRZZ--ZZZZZZZZ...
LIKE THE SOFTEST MUSIC TO ATTENDING EARS, YOUR MAJESTY.

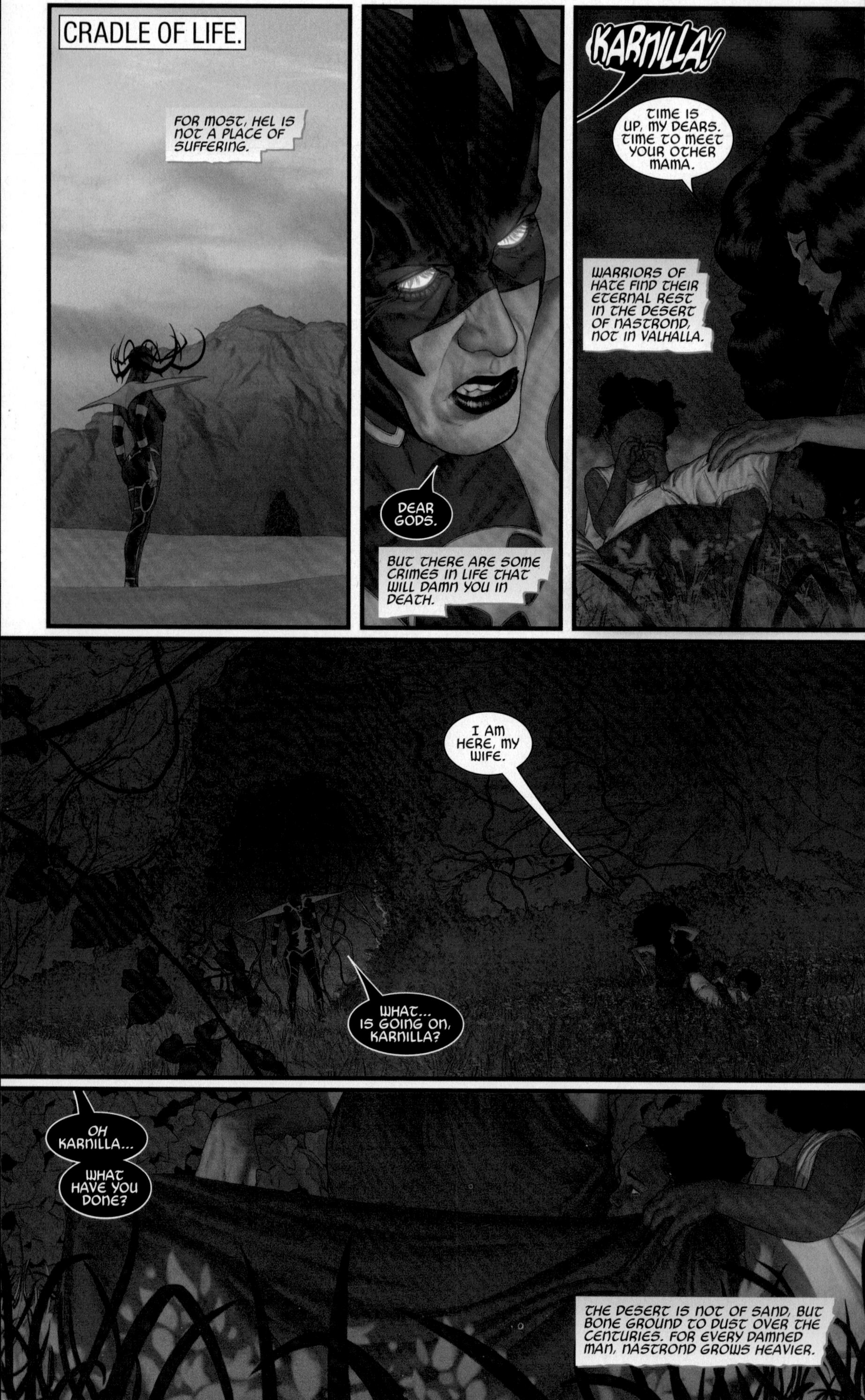
CRADLE OF LIFE.
FOR MOST, HEL IS NOT A PLACE OF SUFFERING.
DEAR GODS.
BUT THERE ARE SOME CRIMES IN LIFE THAT WILL DAMN YOU IN DEATH.
KARNILLA!
TIME IS UP, MY DEARS. TIME TO MEET YOUR OTHER MAMA.
WARRIORS OF HATE FIND THEIR ETERNAL REST IN THE DESERT OF NASTROND, NOT IN VALHALLA.
I AM HERE, MY WIFE.
WHAT... IS GOING ON, KARNILLA?
OH KARNILLA...
WHAT HAVE YOU DONE?
THE DESERT IS NOT OF SAND, BUT BONE GROUND TO DUST OVER THE CENTURIES. FOR EVERY DAMNED MAN, NASTROND GROWS HEAVIER.

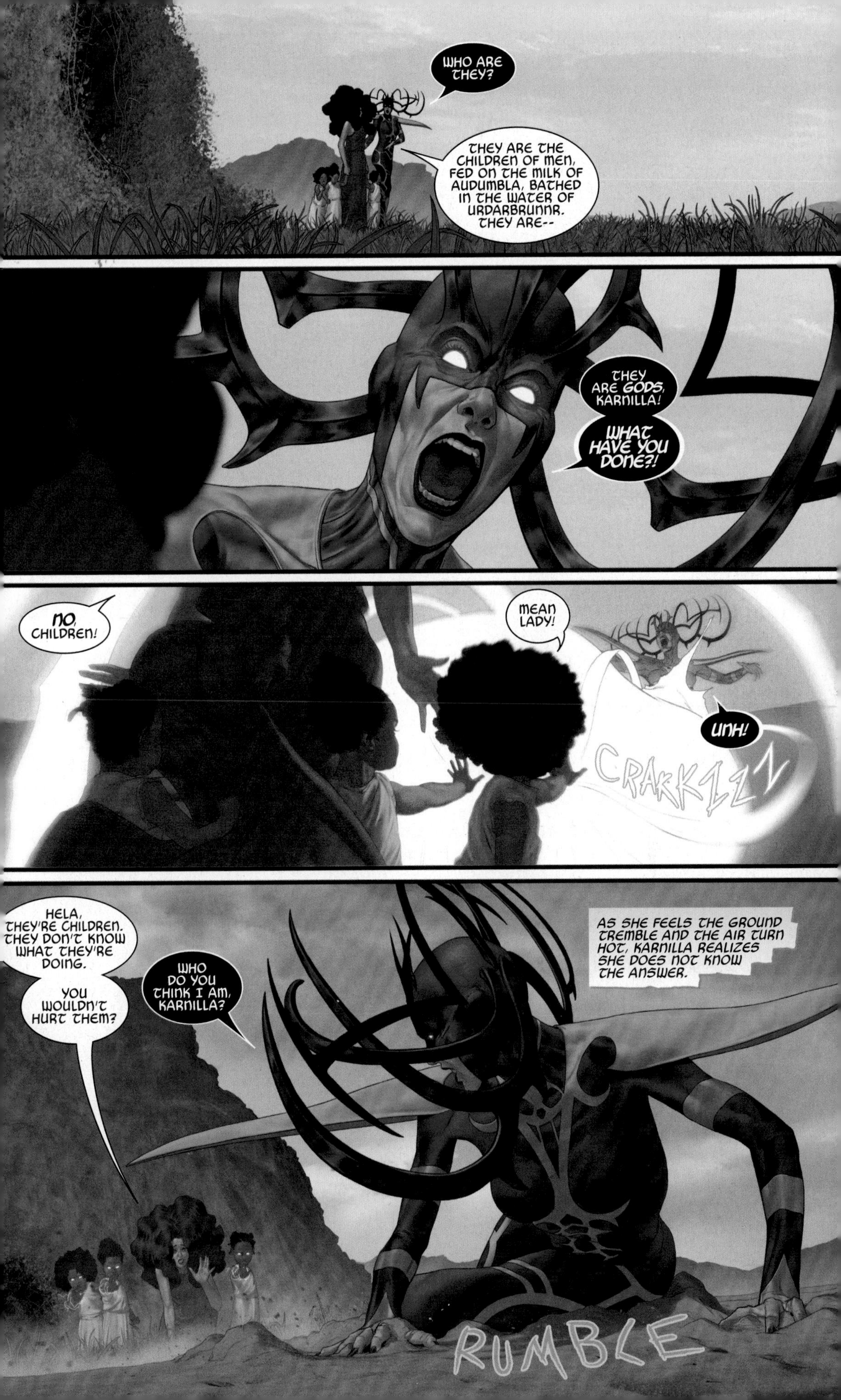

WHO ARE THEY?
THEY ARE THE CHILDREN OF MEN, FED ON THE MILK OF AUDUMBLA, BATHED IN THE WATER OF URDARBRUNNR. THEY ARE--
THEY ARE GODS, KARNILLA!
WHAT HAVE YOU DONE?!
NO, CHILDREN!
MEAN LADY!
UNH!
CRAKKZZZ
HELA, THEY'RE CHILDREN. THEY DON'T KNOW WHAT THEY'RE DOING.
YOU WOULDN'T HURT THEM?
WHO DO YOU THINK I AM, KARNILLA?
AS SHE FEELS THE GROUND TREMBLE AND THE AIR TURN HOT, KARNILLA REALIZES SHE DOES NOT KNOW THE ANSWER.
RUMBLE

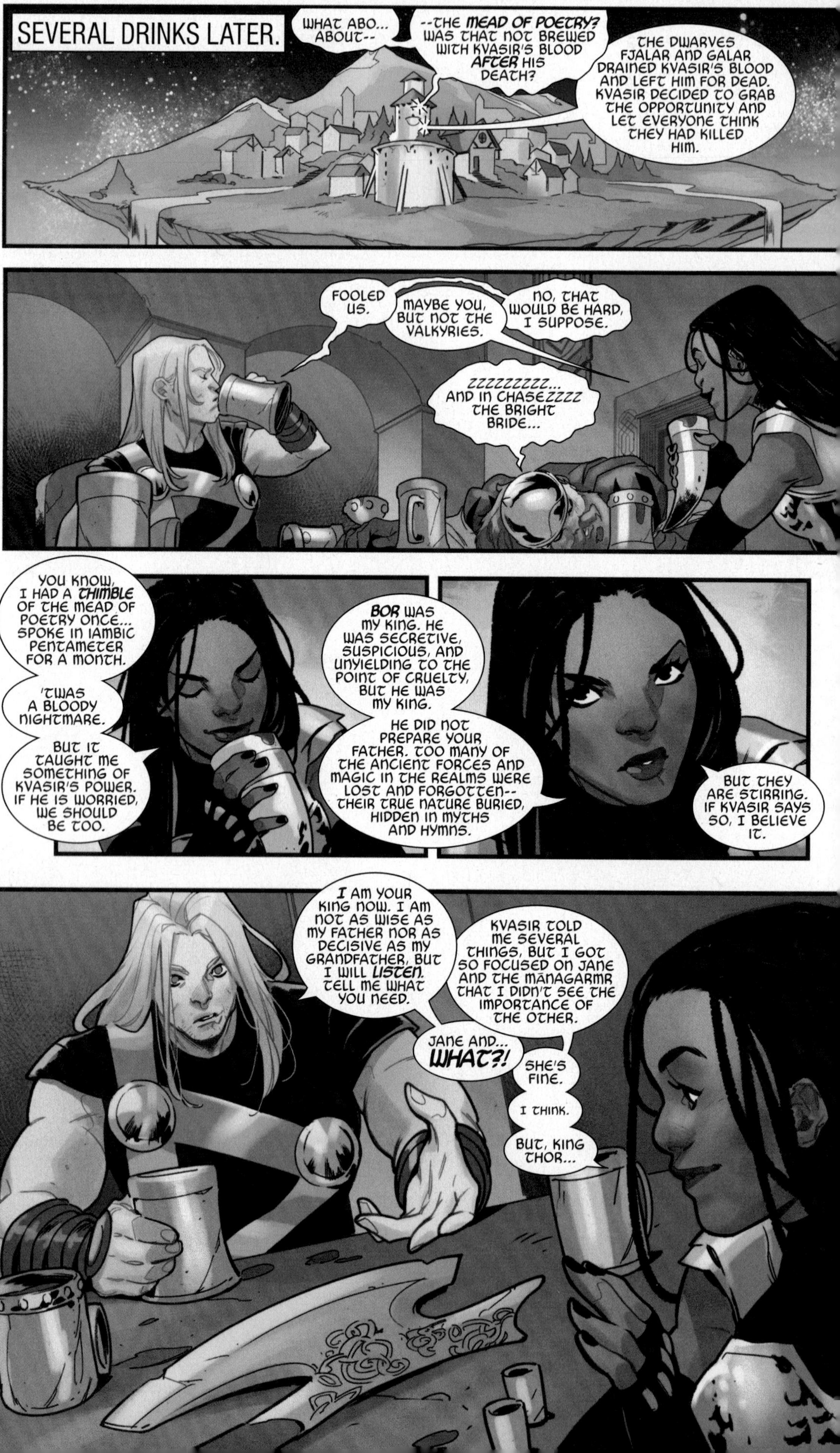

SEVERAL DRINKS LATER.
WHAT ABO... ABOUT--
--THE MEAD OF POETRY? WAS THAT NOT BREWED WITH KVASIR'S BLOOD AFTER HIS DEATH?
THE DWARVES FJALAR AND GALAR DRAINED KVASIR'S BLOOD AND LEFT HIM FOR DEAD. KVASIR DECIDED TO GRAB THE OPPORTUNITY AND LET EVERYONE THINK THEY HAD KILLED HIM.
FOOLED US.
MAYBE YOU, BUT NOT THE VALKYRIES.
NO, THAT WOULD BE HARD, I SUPPOSE.
ZZZZZZZZZ... AND IN CHASEZZZZ THE BRIGHT BRIDE...
YOU KNOW, I HAD A THIMBLE OF THE MEAD OF POETRY ONCE... SPOKE IN IAMBIC PENTAMETER FOR A MONTH.
'TWAS A BLOODY NIGHTMARE.
BUT IT TAUGHT ME SOMETHING OF KVASIR'S POWER. IF HE IS WORRIED, WE SHOULD BE TOO.
BOR WAS MY KING. HE WAS SECRETIVE, SUSPICIOUS, AND UNYIELDING TO THE POINT OF CRUELTY, BUT HE WAS MY KING.
HE DID NOT PREPARE YOUR FATHER. TOO MANY OF THE ANCIENT FORCES AND MAGIC IN THE REALMS WERE LOST AND FORGOTTEN-- THEIR TRUE NATURE BURIED, HIDDEN IN MYTHS AND HYMNS.
BUT THEY ARE STIRRING. IF KVASIR SAYS SO, I BELIEVE IT.
I AM YOUR KING NOW. I AM NOT AS WISE AS MY FATHER NOR AS DECISIVE AS MY GRANDFATHER, BUT I WILL LISTEN. TELL ME WHAT YOU NEED.
KVASIR TOLD ME SEVERAL THINGS, BUT I GOT SO FOCUSED ON JANE AND THE MÁNAGARMR THAT I DIDN'T SEE THE IMPORTANCE OF THE OTHER.
JANE AND... WHAT?!
SHE'S FINE.
I THINK.
BUT, KING THOR...

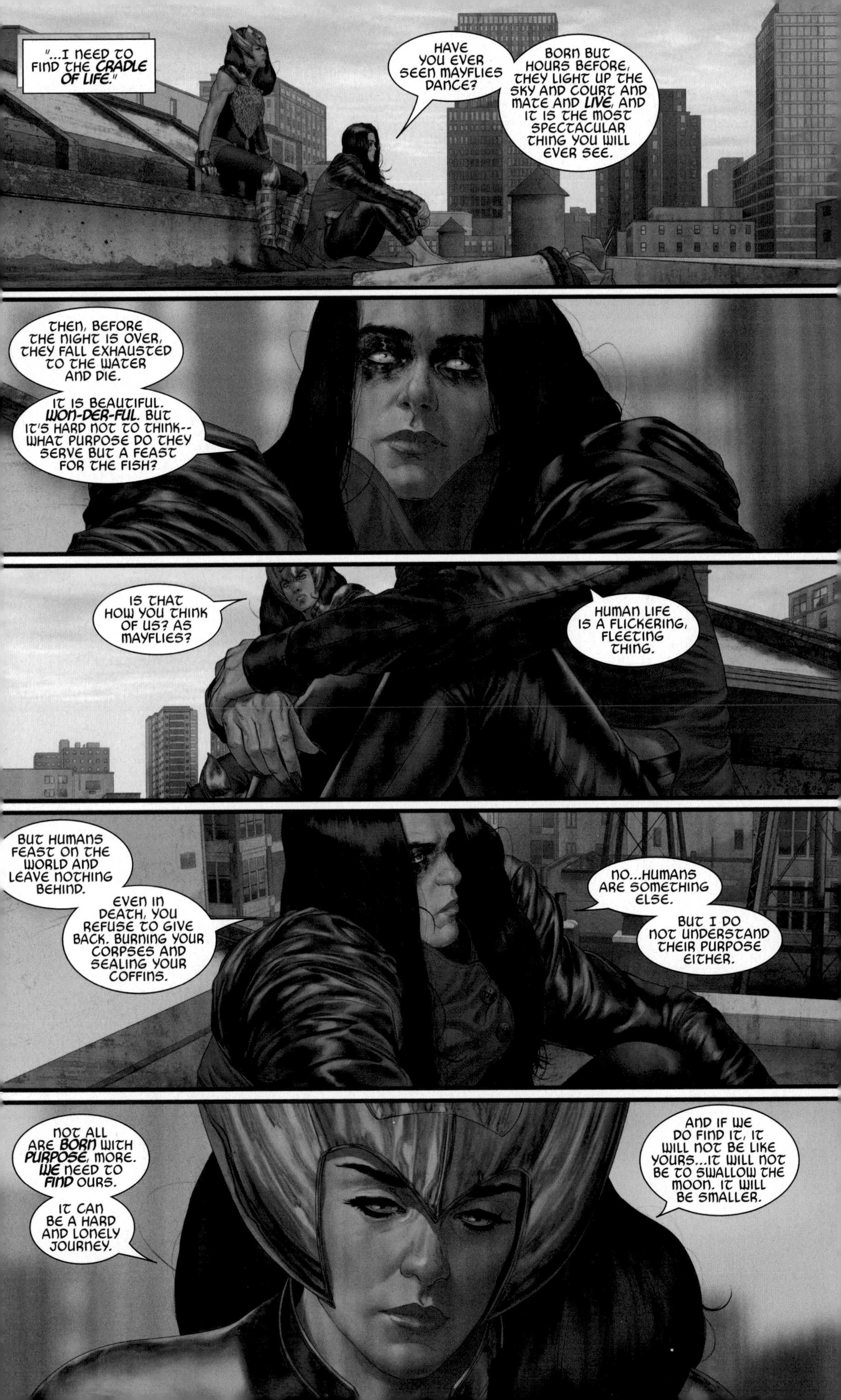
"...I NEED TO FIND THE CRADLE OF LIFE."
HAVE YOU EVER SEEN MAYFLIES DANCE?
BORN BUT HOURS BEFORE, THEY LIGHT UP THE SKY AND COURT AND MATE AND LIVE, AND IT IS THE MOST SPECTACULAR THING YOU WILL EVER SEE.
THEN, BEFORE THE NIGHT IS OVER, THEY FALL EXHAUSTED TO THE WATER AND DIE.
IT IS BEAUTIFUL. WON-DER-FUL. BUT IT'S HARD NOT TO THINK--WHAT PURPOSE DO THEY SERVE BUT A FEAST FOR THE FISH?
IS THAT HOW YOU THINK OF US? AS MAYFLIES?
HUMAN LIFE IS A FLICKERING, FLEETING THING.
BUT HUMANS FEAST ON THE WORLD AND LEAVE NOTHING BEHIND.
EVEN IN DEATH, YOU REFUSE TO GIVE BACK. BURNING YOUR CORPSES AND SEALING YOUR COFFINS.
NO...HUMANS ARE SOMETHING ELSE.
BUT I DO NOT UNDERSTAND THEIR PURPOSE EITHER.
NOT ALL ARE BORN WITH PURPOSE, MORE. WE NEED TO FIND OURS.
IT CAN BE A HARD AND LONELY JOURNEY.
AND IF WE DO FIND IT, IT WILL NOT BE LIKE YOURS...IT WILL NOT BE TO SWALLOW THE MOON. IT WILL BE SMALLER.

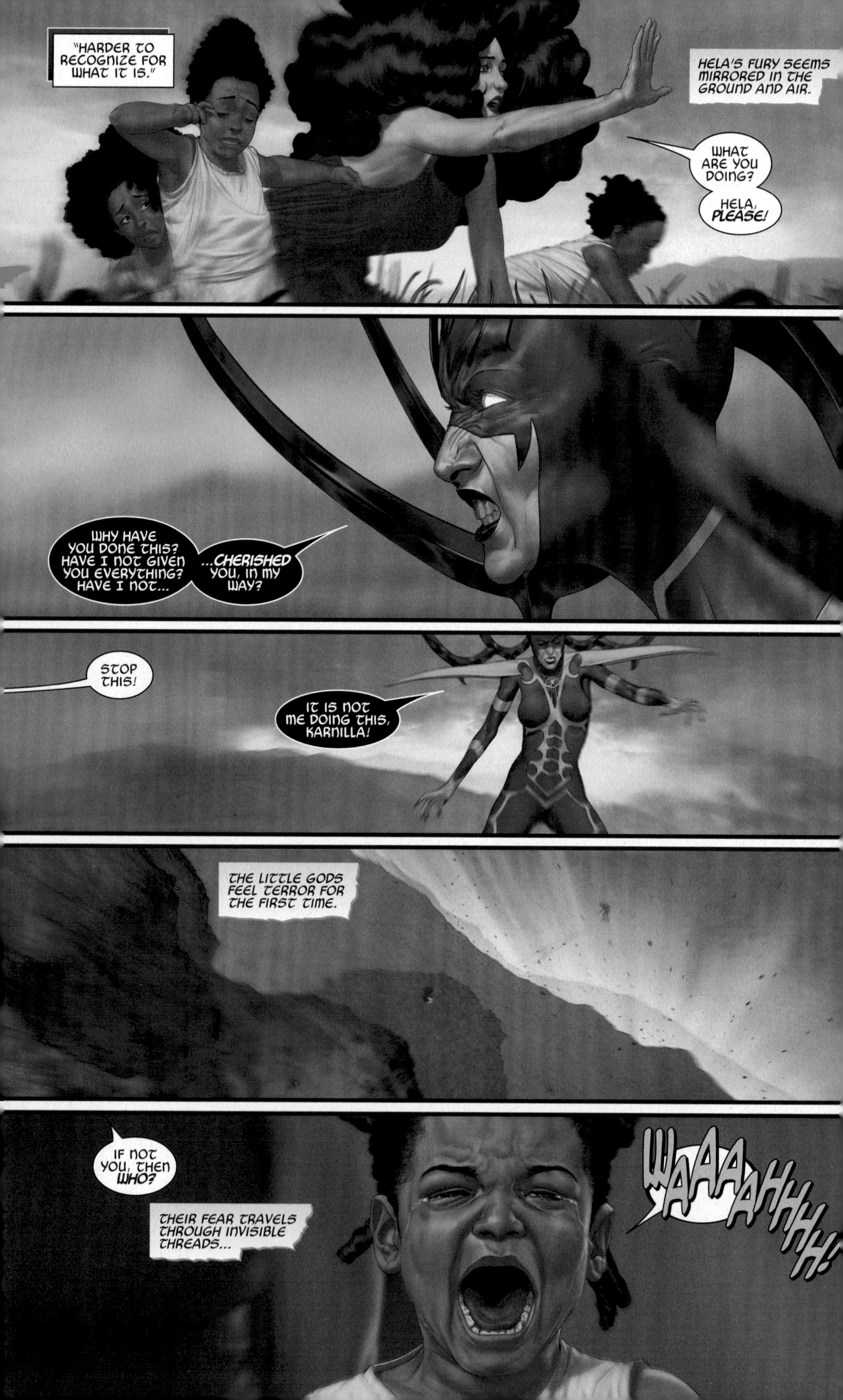
"HARDER TO RECOGNIZE FOR WHAT IT IS."
HELA'S FURY SEEMS MIRRORED IN THE GROUND AND AIR.
WHAT ARE YOU DOING?
HELA, PLEASE!
WHY HAVE YOU DONE THIS? HAVE I NOT GIVEN YOU EVERYTHING? HAVE I NOT...
...CHERISHED YOU, IN MY WAY?
STOP THIS!
IT IS NOT ME DOING THIS, KARNILLA!
THE LITTLE GODS FEEL TERROR FOR THE FIRST TIME.
IF NOT YOU, THEN WHO?
THEIR FEAR TRAVELS THROUGH INVISIBLE THREADS...
WAAAAHHHH!

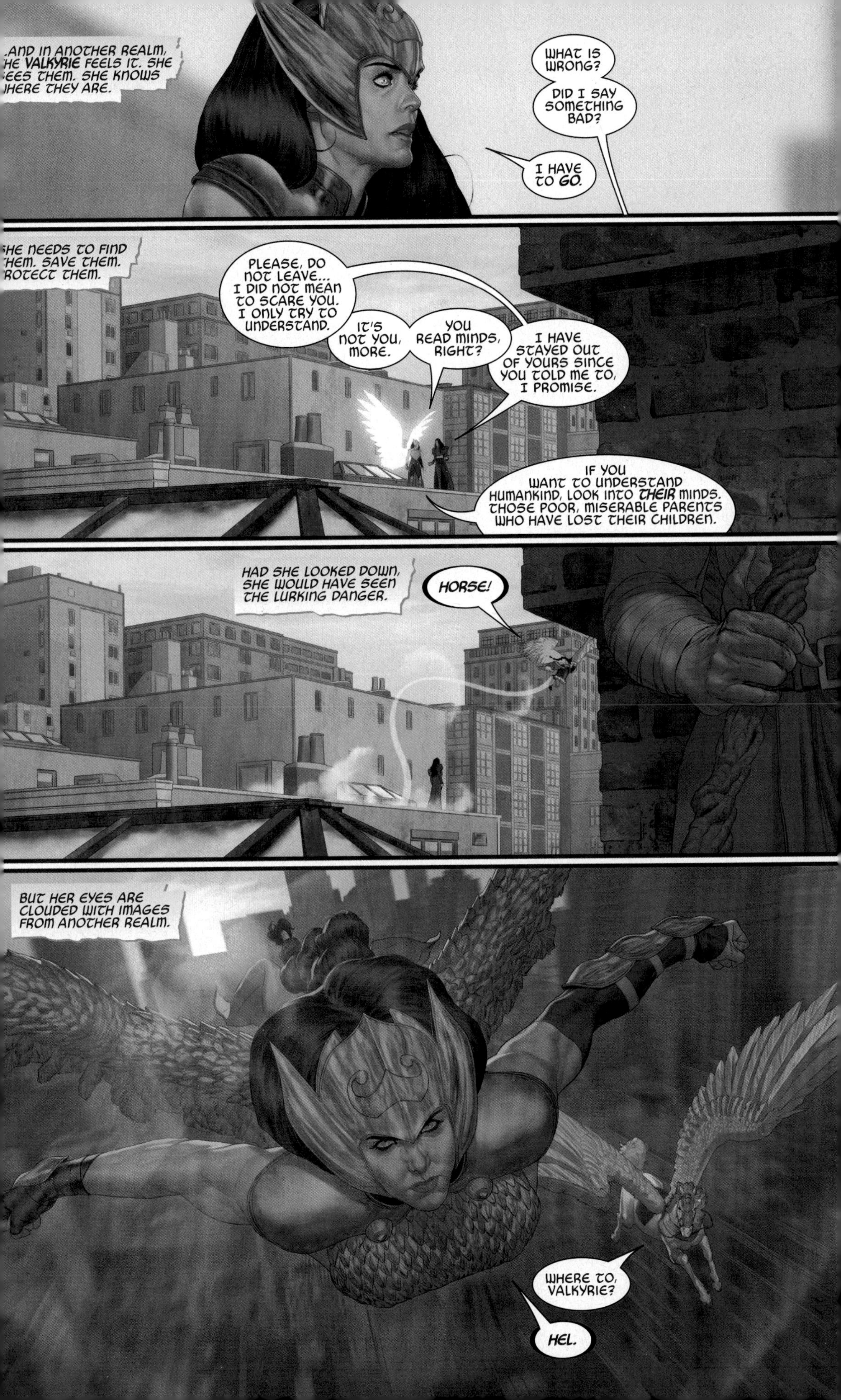
...AND IN ANOTHER REALM, THE VALKYRIE FEELS IT. SHE SEES THEM. SHE KNOWS WHERE THEY ARE.
WHAT IS WRONG?
DID I SAY SOMETHING BAD?
I HAVE TO GO.
SHE NEEDS TO FIND THEM. SAVE THEM. PROTECT THEM.
PLEASE, DO NOT LEAVE... I DID NOT MEAN TO SCARE YOU. I ONLY TRY TO UNDERSTAND.
IT'S NOT YOU, MORE.
YOU READ MINDS, RIGHT?
I HAVE STAYED OUT OF YOURS SINCE YOU TOLD ME TO, I PROMISE.
IF YOU WANT TO UNDERSTAND HUMANKIND, LOOK INTO THEIR MINDS. THOSE POOR, MISERABLE PARENTS WHO HAVE LOST THEIR CHILDREN.
HAD SHE LOOKED DOWN, SHE WOULD HAVE SEEN THE LURKING DANGER.
HORSE!
BUT HER EYES ARE CLOUDED WITH IMAGES FROM ANOTHER REALM.
WHERE TO, VALKYRIE?
HEL.

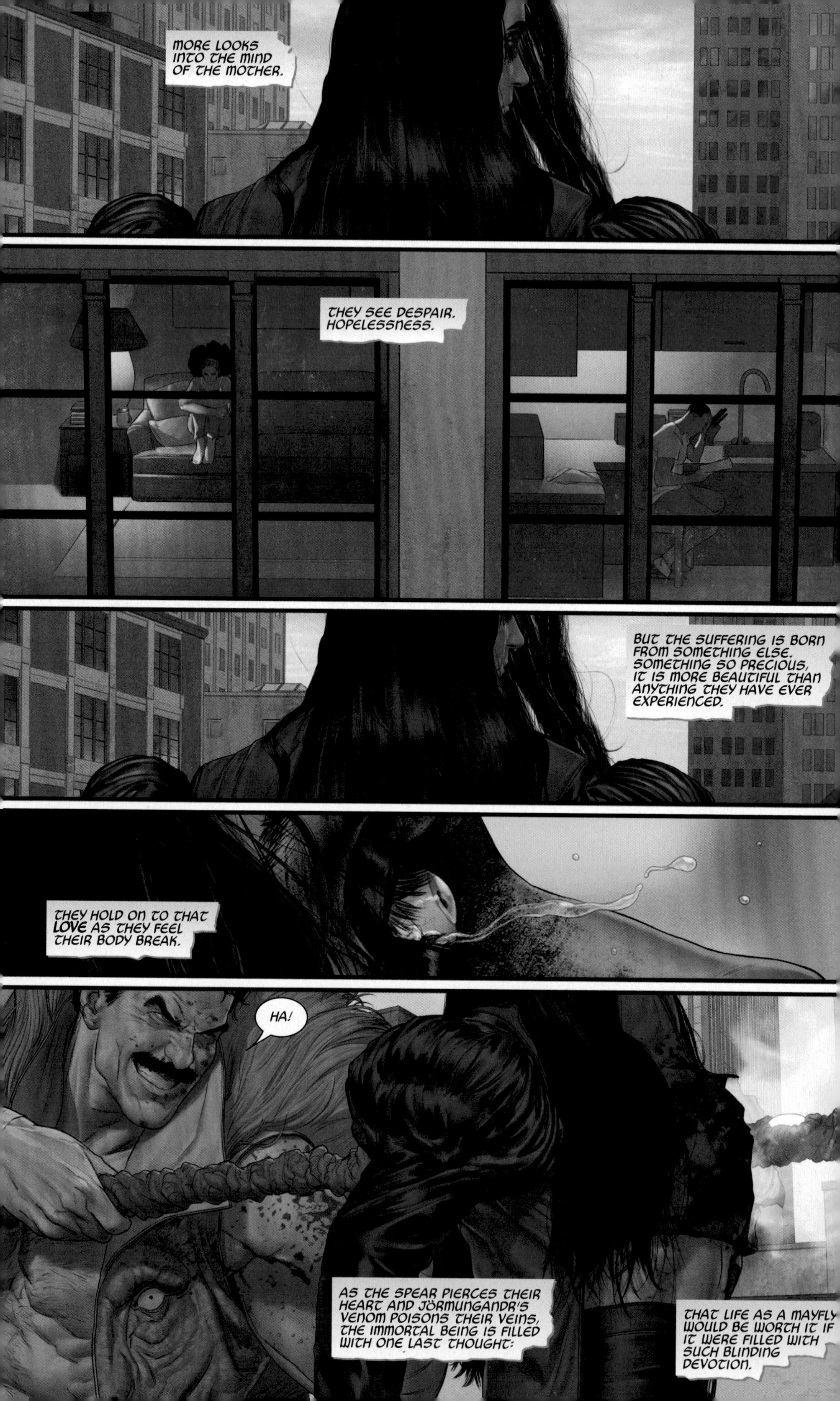
MORE LOOKS INTO THE MIND OF THE MOTHER.
THEY SEE DESPAIR. HOPELESSNESS.
BUT THE SUFFERING IS BORN FROM SOMETHING ELSE. SOMETHING SO PRECIOUS, IT IS MORE BEAUTIFUL THAN ANYTHING THEY HAVE EVER EXPERIENCED.
THEY HOLD ON TO THAT LOVE AS THEY FEEL THEIR BODY BREAK.
HA!
AS THE SPEAR PIERCES THEIR HEART AND JÖRMUNGANDR'S VENOM POISONS THEIR VEINS, THE IMMORTAL BEING IS FILLED WITH ONE LAST THOUGHT:
THAT LIFE AS A MAYFLY WOULD BE WORTH IT IF IT WERE FILLED WITH SUCH BLINDING DEVOTION.

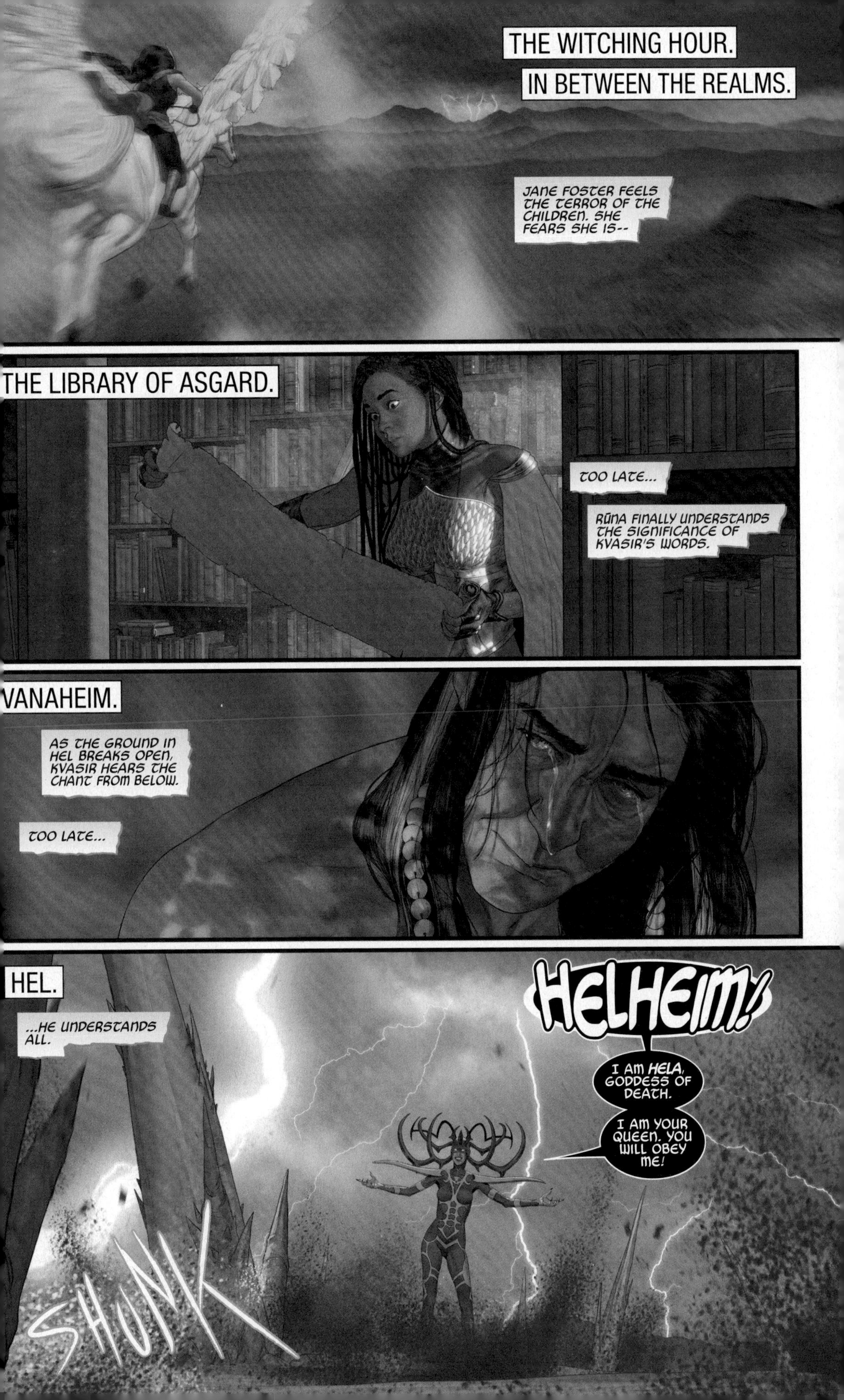

THE WITCHING HOUR.
IN BETWEEN THE REALMS.
JANE FOSTER FEELS THE TERROR OF THE CHILDREN. SHE FEARS SHE IS--
THE LIBRARY OF ASGARD.
TOO LATE...
RŪNA FINALLY UNDERSTANDS THE SIGNIFICANCE OF KVASIR'S WORDS.
VANAHEIM.
AS THE GROUND IN HEL BREAKS OPEN, KVASIR HEARS THE CHANT FROM BELOW.
TOO LATE...
HEL.
...HE UNDERSTANDS ALL.
HELHEIM!
I AM HELA, GODDESS OF DEATH.
I AM YOUR QUEEN. YOU WILL OBEY ME!
SHUNK

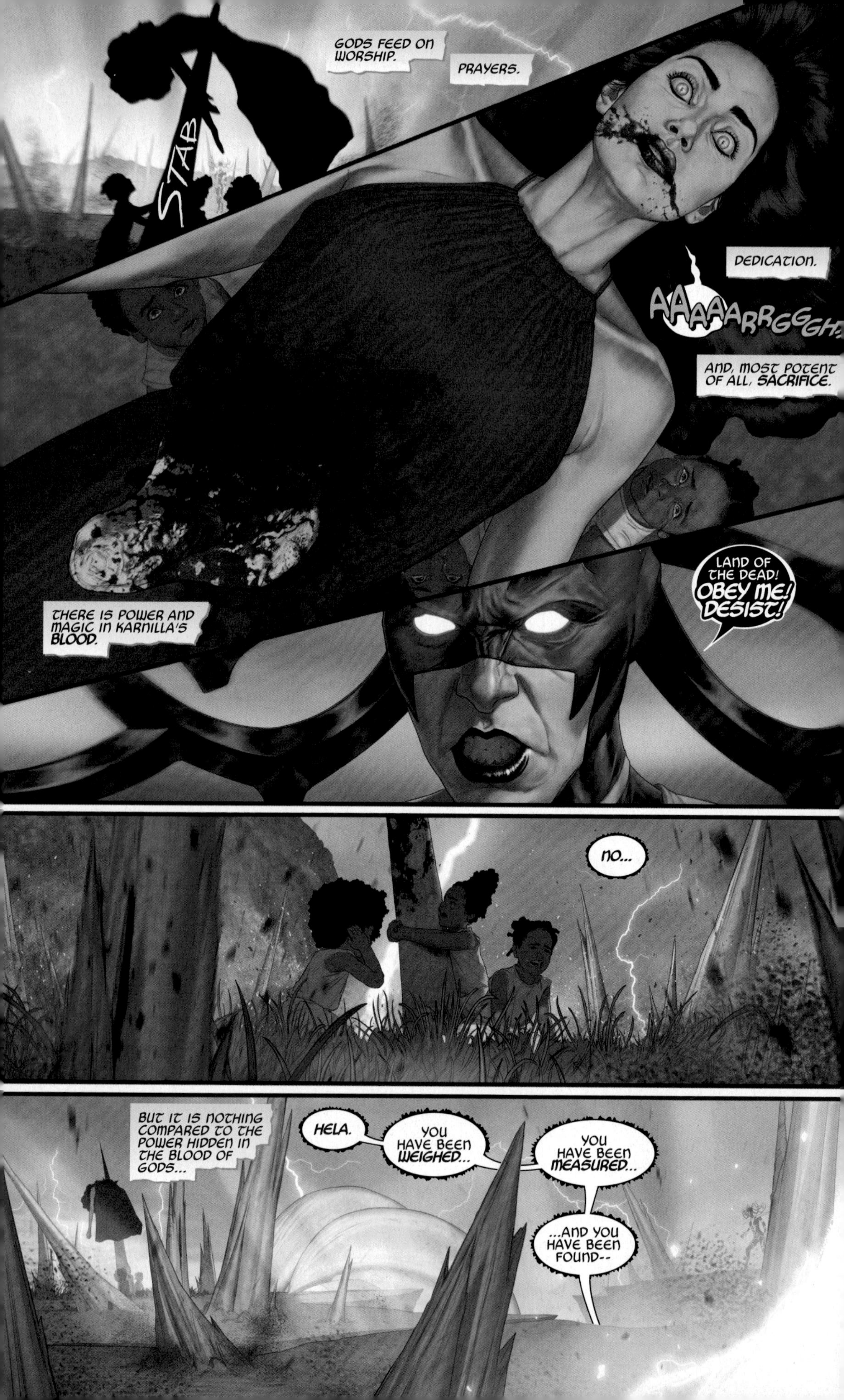

STAB
GODS FEED ON WORSHIP.
PRAYERS.
DEDICATION.
AAAAAARRGGGH!
AND, MOST POTENT OF ALL, SACRIFICE.
THERE IS POWER AND MAGIC IN KARNILLA'S BLOOD.
LAND OF THE DEAD! OBEY ME! DESIST!
NO...
BUT IT IS NOTHING COMPARED TO THE POWER HIDDEN IN THE BLOOD OF GODS...
HELA.
YOU HAVE BEEN WEIGHED...
YOU HAVE BEEN MEASURED...
...AND YOU HAVE BEEN FOUND--

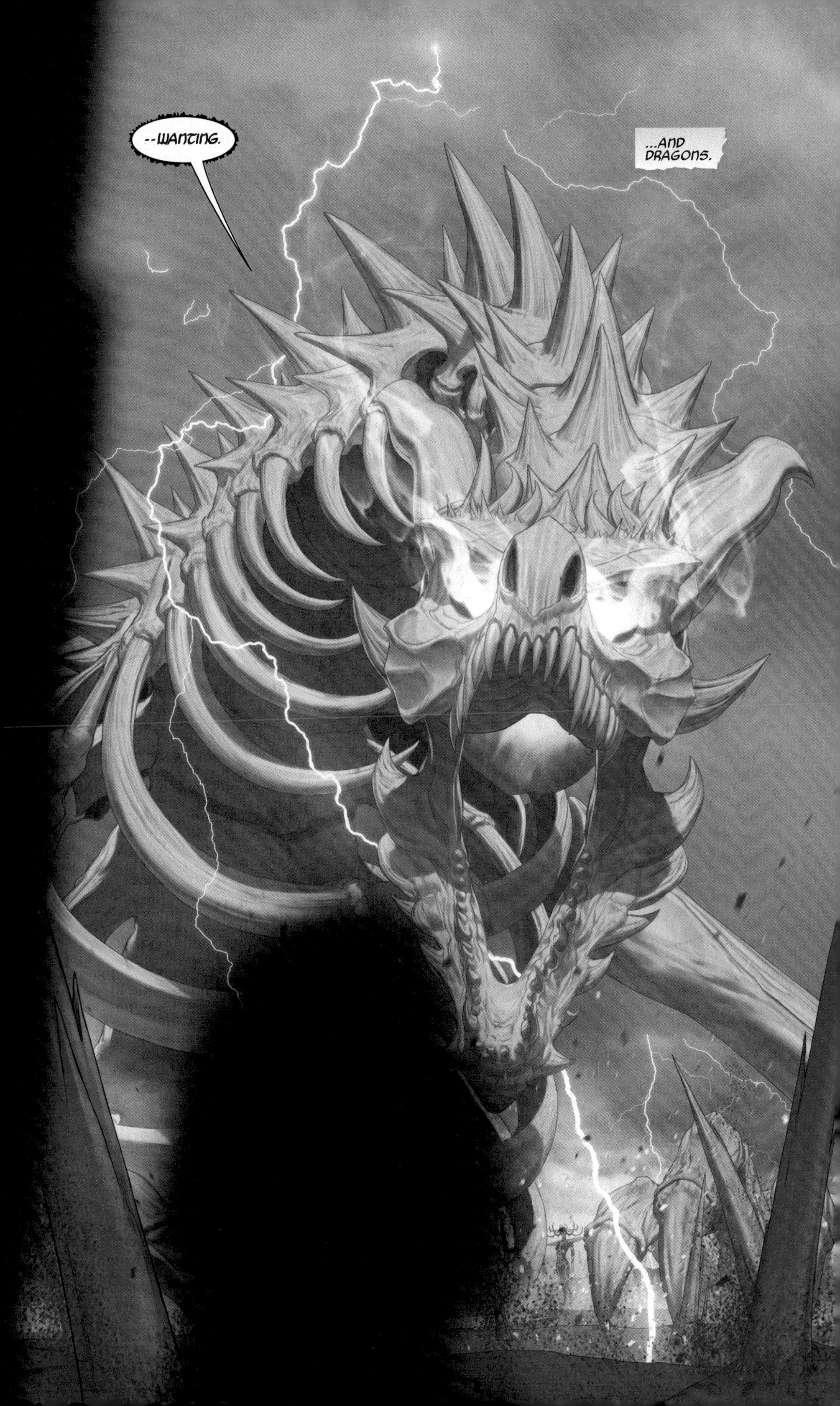
--WANTING.
...AND DRAGONS.

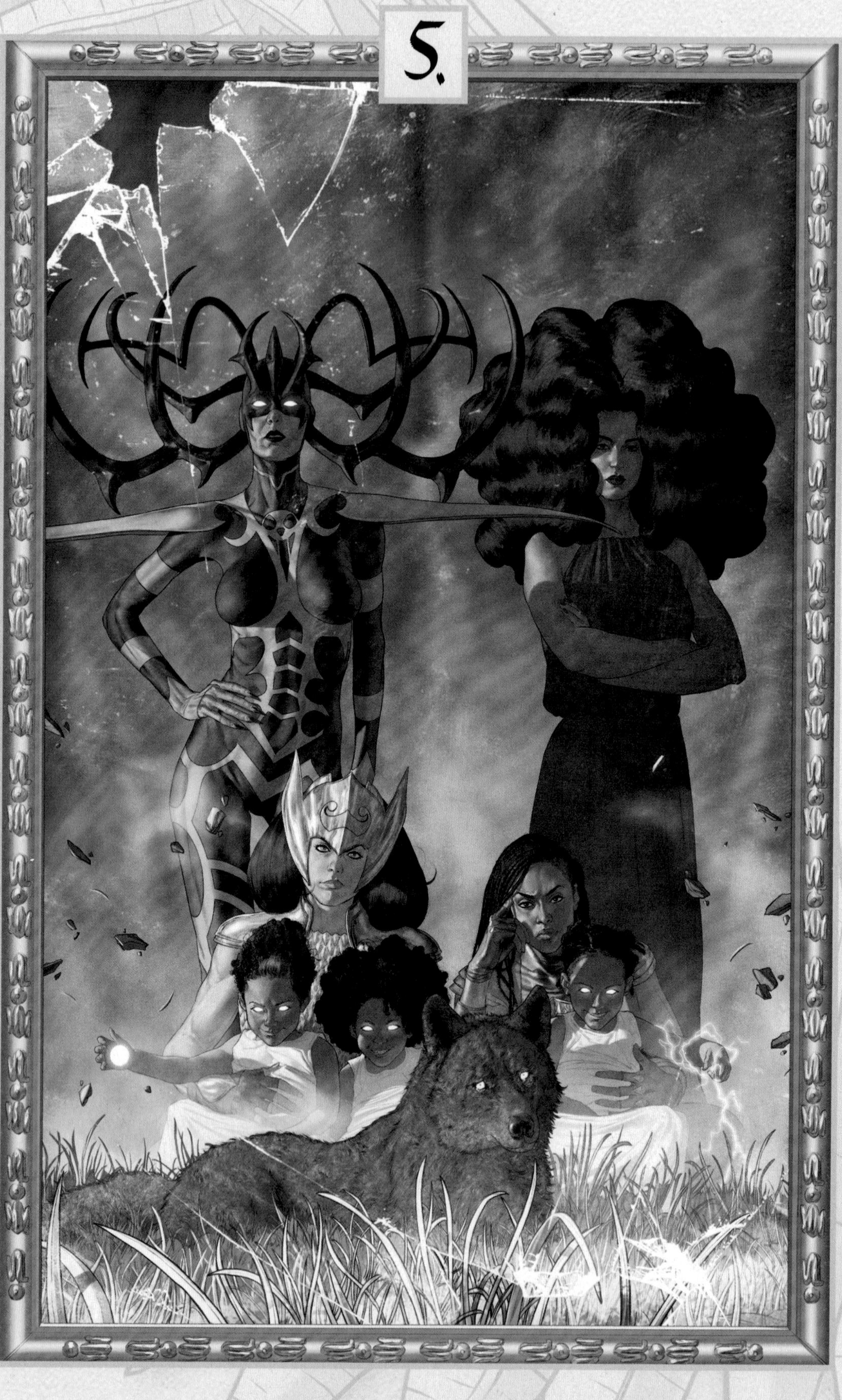
5.

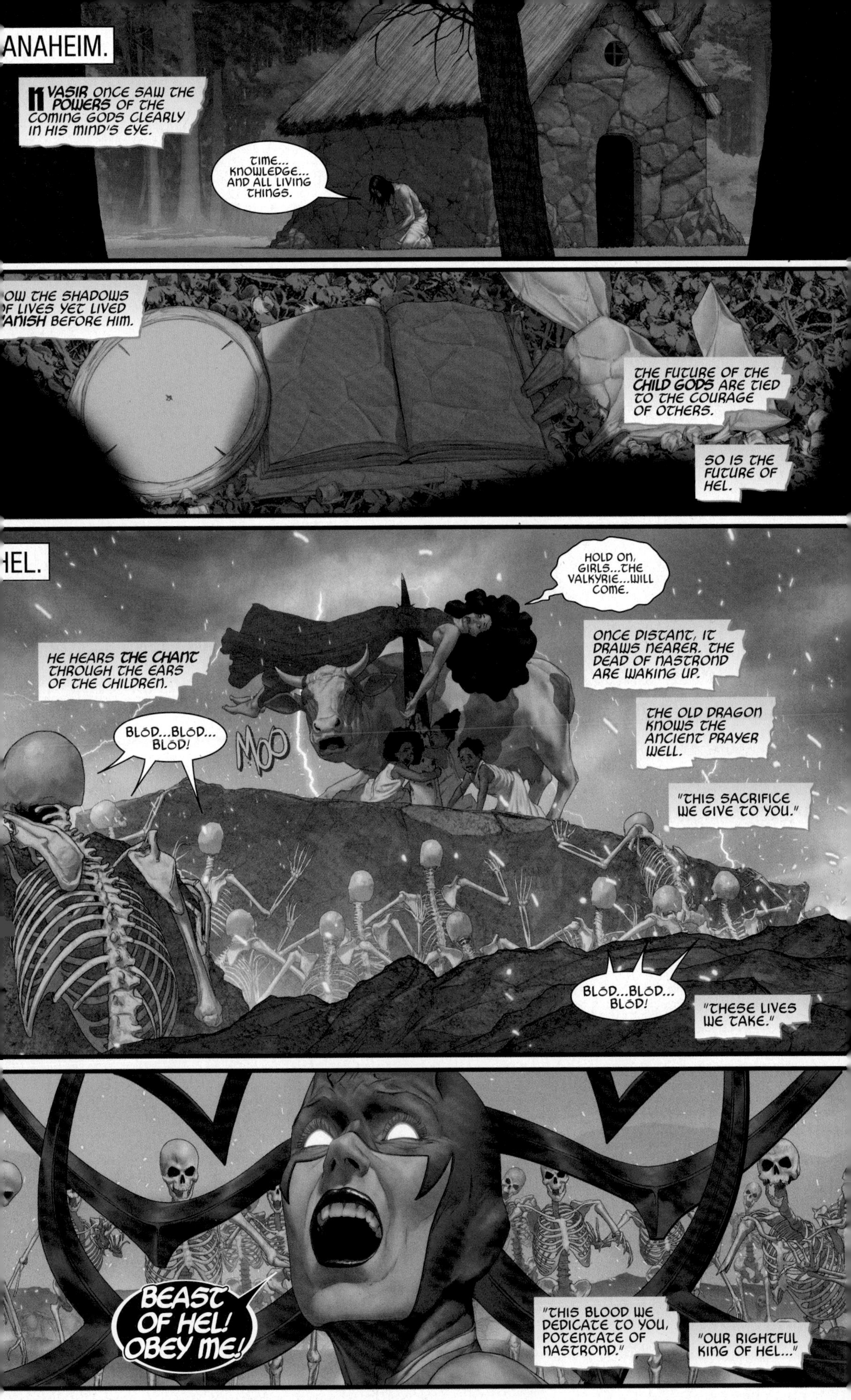

ANAHEIM.
KVASIR ONCE SAW THE POWERS OF THE COMING GODS CLEARLY IN HIS MIND'S EYE.
TIME... KNOWLEDGE... AND ALL LIVING THINGS.
OW THE SHADOWS F LIVES YET LIVED ANISH BEFORE HIM.
THE FUTURE OF THE CHILD GODS ARE TIED TO THE COURAGE OF OTHERS.
SO IS THE FUTURE OF HEL.
HEL.
HOLD ON, GIRLS...THE VALKYRIE...WILL COME.
HE HEARS THE CHANT THROUGH THE EARS OF THE CHILDREN.
ONCE DISTANT, IT DRAWS NEARER. THE DEAD OF NASTROND ARE WAKING UP.
BLŌD...BLŌD... BLŌD!
MOO
THE OLD DRAGON KNOWS THE ANCIENT PRAYER WELL.
"THIS SACRIFICE WE GIVE TO YOU."
BLŌD...BLŌD... BLŌD!
"THESE LIVES WE TAKE."
BEAST OF HEL! OBEY ME!
"THIS BLOOD WE DEDICATE TO YOU, POTENTATE OF NASTROND."
"OUR RIGHTFUL KING OF HEL..."

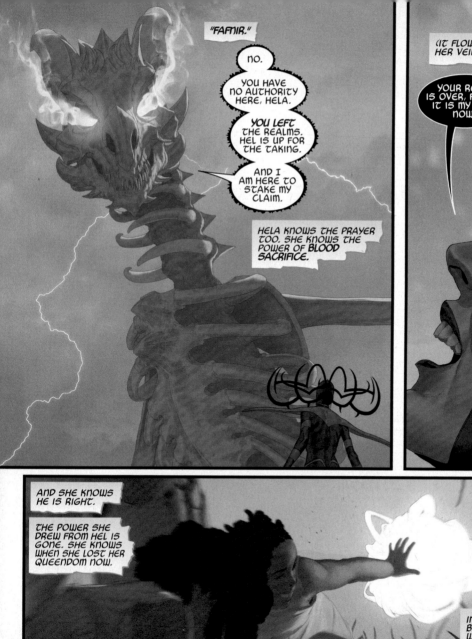

"FAFNIR."

NO.

YOU HAVE NO AUTHORITY HERE, HELA.

YOU LEFT THE REALMS. HEL IS UP FOR THE TAKING.

AND I AM HERE TO STAKE MY CLAIM.

HELA KNOWS THE PRAYER TOO. SHE KNOWS THE POWER OF **BLOOD SACRIFICE.**

(IT FLOWS THROUGH HER VEINS AS WELL.)

YOUR REIGN IS OVER, FAFNIR. IT IS MY TIME NOW.

EVERY DROP OF BLOOD SPILLED IN THIS BATTLE WILL MAKE HIM STRONGER.

AND SHE KNOWS HE IS RIGHT.

THE POWER SHE DREW FROM HEL IS GONE. SHE KNOWS WHEN SHE LOST HER QUEENDOM NOW.

IN THE CHAOS OF THE BLACK HOLE, THERE WAS A MOMENT WHEN SHE LEFT NOT ONLY THE REALMS, BUT REALITY ITSELF.*

I AM HELA. I AM THE GODDESS OF DEATH AND THE QUEEN OF HEL.

WHEN SHE RETURNED, HEL HAD CHANGED.

AND I GO WHERE I DAMN WELL PLEASE!

REGRESSED INTO WHAT IT USED TO BE.

*GUARDIANS OF THE GALAXY (2019) #6!

A HOPELESS PLACE OF ANGER.
HATRED.
AND FEAR.
DEAD! LIVING! WHAT-THE-HEL-EVER!
ALL OF YOU, STAND DOWN!
IN THE NAME OF THE VALKYRIES!

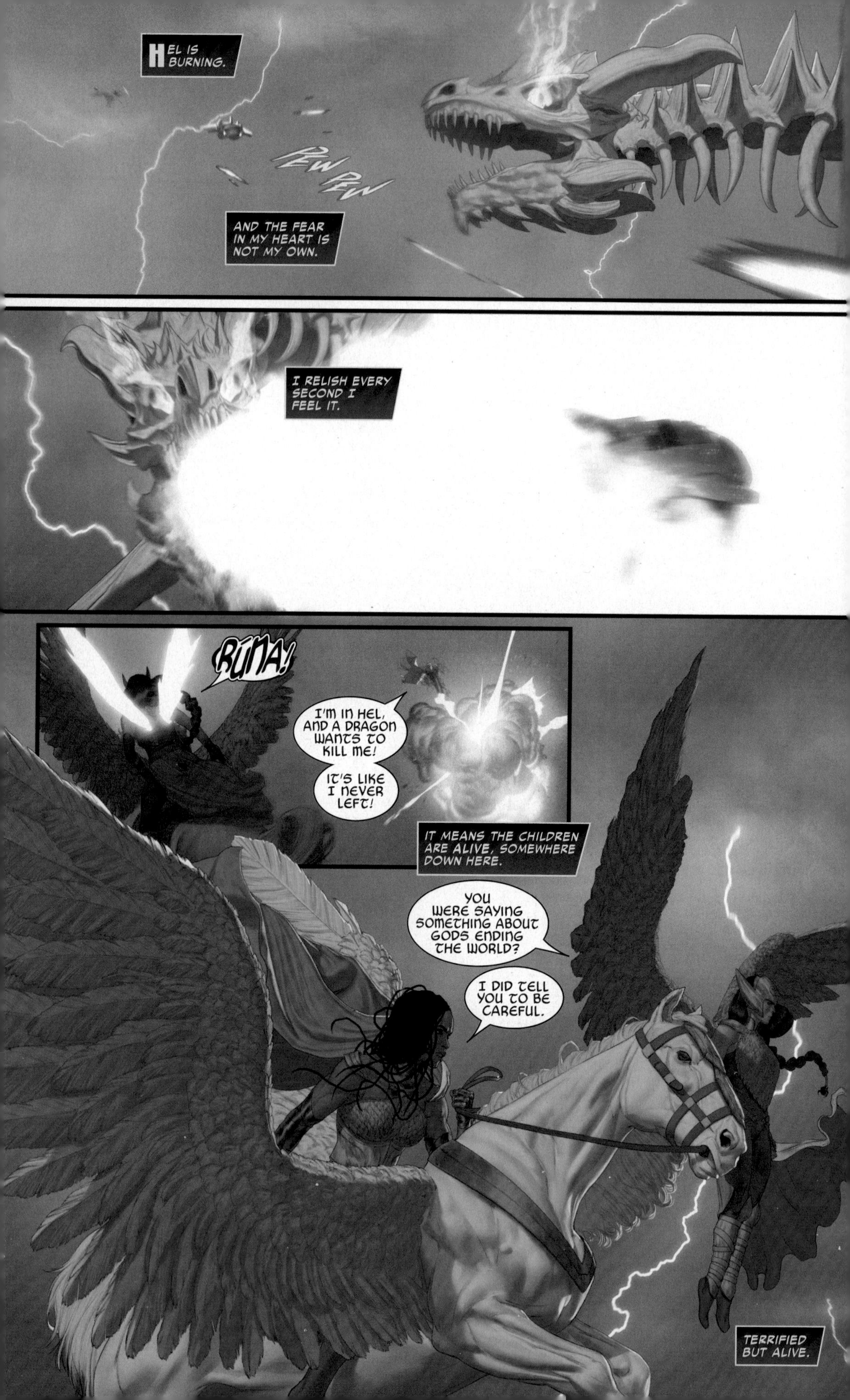
HEL IS BURNING.
PEW PEW
AND THE FEAR IN MY HEART IS NOT MY OWN.
I RELISH EVERY SECOND I FEEL IT.
RUNA!
I'M IN HEL, AND A DRAGON WANTS TO KILL ME!
IT'S LIKE I NEVER LEFT!
IT MEANS THE CHILDREN ARE ALIVE, SOMEWHERE DOWN HERE.
YOU WERE SAYING SOMETHING ABOUT GODS ENDING THE WORLD?
I DID TELL YOU TO BE CAREFUL.
TERRIFIED BUT ALIVE.

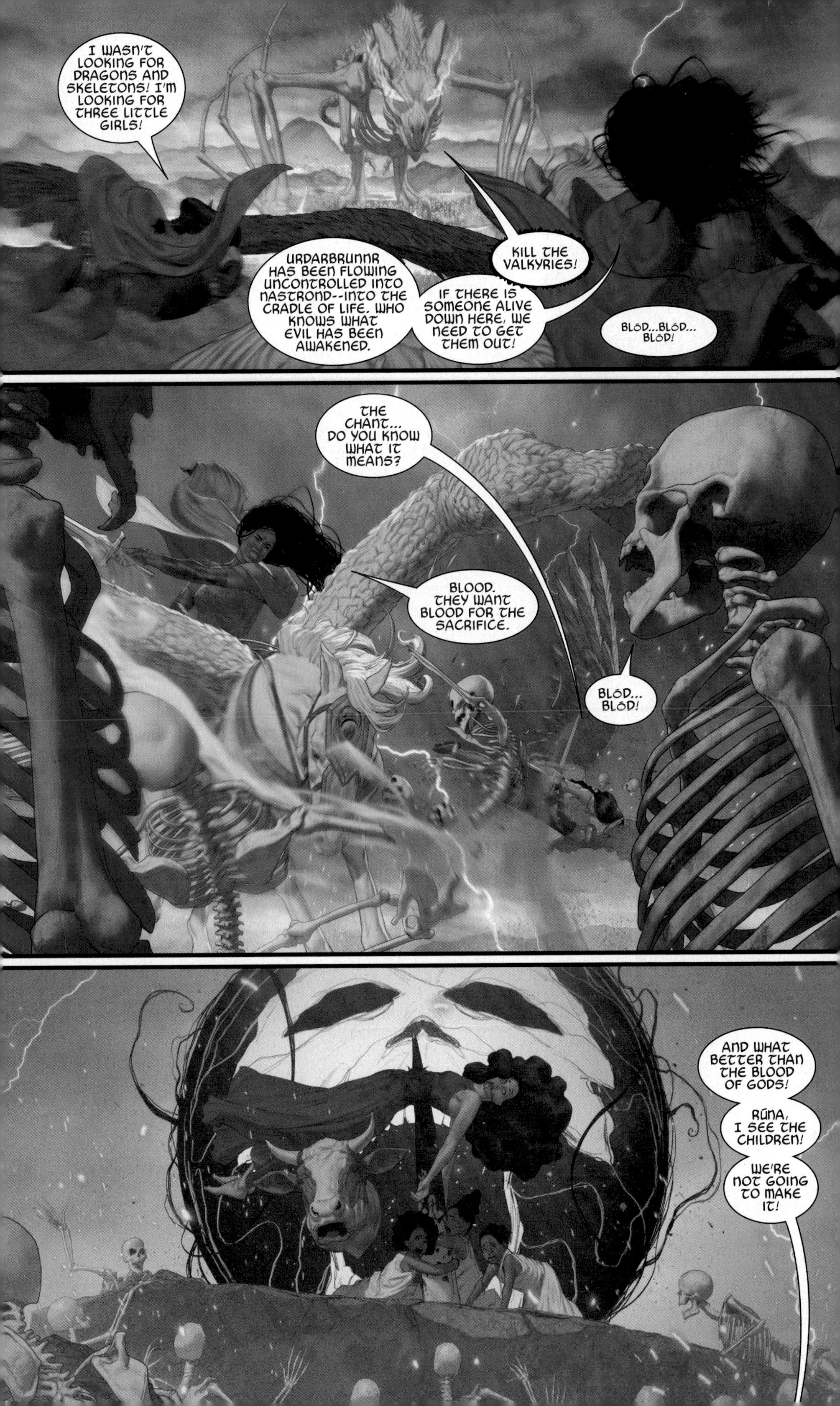

I WASN'T LOOKING FOR DRAGONS AND SKELETONS! I'M LOOKING FOR THREE LITTLE GIRLS!
URDARBRUNNR HAS BEEN FLOWING UNCONTROLLED INTO NASTROND--INTO THE CRADLE OF LIFE. WHO KNOWS WHAT EVIL HAS BEEN AWAKENED.
KILL THE VALKYRIES!
IF THERE IS SOMEONE ALIVE DOWN HERE, WE NEED TO GET THEM OUT!
BLŌD...BLŌD... BLŌD!
THE CHANT... DO YOU KNOW WHAT IT MEANS?
BLOOD. THEY WANT BLOOD FOR THE SACRIFICE.
BLŌD... BLŌD!
AND WHAT BETTER THAN THE BLOOD OF GODS!
RÚNA, I SEE THE CHILDREN!
WE'RE NOT GOING TO MAKE IT!

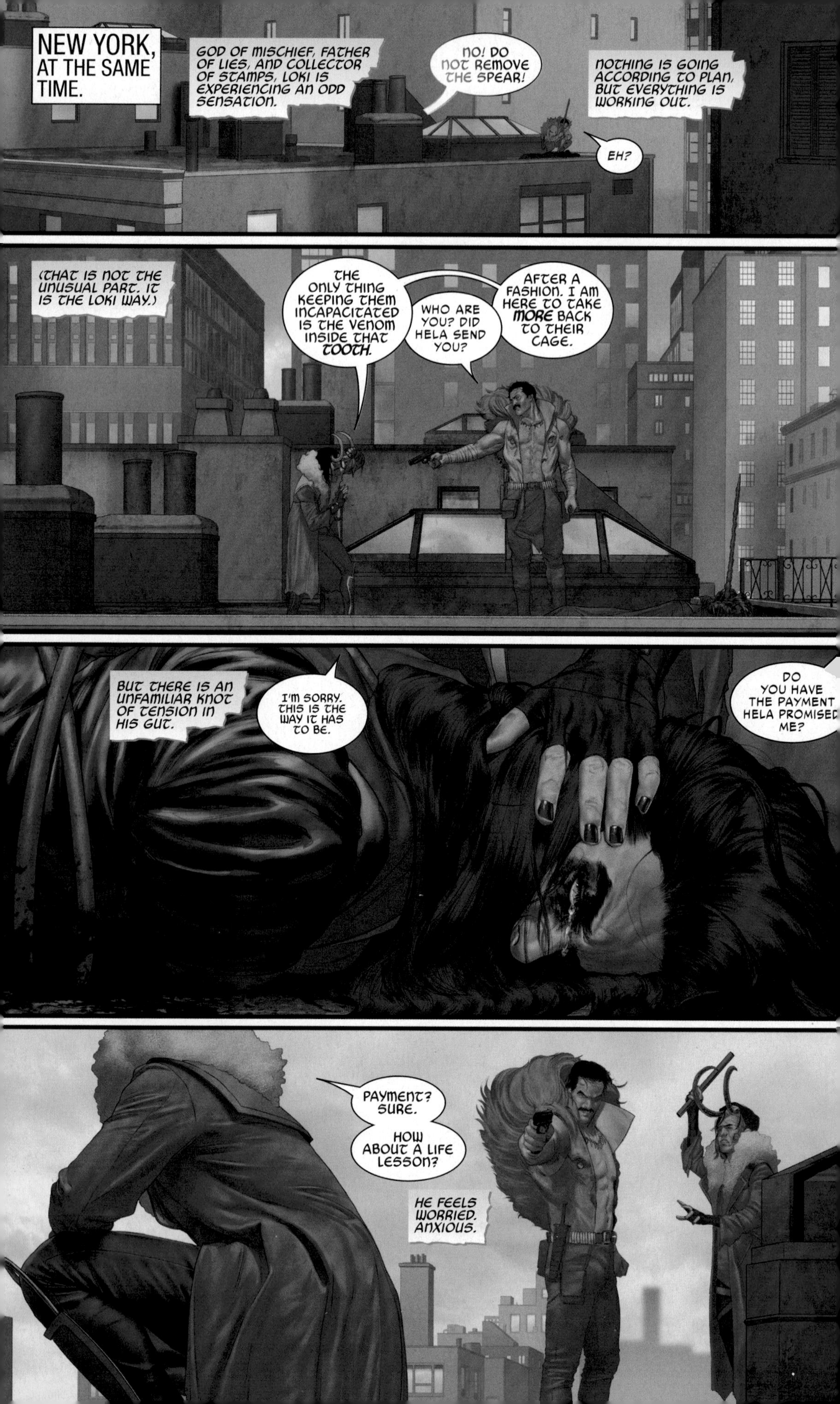

NEW YORK, AT THE SAME TIME.
GOD OF MISCHIEF, FATHER OF LIES, AND COLLECTOR OF STAMPS, LOKI IS EXPERIENCING AN ODD SENSATION.
NO! DO NOT REMOVE THE SPEAR!
NOTHING IS GOING ACCORDING TO PLAN, BUT EVERYTHING IS WORKING OUT.
EH?
(THAT IS NOT THE UNUSUAL PART. IT IS THE LOKI WAY.)
THE ONLY THING KEEPING THEM INCAPACITATED IS THE VENOM INSIDE THAT TOOTH.
WHO ARE YOU? DID HELA SEND YOU?
AFTER A FASHION. I AM HERE TO TAKE MORE BACK TO THEIR CAGE.
BUT THERE IS AN UNFAMILIAR KNOT OF TENSION IN HIS GUT.
I'M SORRY. THIS IS THE WAY IT HAS TO BE.
DO YOU HAVE THE PAYMENT HELA PROMISED ME?
PAYMENT? SURE.
HOW ABOUT A LIFE LESSON?
HE FEELS WORRIED. ANXIOUS.

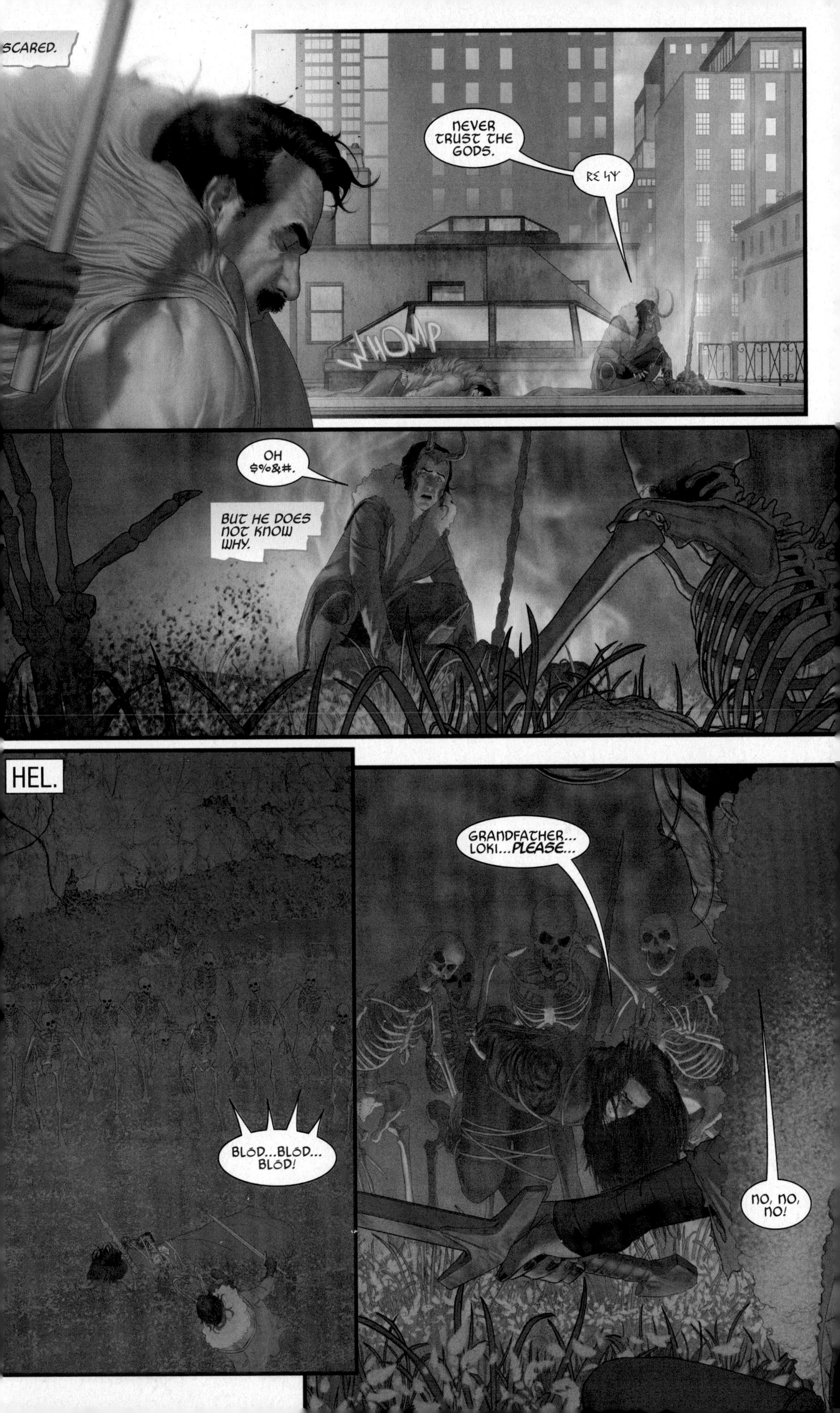
SCARED.
NEVER TRUST THE GODS.
WHOMP
OH $%&#.
BUT HE DOES NOT KNOW WHY.
HEL.
BLŌD...BLŌD... BLŌD!
GRANDFATHER... LOKI...*PLEASE*...
no, no, no!

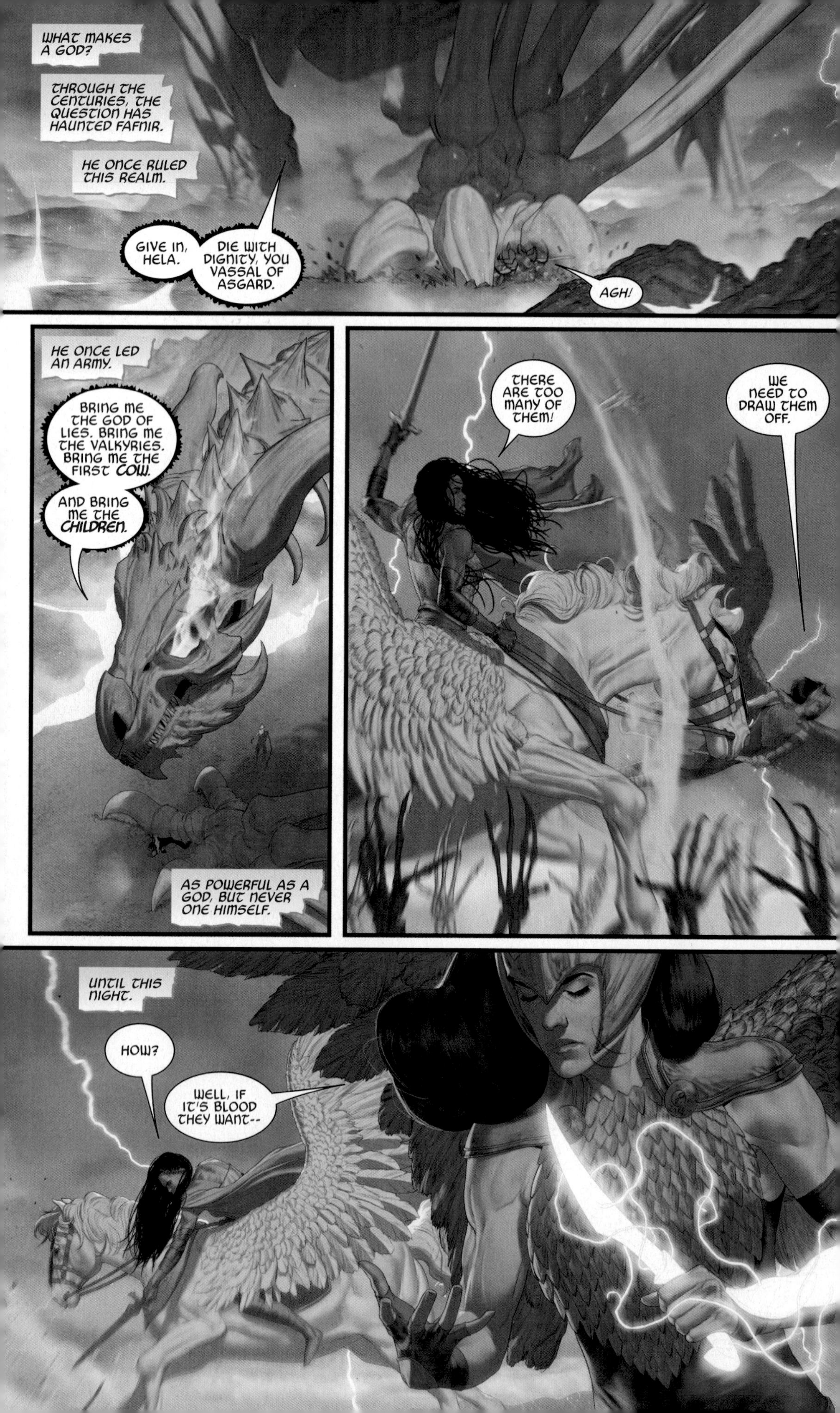
WHAT MAKES A GOD?
THROUGH THE CENTURIES, THE QUESTION HAS HAUNTED FAFNIR.
HE ONCE RULED THIS REALM.
GIVE IN, HELA.
DIE WITH DIGNITY, YOU VASSAL OF ASGARD.
AGH!
HE ONCE LED AN ARMY.
BRING ME THE GOD OF LIES. BRING ME THE VALKYRIES. BRING ME THE FIRST COW.
AND BRING ME THE CHILDREN.
AS POWERFUL AS A GOD, BUT NEVER ONE HIMSELF.
THERE ARE TOO MANY OF THEM!
WE NEED TO DRAW THEM OFF.
UNTIL THIS NIGHT.
HOW?
WELL, IF IT'S BLOOD THEY WANT--

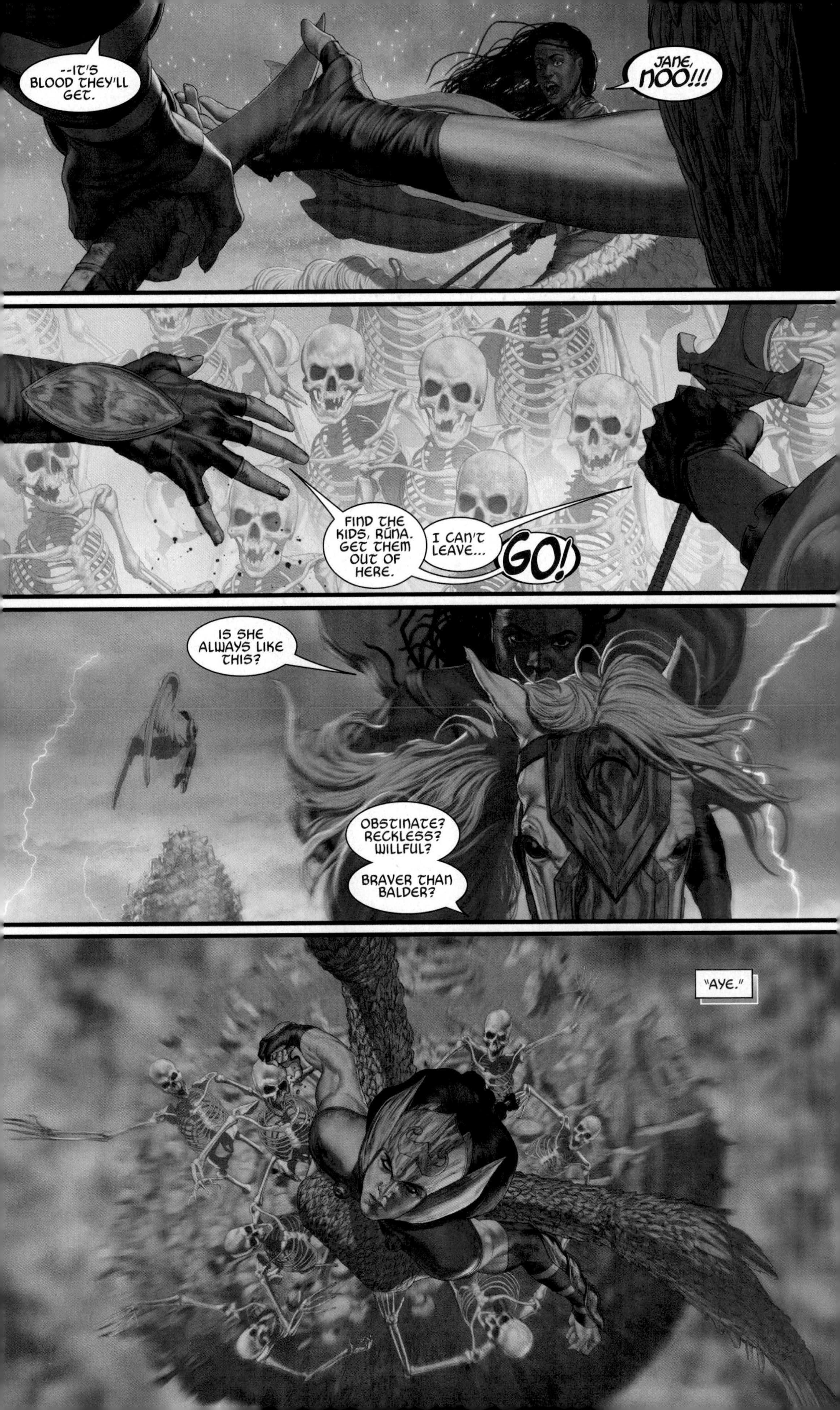
--IT'S BLOOD THEY'LL GET.
JANE, NOO!!!
FIND THE KIDS, RÚNA. GET THEM OUT OF HERE.
I CAN'T LEAVE...
GO!
IS SHE ALWAYS LIKE THIS?
OBSTINATE? RECKLESS? WILLFUL?
BRAVER THAN BALDER?
"AYE."

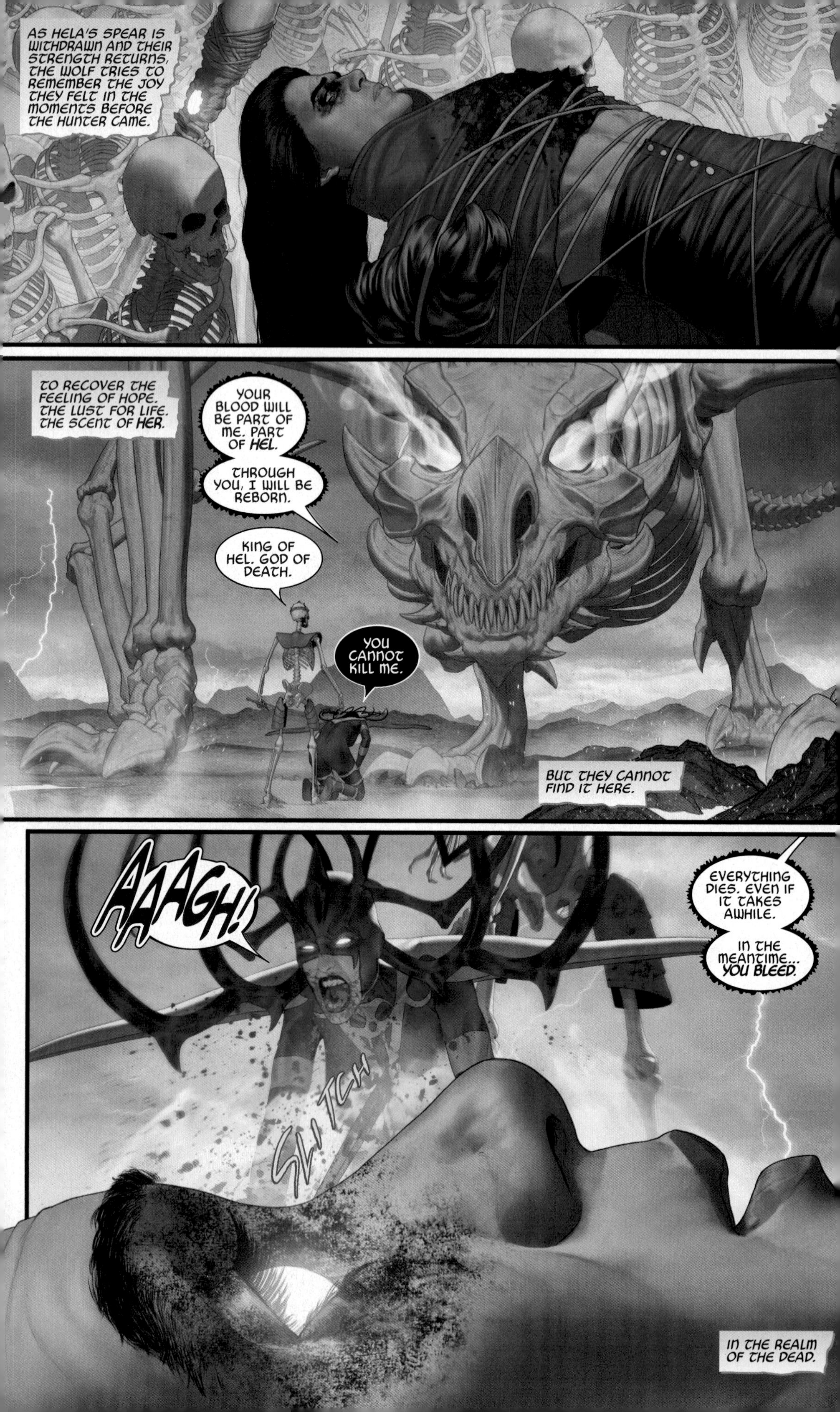
AS HELA'S SPEAR IS WITHDRAWN AND THEIR STRENGTH RETURNS, THE WOLF TRIES TO REMEMBER THE JOY THEY FELT IN THE MOMENTS BEFORE THE HUNTER CAME.
TO RECOVER THE FEELING OF HOPE. THE LUST FOR LIFE. THE SCENT OF HER.
YOUR BLOOD WILL BE PART OF ME. PART OF HEL.
THROUGH YOU, I WILL BE REBORN.
KING OF HEL. GOD OF DEATH.
YOU CANNOT KILL ME.
BUT THEY CANNOT FIND IT HERE.
AAAGH!
EVERYTHING DIES. EVEN IF IT TAKES AWHILE.
IN THE MEANTIME... YOU BLEED.
SHLITCH
IN THE REALM OF THE DEAD.

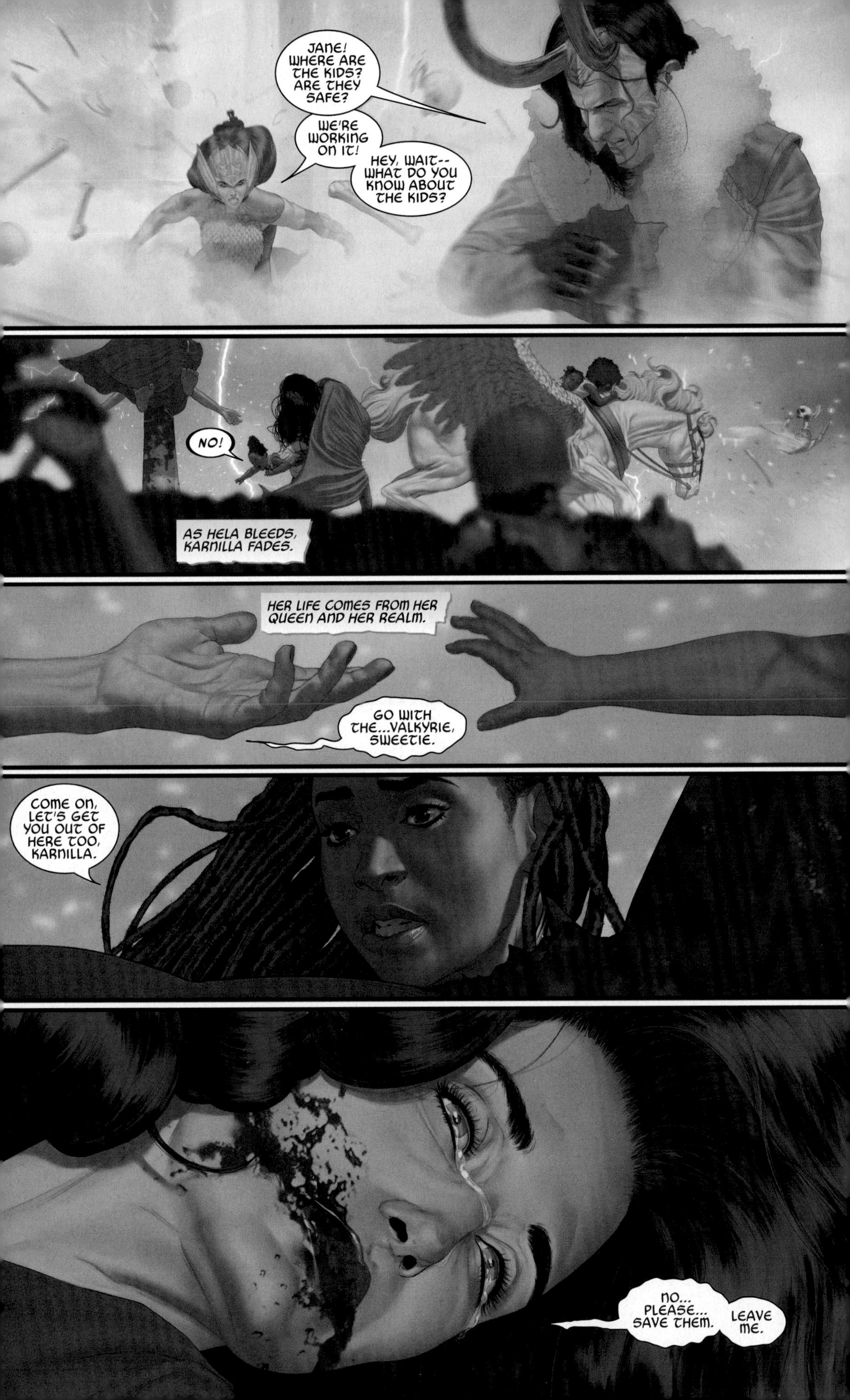
JANE! WHERE ARE THE KIDS? ARE THEY SAFE?
WE'RE WORKING ON IT!
HEY, WAIT-- WHAT DO YOU KNOW ABOUT THE KIDS?
NO!
AS HELA BLEEDS, KARNILLA FADES.
HER LIFE COMES FROM HER QUEEN AND HER REALM.
GO WITH THE...VALKYRIE, SWEETIE.
COME ON, LET'S GET YOU OUT OF HERE TOO, KARNILLA.
NO... PLEASE... SAVE THEM.
LEAVE ME.

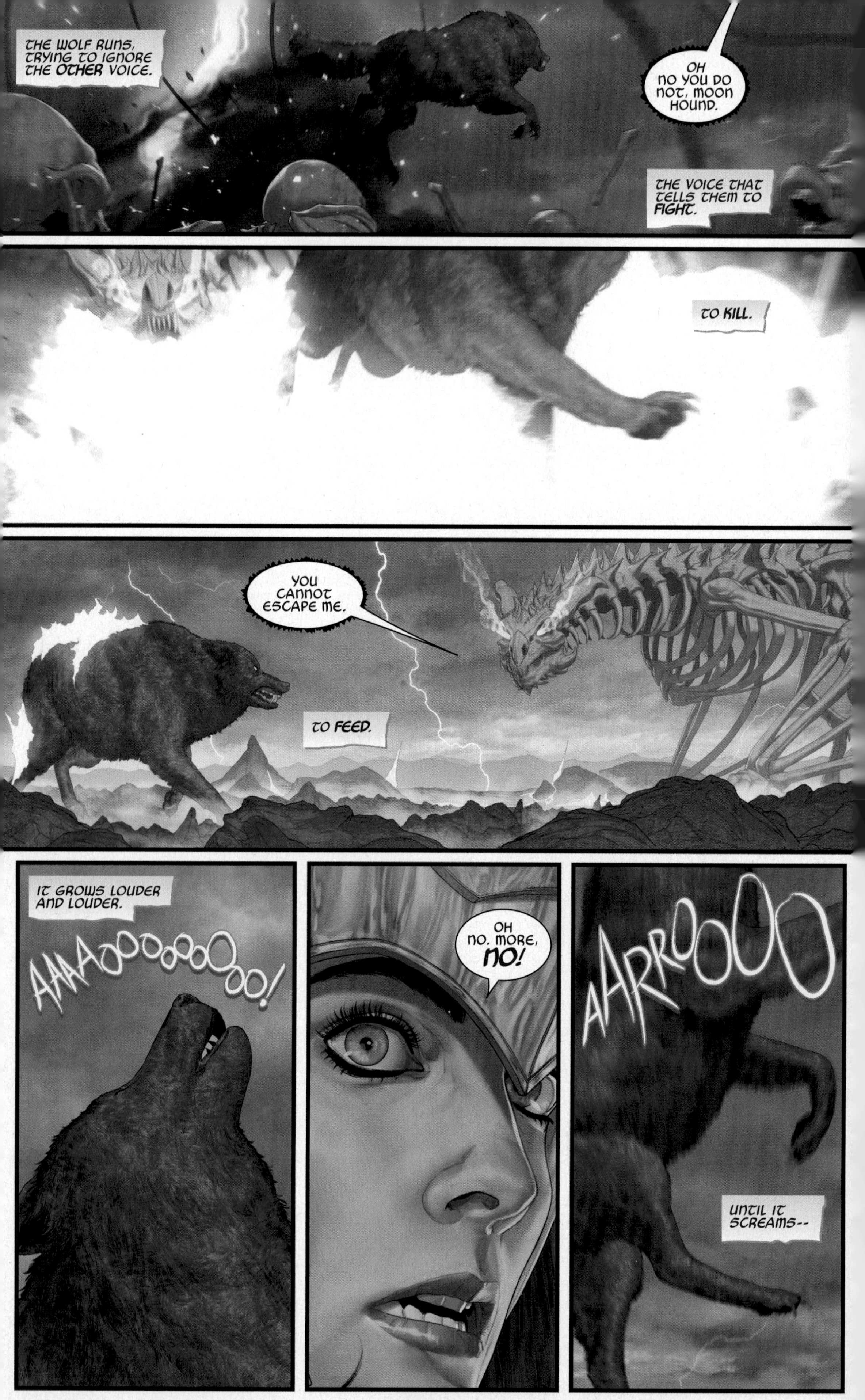
THE WOLF RUNS, TRYING TO IGNORE THE OTHER VOICE.
OH NO YOU DO NOT, MOON HOUND.
THE VOICE THAT TELLS THEM TO FIGHT.
TO KILL.
YOU CANNOT ESCAPE ME.
TO FEED.
IT GROWS LOUDER AND LOUDER.
AAAAOOOOOOOOOO!
OH NO. MORE, NO!
AARROOOO
UNTIL IT SCREAMS--

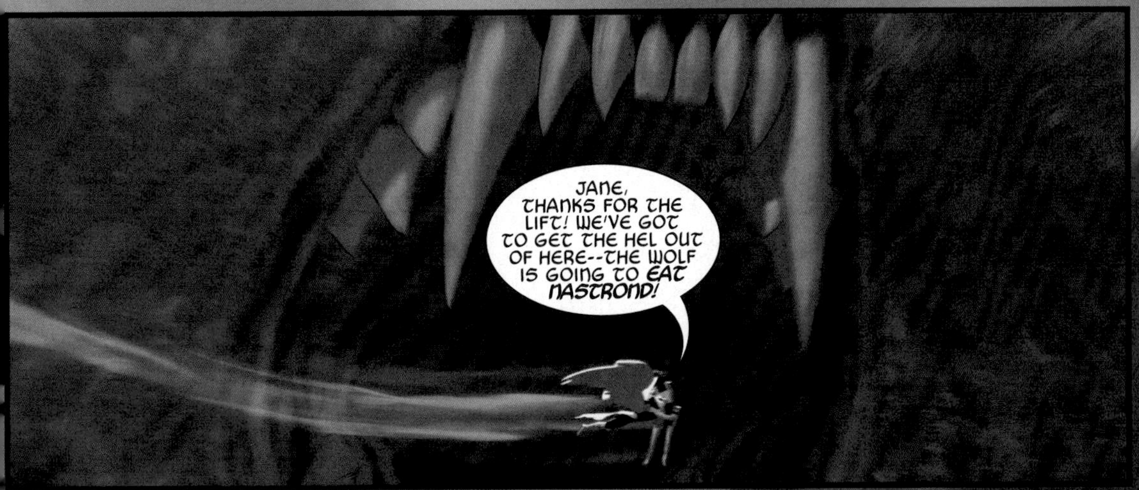
JANE, THANKS FOR THE LIFT! WE'VE GOT TO GET THE HEL OUT OF HERE--THE WOLF IS GOING TO EAT NASTROND!

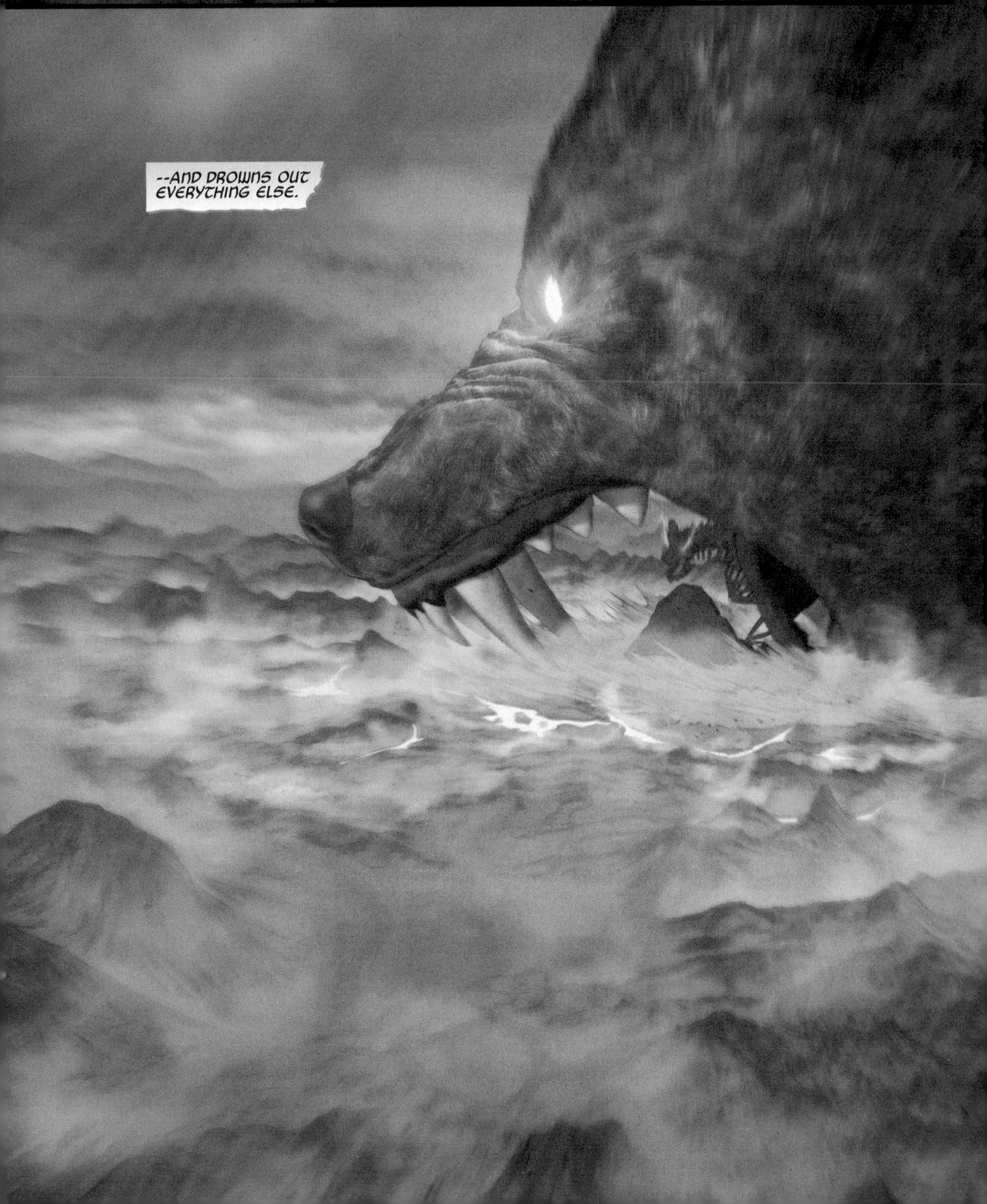
--AND DROWNS OUT EVERYTHING ELSE.

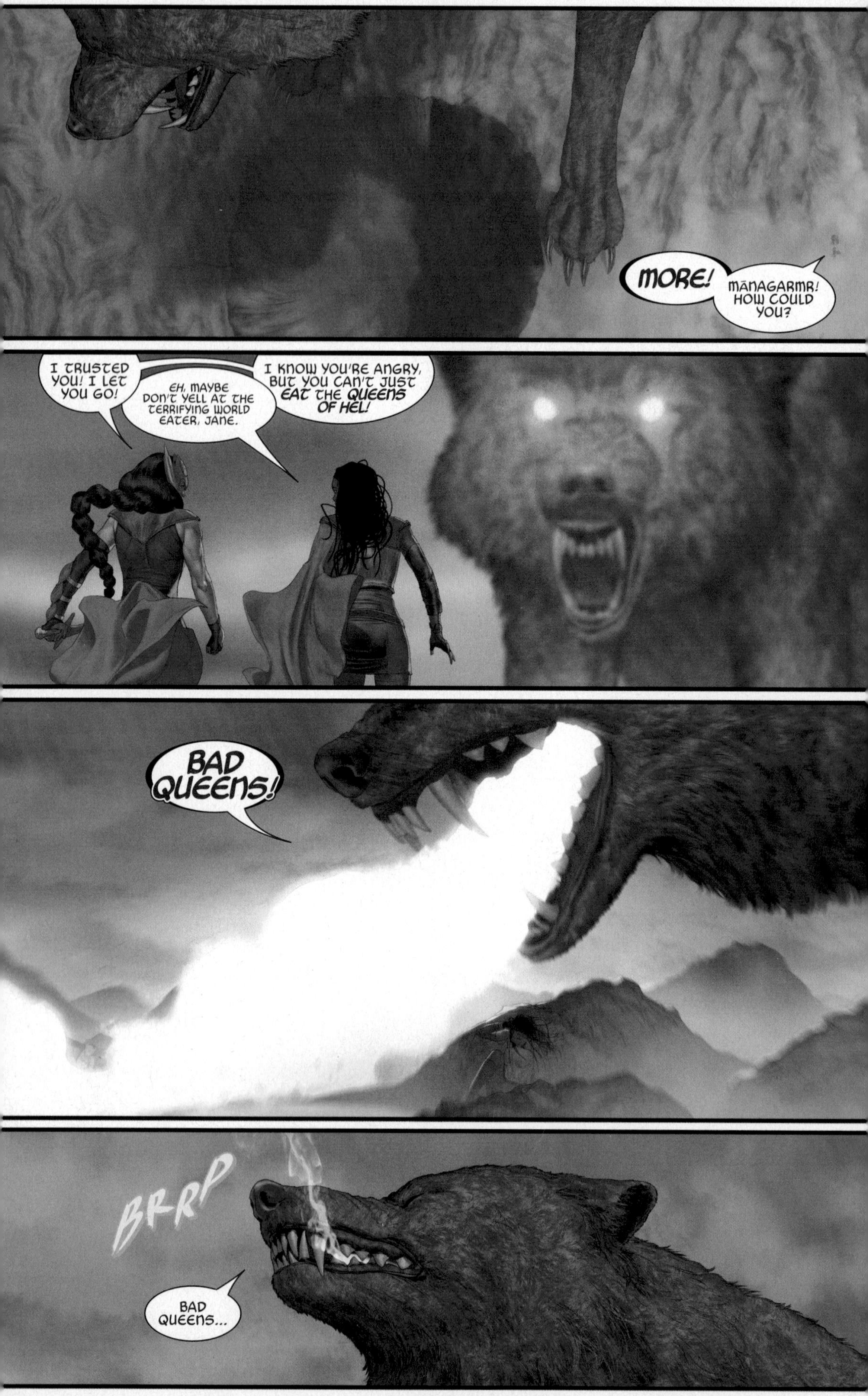
MORE!
MĀNAGARMR! HOW COULD YOU?
I TRUSTED YOU! I LET YOU GO!
EH, MAYBE DON'T YELL AT THE TERRIFYING WORLD EATER, JANE.
I KNOW YOU'RE ANGRY, BUT YOU CAN'T JUST EAT THE QUEENS OF HEL!
BAD QUEENS!
BRRP
BAD QUEENS...

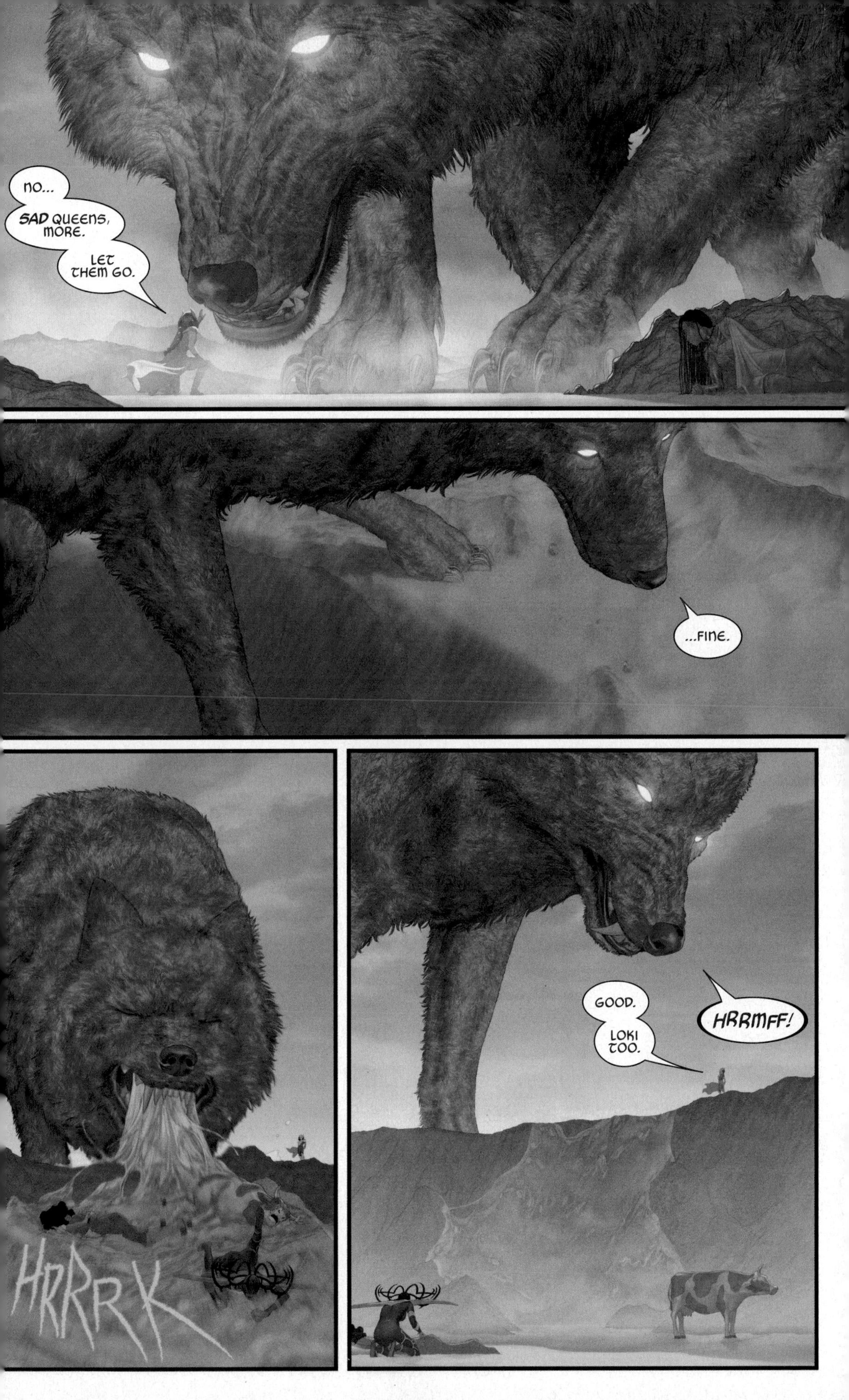
NO...
SAD QUEENS, MORE.
LET THEM GO.
...FINE.
HRRRK
GOOD.
LOKI TOO.
HRRMFF!

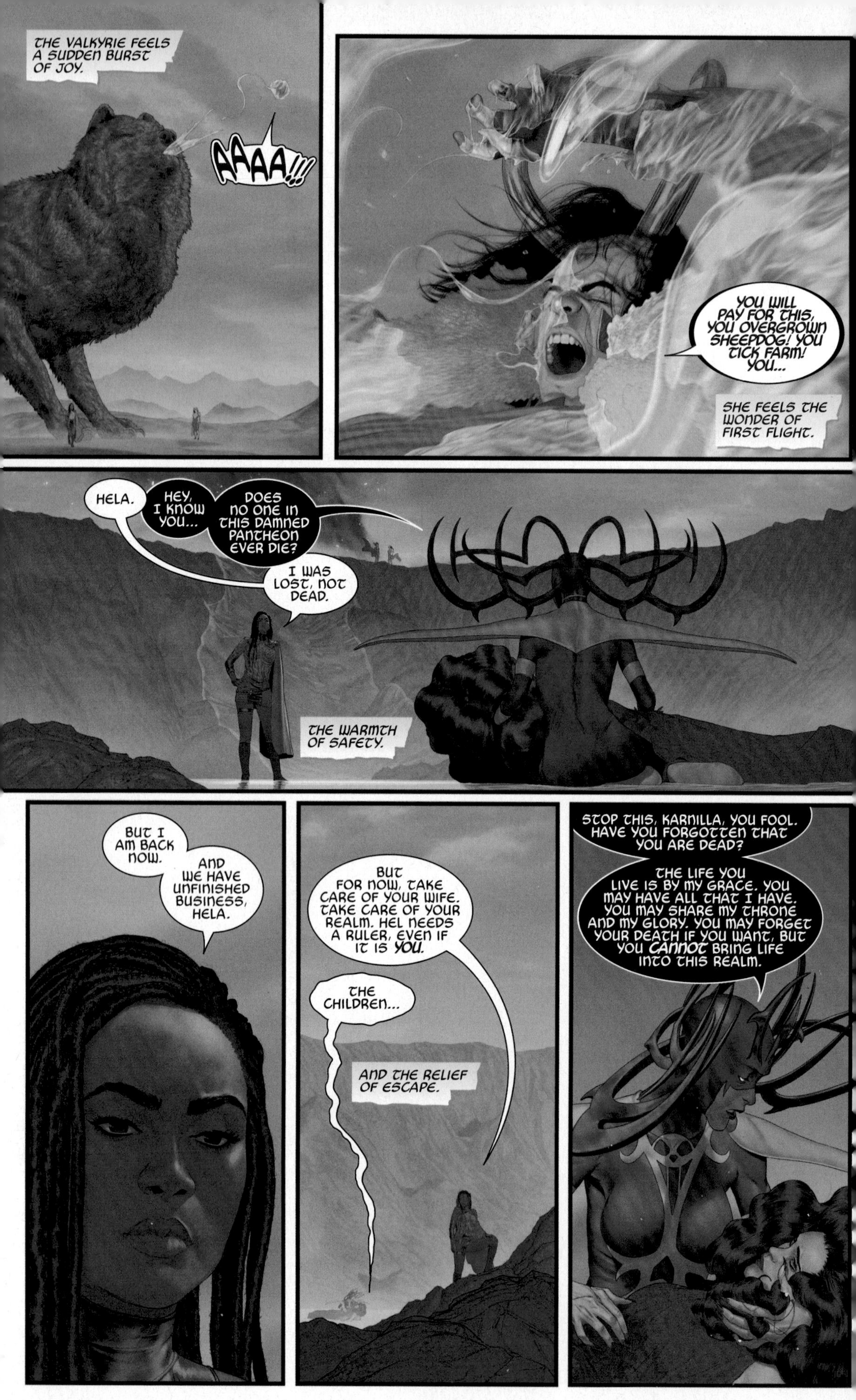

THE VALKYRIE FEELS A SUDDEN BURST OF JOY.
AAAA!!!
YOU WILL PAY FOR THIS, YOU OVERGROWN SHEEPDOG! YOU TICK FARM! YOU...
SHE FEELS THE WONDER OF FIRST FLIGHT.
HELA.
HEY, I KNOW YOU...
DOES NO ONE IN THIS DAMNED PANTHEON EVER DIE?
I WAS LOST, NOT DEAD.
THE WARMTH OF SAFETY.
BUT I AM BACK NOW.
AND WE HAVE UNFINISHED BUSINESS, HELA.
BUT FOR NOW, TAKE CARE OF YOUR WIFE. TAKE CARE OF YOUR REALM. HEL NEEDS A RULER, EVEN IF IT IS YOU.
THE CHILDREN...
AND THE RELIEF OF ESCAPE.
STOP THIS, KARNILLA, YOU FOOL. HAVE YOU FORGOTTEN THAT YOU ARE DEAD?
THE LIFE YOU LIVE IS BY MY GRACE. YOU MAY HAVE ALL THAT I HAVE. YOU MAY SHARE MY THRONE AND MY GLORY. YOU MAY FORGET YOUR DEATH IF YOU WANT, BUT YOU CANNOT BRING LIFE INTO THIS REALM.

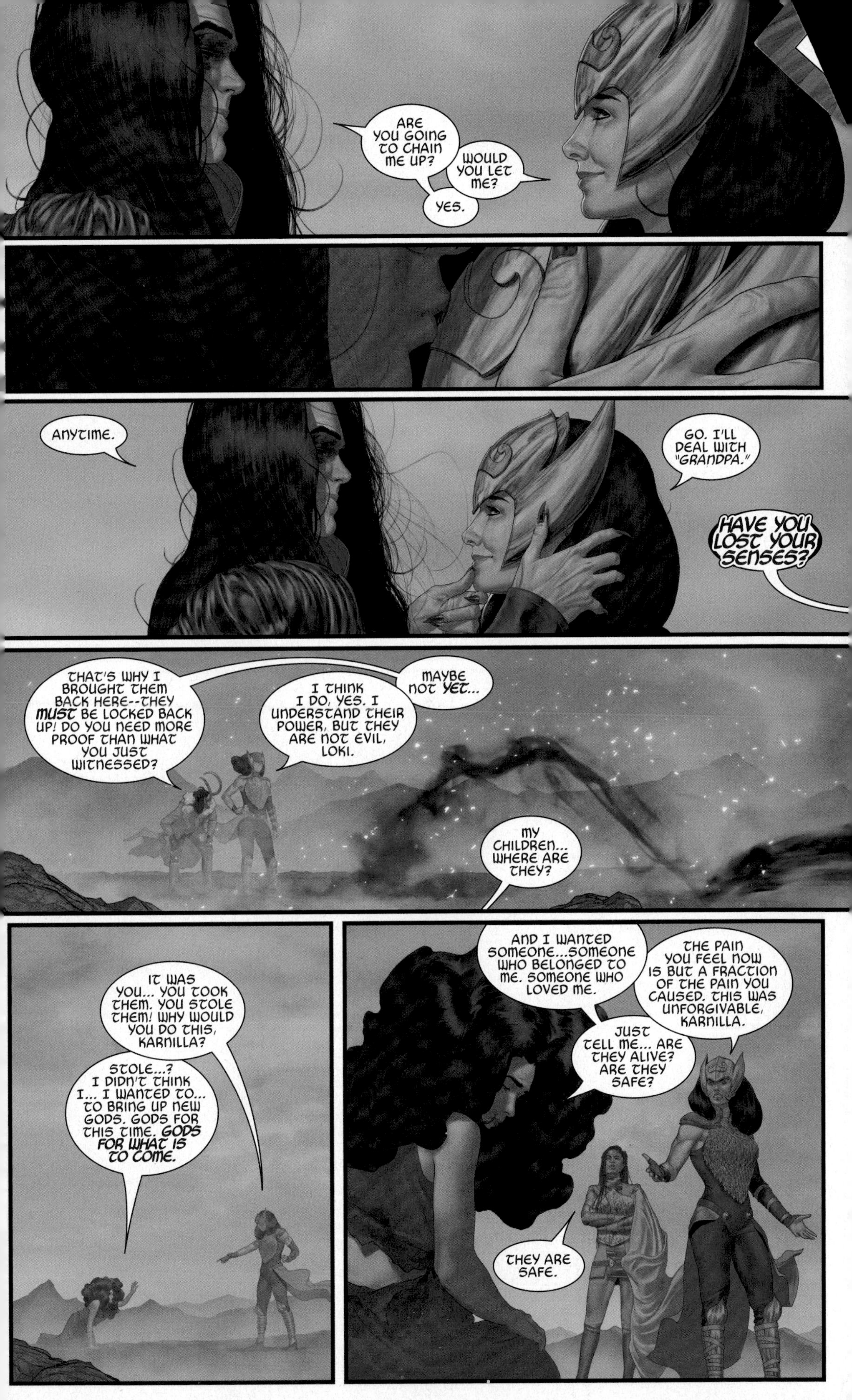
ARE YOU GOING TO CHAIN ME UP?
WOULD YOU LET ME?
YES.
ANYTIME.
GO. I'LL DEAL WITH "GRANDPA."
HAVE YOU LOST YOUR SENSES?
THAT'S WHY I BROUGHT THEM BACK HERE--THEY MUST BE LOCKED BACK UP! DO YOU NEED MORE PROOF THAN WHAT YOU JUST WITNESSED?
MAYBE NOT YET...
I THINK I DO, YES. I UNDERSTAND THEIR POWER, BUT THEY ARE NOT EVIL, LOKI.
MY CHILDREN... WHERE ARE THEY?
IT WAS YOU... YOU TOOK THEM. YOU STOLE THEM! WHY WOULD YOU DO THIS, KARNILLA?
STOLE...? I DIDN'T THINK I... I WANTED TO... TO BRING UP NEW GODS. GODS FOR THIS TIME. GODS FOR WHAT IS TO COME.
AND I WANTED SOMEONE...SOMEONE WHO BELONGED TO ME. SOMEONE WHO LOVED ME.
THE PAIN YOU FEEL NOW IS BUT A FRACTION OF THE PAIN YOU CAUSED. THIS WAS UNFORGIVABLE, KARNILLA.
JUST TELL ME... ARE THEY ALIVE? ARE THEY SAFE?
THEY ARE SAFE.

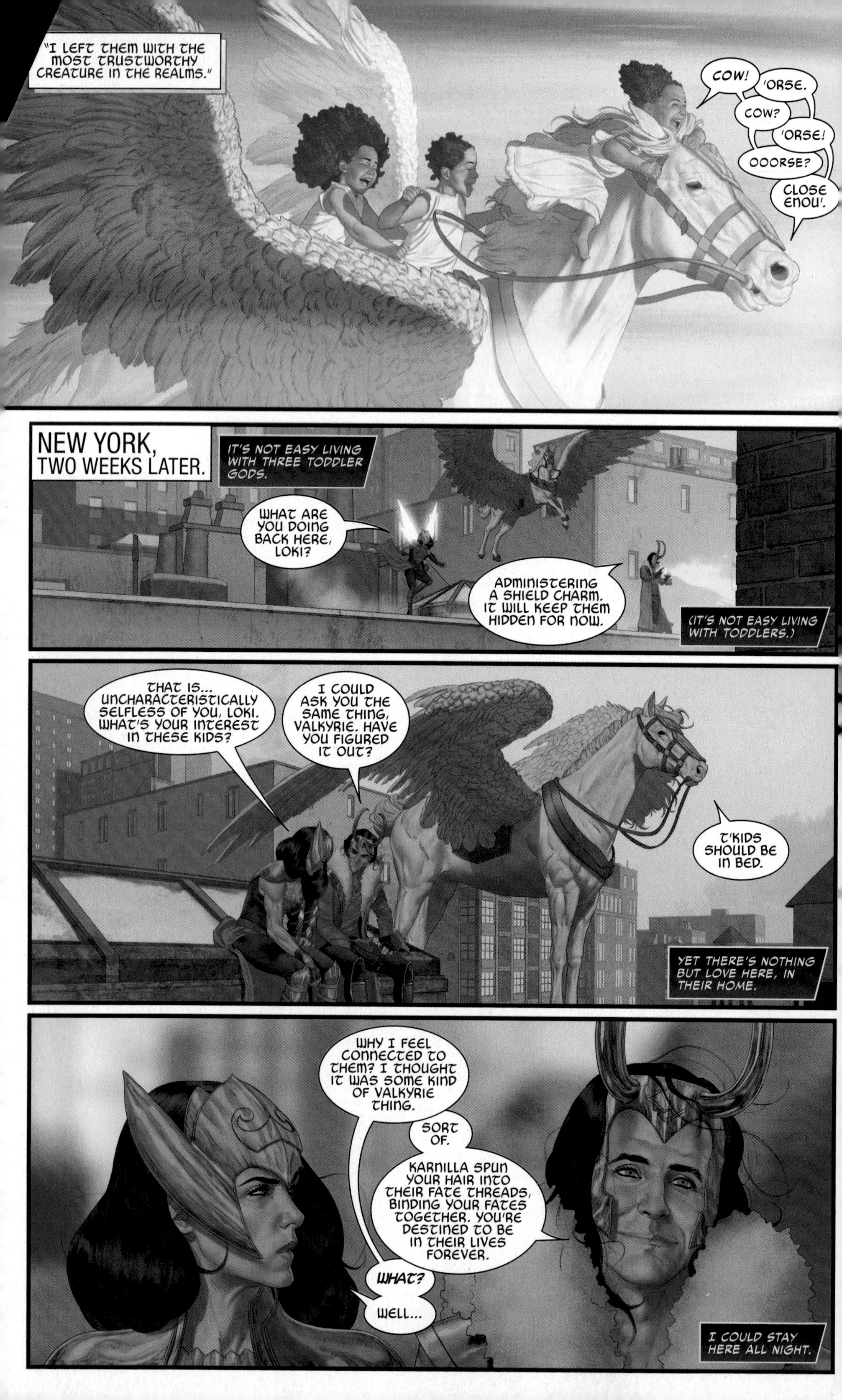

"I LEFT THEM WITH THE MOST TRUSTWORTHY CREATURE IN THE REALMS."
COW!
'ORSE.
COW?
'ORSE!
OOORSE?
CLOSE ENOU'.
NEW YORK, TWO WEEKS LATER.
IT'S NOT EASY LIVING WITH THREE TODDLER GODS.
WHAT ARE YOU DOING BACK HERE, LOKI?
ADMINISTERING A SHIELD CHARM. IT WILL KEEP THEM HIDDEN FOR NOW.
(IT'S NOT EASY LIVING WITH TODDLERS.)
THAT IS... UNCHARACTERISTICALLY SELFLESS OF YOU, LOKI. WHAT'S YOUR INTEREST IN THESE KIDS?
I COULD ASK YOU THE SAME THING, VALKYRIE. HAVE YOU FIGURED IT OUT?
T'KIDS SHOULD BE IN BED.
YET THERE'S NOTHING BUT LOVE HERE, IN THEIR HOME.
WHY I FEEL CONNECTED TO THEM? I THOUGHT IT WAS SOME KIND OF VALKYRIE THING.
SORT OF.
KARNILLA SPUN YOUR HAIR INTO THEIR FATE THREADS, BINDING YOUR FATES TOGETHER. YOU'RE DESTINED TO BE IN THEIR LIVES FOREVER.
WHAT?
WELL...
I COULD STAY HERE ALL NIGHT.

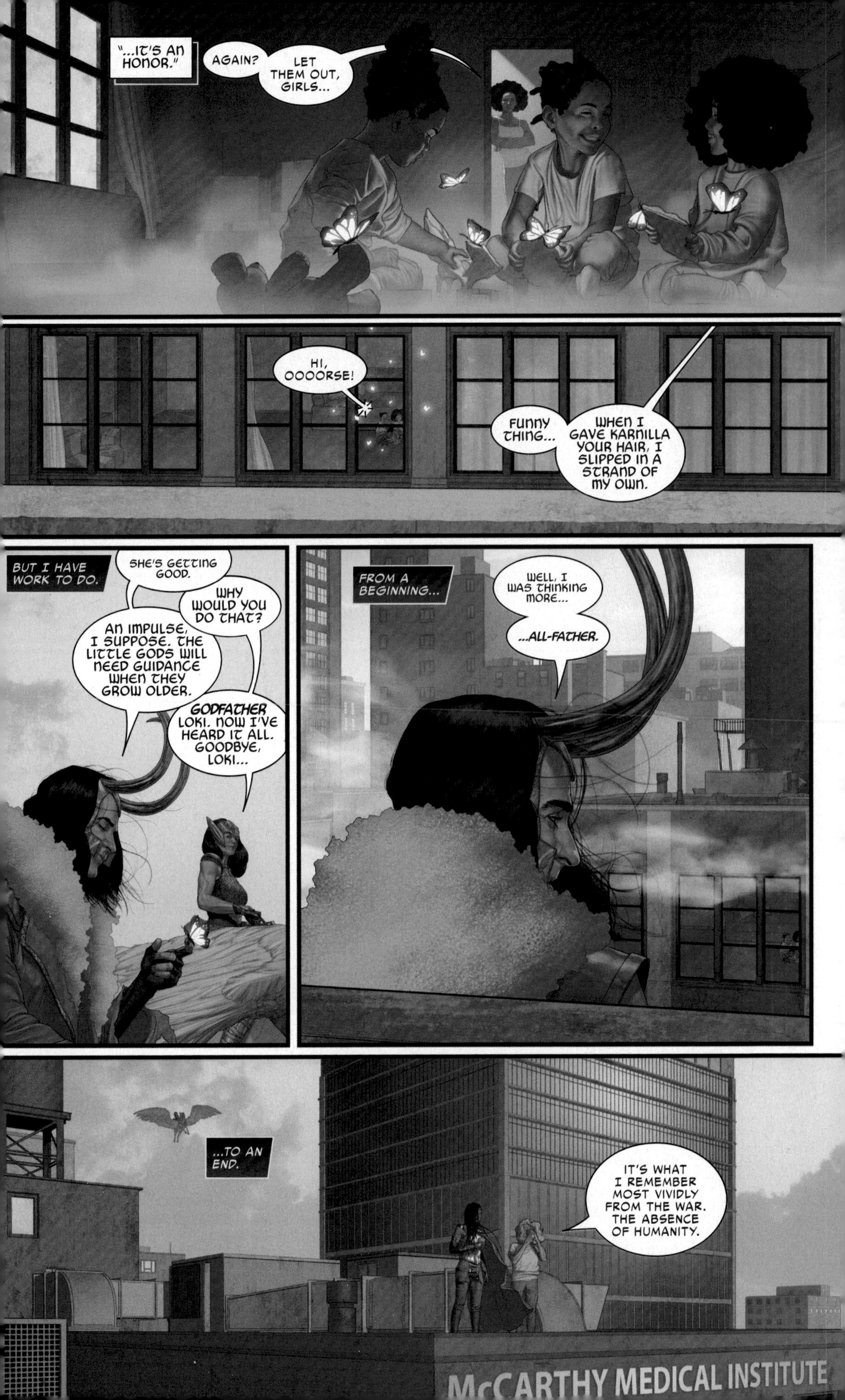
"...IT'S AN HONOR."
AGAIN?
LET THEM OUT, GIRLS...
HI, OOOORSE!
FUNNY THING...
WHEN I GAVE KARNILLA YOUR HAIR, I SLIPPED IN A STRAND OF MY OWN.
BUT I HAVE WORK TO DO.
SHE'S GETTING GOOD.
WHY WOULD YOU DO THAT?
AN IMPULSE, I SUPPOSE. THE LITTLE GODS WILL NEED GUIDANCE WHEN THEY GROW OLDER.
GODFATHER LOKI. NOW I'VE HEARD IT ALL. GOODBYE, LOKI...
FROM A BEGINNING...
WELL, I WAS THINKING MORE...
...ALL-FATHER.
...TO AN END.
IT'S WHAT I REMEMBER MOST VIVIDLY FROM THE WAR. THE ABSENCE OF HUMANITY.
McCARTHY MEDICAL INSTITUTE

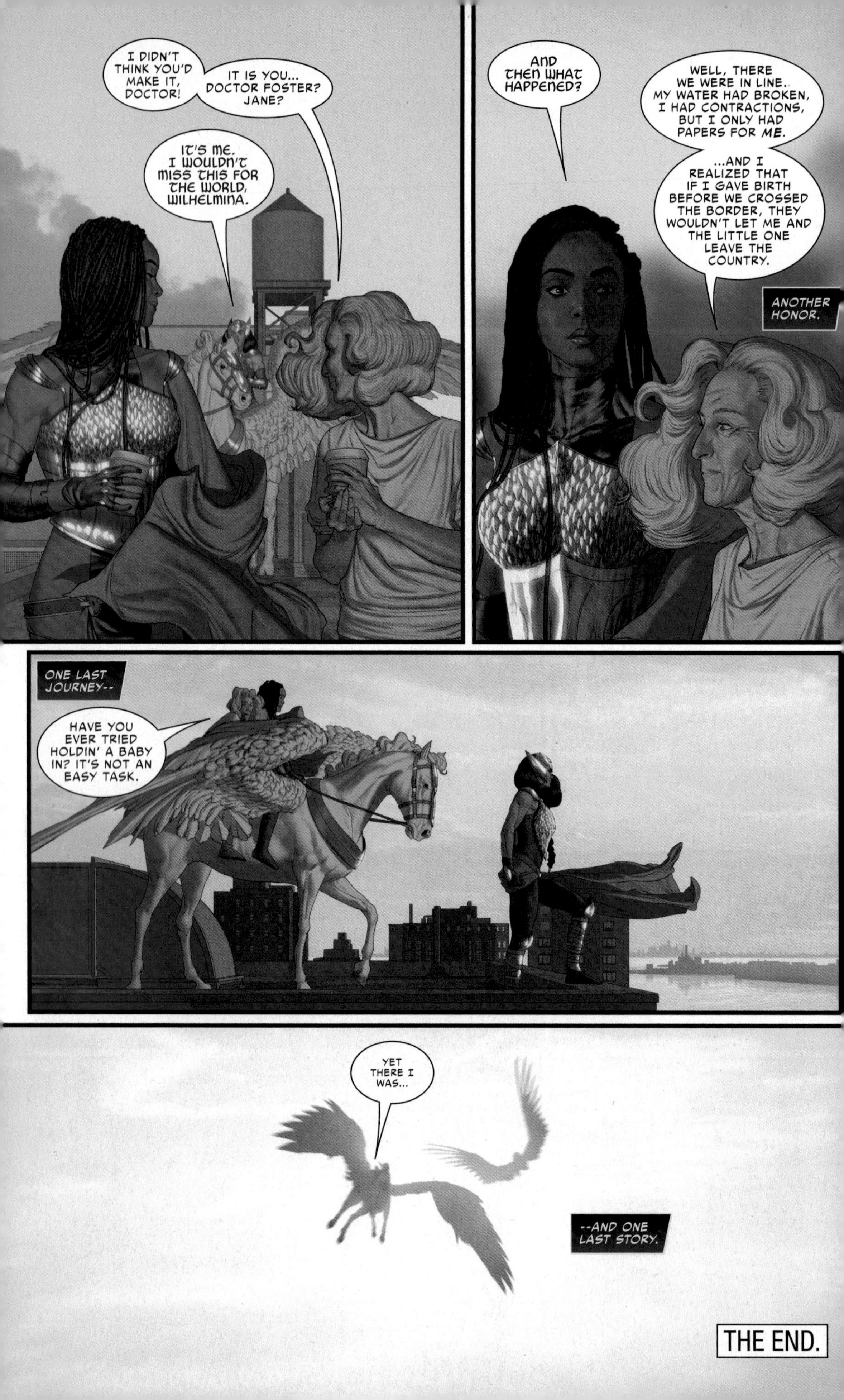
I DIDN'T THINK YOU'D MAKE IT, DOCTOR!
IT IS YOU... DOCTOR FOSTER? JANE?
IT'S ME. I WOULDN'T MISS THIS FOR THE WORLD, WILHELMINA.
AND THEN WHAT HAPPENED?
WELL, THERE WE WERE IN LINE. MY WATER HAD BROKEN, I HAD CONTRACTIONS, BUT I ONLY HAD PAPERS FOR *ME*.
...AND I REALIZED THAT IF I GAVE BIRTH BEFORE WE CROSSED THE BORDER, THEY WOULDN'T LET ME AND THE LITTLE ONE LEAVE THE COUNTRY.
ANOTHER HONOR.
ONE LAST JOURNEY--
HAVE YOU EVER TRIED HOLDIN' A BABY IN? IT'S NOT AN EASY TASK.
YET THERE I WAS...
--AND ONE LAST STORY.
THE END.

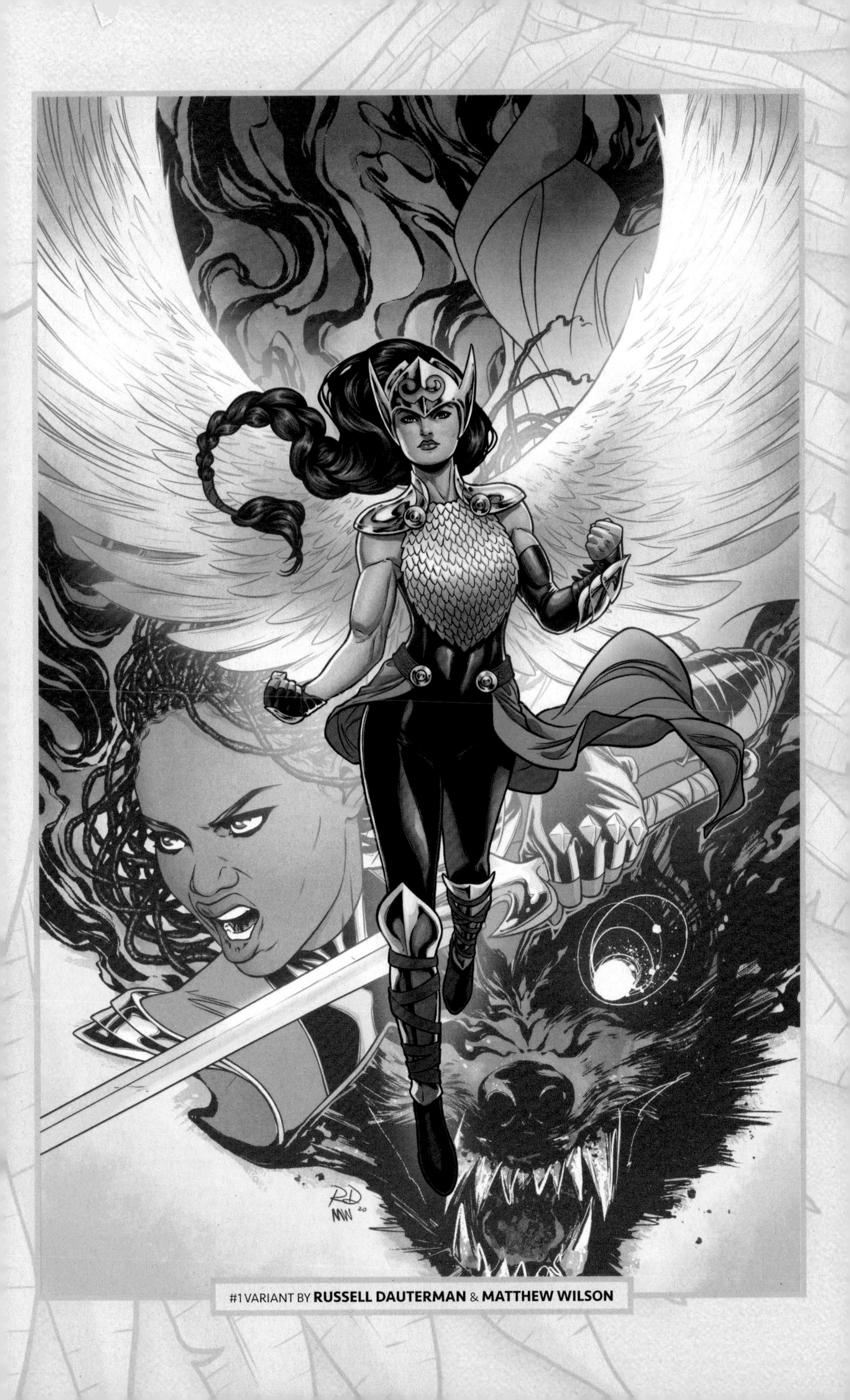

#1 VARIANT BY **RUSSELL DAUTERMAN** & **MATTHEW WILSON**

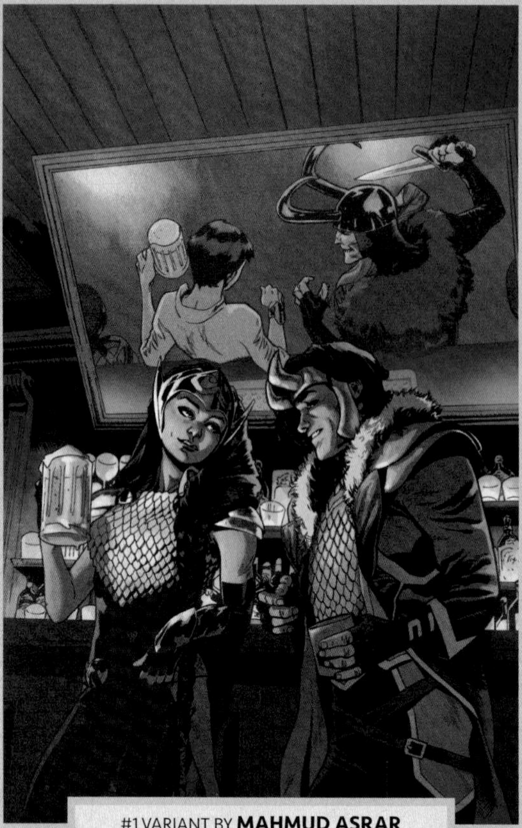

#1 VARIANT BY **MAHMUD ASRAR** & **MATTHEW WILSON**

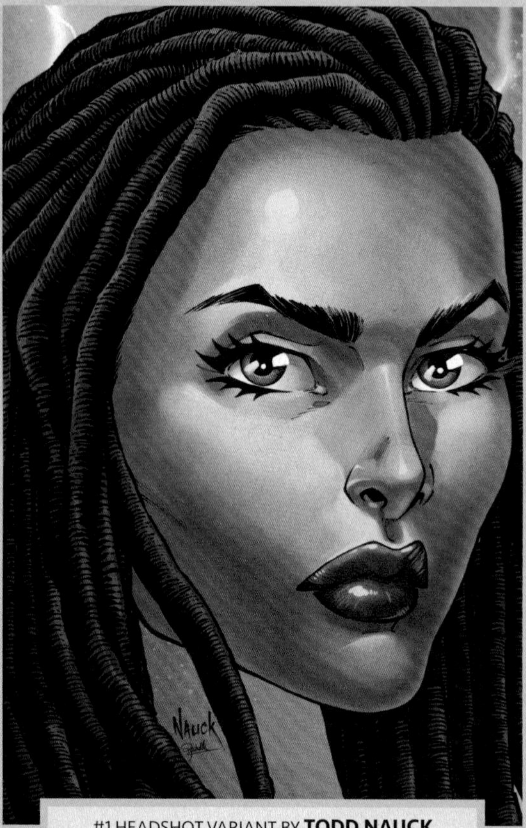
NAUCK

#1 HEADSHOT VARIANT BY **TODD NAUCK** & **RACHELLE ROSENBERG**

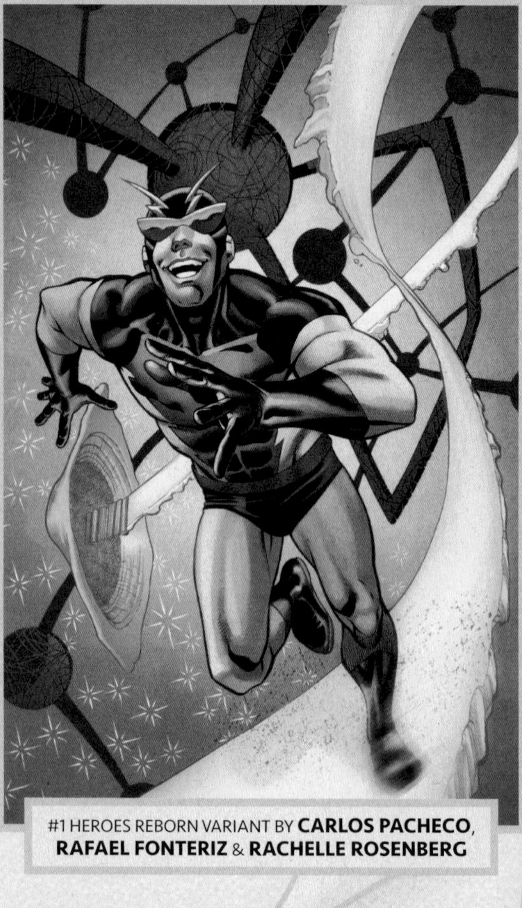

#1 HEROES REBORN VARIANT BY **CARLOS PACHECO, RAFAEL FONTERIZ** & **RACHELLE ROSENBERG**

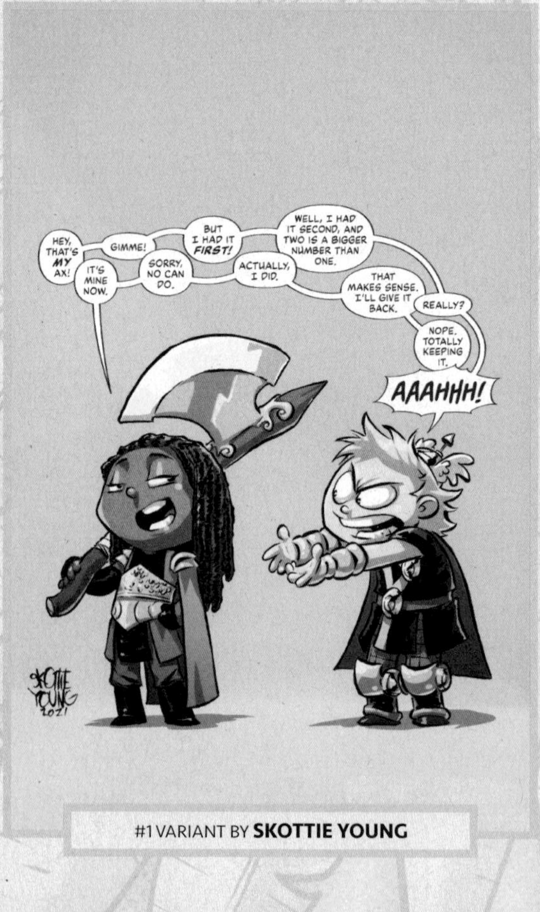
HEY, THAT'S MY AX!
IT'S MINE NOW.
GIMME!
SORRY, NO CAN DO.
BUT I HAD IT FIRST!
ACTUALLY, I DID.
WELL, I HAD IT SECOND, AND TWO IS A BIGGER NUMBER THAN ONE.
THAT MAKES SENSE. I'LL GIVE IT BACK.
REALLY?
NOPE. TOTALLY KEEPING IT.
AAAHHH!
SKOTTIE YOUNG 2021

#1 VARIANT BY **SKOTTIE YOUNG**

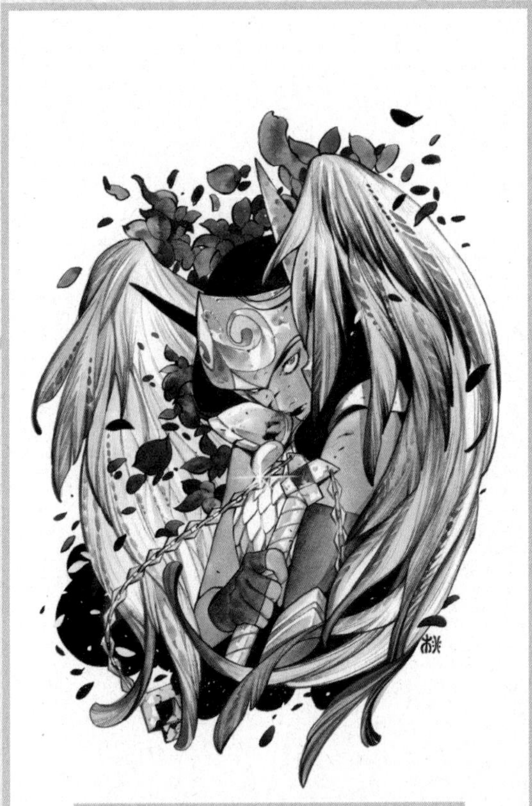

#2 VARIANT BY **PEACH MOMOKO**

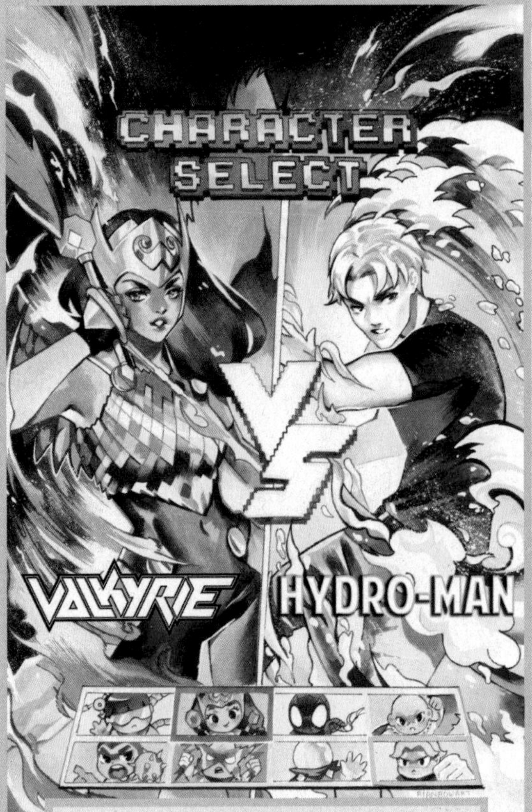
CHARACTER
SELECT
VALKYRIE
HYDRO-MAN

#3 SPIDER-MAN VILLAINS VARIANT
BY **RIAN GONZALES**

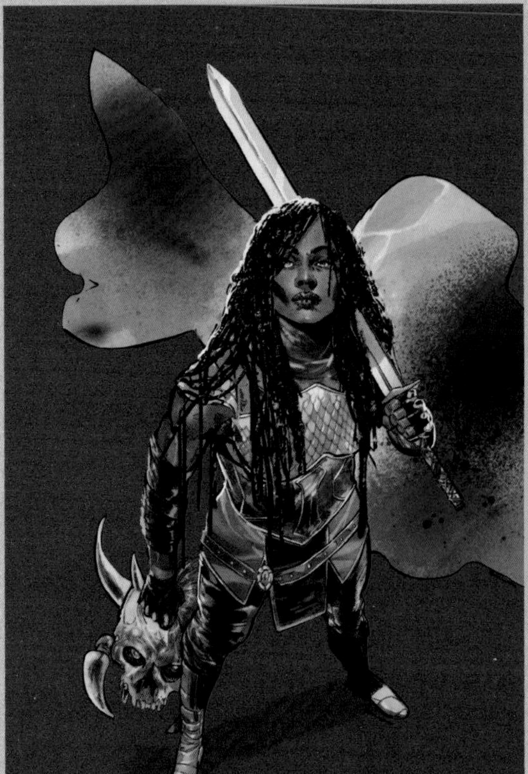

#3 PRIDE VARIANT BY **PHIL JIMENEZ**
& **FEDERICO BLEE**

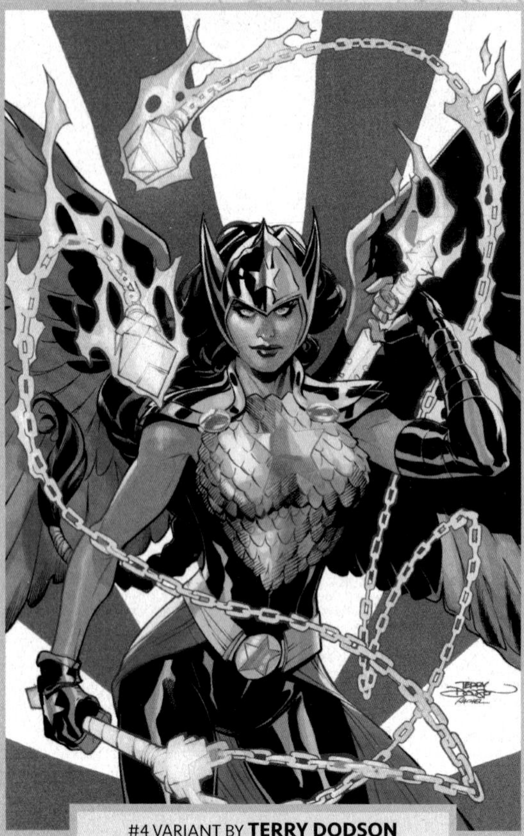

#4 VARIANT BY **TERRY DODSON**
& **RACHEL DODSON**

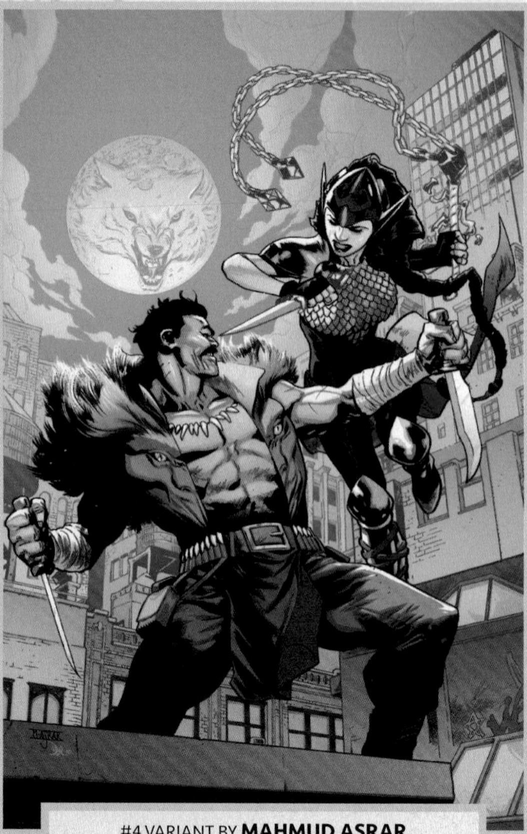

#4 VARIANT BY **MAHMUD ASRAR**
& **MATTHEW WILSON**

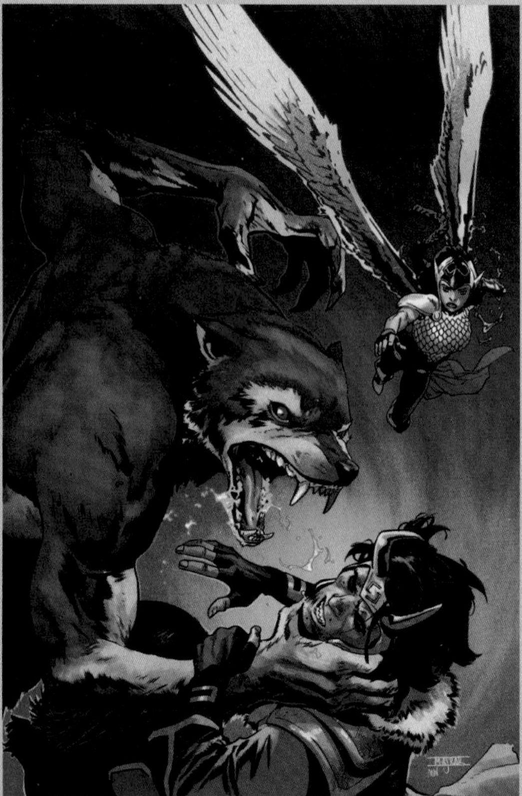

#5 VARIANT BY **MAHMUD ASRAR**
& **MATTHEW WILSON**